Notes on Spiritual Discourses of Shrī Ātmānanda

Notes on Spiritual Discourses of Shrī Ātmānanda

TAKEN BY NITYA TṚIPTA

Volume 1 of 3

Notes 1 to 472

NON-DUALITY PRESS
& STILLNESS SPEAKS

2nd edition published December 2009 by Non-Duality Press
& Stillness Speaks

Non-Duality Press | PO Box 2228 | Salisbury | SP2 2GZ
United Kingdom

www.non-dualitypress.com
www.stillnessspeaks.com

ISBN: 978-0-9563091-2-9

Contents
(of all 3 volumes)

Volume 1

Changes in the second edition vii
Transliteration scheme viii
Preface ix
Foreword xi
My indebtedness xiii
Introduction xiv
Why such open talk? xviii
On the life sketch of the Sage, Shrī Ātmānanda xix
On devotion to a living Guru xx

Notes on discourses (1 to 472) 1-234

Volume 2

Notes on discourses (473 to 1121) 1-251

Volume 3

Notes on discourses (1122 to 1451) 1-160

Some spiritual statements of Shrī Ātmānanda 161
Life sketch of Shrī Kṛiṣhṇa Mēnōn (Shrī Ātmānanda) 203
Glossary 241
Index (for all 3 volumes) 253

Changes in the second edition

In this second edition of *Notes on Spiritual Discourses of Shrī Ātmānanda*, there has been some minor editing (particularly of punctuation), to make the text more readable.

The notes are now numbered in a continuous sequence throughout the book, instead of the year by year numbering in the first edition.

The original 'subject war grouping' before the main body of notes has been replaced by an index at the end. The reader should note, however, that the index refers to note numbers, not page numbers.

Some added notes, explanations and translations are given in square brackets. Wherever square brackets occur, the contents are added by the second edition editor.

Editor of second edition, August 2009

Transliteration scheme

For ordinary readers, a simplified transliteration has been used for Sanskrit and Malayalam names and even for the titles of cited texts. But, for detailed quotations, a more exact transliteration has been used, for the sake of textual accuracy.

For Sanskrit, the exact transliteration is the standard one, using the usual diacritical marks, except that ‘e’ is written as ‘ē’ and ‘o’ as ‘ō’. This slight modification is needed to have a common transliteration scheme which applies to both Sanskrit and Malayalam.

For the simplified transliteration of Sanskrit characters, there are the following departures from standard academic practice: ‘ṛ’ is written as ‘ṛi’, ‘ṝ’ as ‘ṛī’, ‘ḷ’ as ‘ḷi’, ‘ḹ’ as ‘ḷī’, ‘ṅ’ as ‘n’ or ‘ng’, ‘ñ’ as ‘n’ or ‘ny’, ‘ś’ as ‘sh’, ‘ṣ’ as ‘ṣh’.

For Malayalam characters that don’t occur in Sanskrit, the following transliterations are used:

‘ള’ is written as ‘ḷ’. Thus, ‘ഉള്ളിൽ’ is written as ‘uḷḷil’.

‘ഴ’ is written as ‘ṟ’. Thus, ‘എപ്പോഴും’ is written as ‘eppōṟum’.

‘റ’ is written as ‘ŕ’. Thus, ‘അറിവ്’ is written as ‘aŕivŭ’.

‘റ്റ’ is written as ‘ŕŕ’. Thus, ‘പറ്റി’ is written as ‘paŕŕi’.

I apologize to Malayalam speakers for whom some of these usages will be unfamiliar. But I think that they are needed for the sake of those who do not know Malayalam.

For the ordinary reader, this scheme of transliteration is meant to indicate an approximate pronunciation, even if the diacritical marks are ignored. However, it may help to note that unmarked ‘c’, ‘t’ and ‘d’ are soft. In particular, ‘c’ is pronounced like ‘ch’ in ‘chat’; and ‘t’ and ‘d’ are pronounced as in the Italian ‘pasta’ and ‘dolce’. By contrast, ‘ṭ’ and ‘ŕ’ are pronounced more like the hard ‘t’ in ‘table’, and ‘ḍ’ like the hard ‘d’ in ‘donkey’. Where ‘h’ occurs after a preceding consonant, it does not indicate a softening of the consonant (as it may in English). Instead, it indicates an aspirated sound that occurs immediately after the consonant.

Second edition editor

Preface

Though I have been closely attached to Shrī Ātmānanda Guru ever since 1927 (when I was accepted as his disciple and initiated), it was only in November 1950 that I made bold one day – at the instance of a distinguished friend of mine – to make an attempt to take some notes on that day's talk, which had been particularly compelling. The friend left the same night. I wrote down the notes the next day and most hesitatingly submitted them at Gurunāthan's feet, to see if they could be sent to the friend.

He gladly ordered me to read them and I obeyed rather nervously. He listened to them patiently, and suggested some small deletions to avoid controversy. At the end, he asked me with a luminous smile on his face: 'How did you do this?' I humbly replied, 'I do not know', and told him the circumstances. He laughed, and said: 'I am pleased with them. You may send them to her and also continue the practice.'

I realized immediately how I was a simple tool at the merciful hands of the Absolute, and prostrated at his feet. He blessed me with both hands, and I stood up in tears. Thus encouraged and enriched, I continued the practice till the middle of April 1959.

That was how these notes came to be. Subsequently, they were twice read out to Gurunāthan [Shrī Ātmānanda] himself, and finally approved by him – as true to his exposition, both in idea and in rendering.

Though intended originally for the benefit of the disciples alone, who already had received directly from him the fundamentals of his exposition, they are now printed and published for the benefit of the general public as well. They have been found to be helpful to all those who have acquired at least a modest acquaintance with his method of direct approach to the ultimate Truth.

A preliminary knowledge of his book *Ātmānandōpaniṣhad* – in two parts, separately called *Ātma-darshan* and *Ātma-nirvṛiti* – is almost indispensable for understanding these notes, not only for those who have had no direct contact with Shrī Ātmānanda Guru, but also for those who are already his disciples.

A word too has to be said about the English language used here. Born in a different climate and designed to describe experiences somewhat different from those obtaining in spiritual India, the English language (now almost an international language) has perforce to undergo certain local modifications of idiom and punctuation. Sometimes, a bold departure from the accepted usage of a word or a phrase could alone yield the right meaning of Vēdānta. Such departures are inevitable, and they give force to the ideas and enrich the language.

He was insisting upon me ever since 1956 to print and publish these notes. It required a lot of time to compile and edit them. I was proudly privileged to utilize all my available time for direct services to his person. I was reluctant to divert any part of my time to other work which could well afford to wait. Therefore I could not take up this work of publication till he passed away. If any mistakes of expression or of any other kind have slipped into these notes without his knowledge, I am solely responsible. All the rest belongs to my Guru, the Truth.*

Nitya Tṛipta

---

*A word of caution in this context has become necessary. There are other persons and sannyāsins of different orders known by the identical name Ātmānanda. Let not the views or writings of any of them be mistaken for those of Shrī Ātmānanda of Trivandrum.

Foreword

A NOTE TO THE READERS

The subject matter of this book being notes of discourses, certain conversational mannerisms, peculiar usages, repetitions etc. – though not strictly literary – have necessarily been retained. Their force, freshness and naturalness appeal particularly to those who have listened to the discourses direct.

I had to fight against odds in this maiden enterprise of mine in the field of publication, and I am conscious of the innumerable imperfections and oversights that have crept into these pages. Therefore, as an immediate remedy, I have added just a modest errata at the close of every year, for such mistakes alone that affect the sense directly. Minor imperfections can be rectified only in the next impression.

A subject war grouping and tabulation of the titles by numbers added after the contents would enable the reader to have an exhaustive idea of any particular topic whenever necessary. [In this second edition, the subject war grouping is replaced by an index, at the end of the volume.]

A glossary is added towards the end of the volume, in alphabetic order, giving simple Advaitic explanations of the important technical and philosophical terms and expressions occurring in the course of the book.

A list of about five hundred of Shrī Ātmānanda's spiritual statements (collected from these talks and from elsewhere, and added towards the end of the volume) will be particularly useful to those who had any direct contact with him, and will feed the spiritual inquisitiveness of many a thinking person.

A list of the original Sanskrit quotations referred to in the course of the talks is added in Sanskrit script at the end of the volume and the particular number is given for reference at the places where it is mentioned. [In this second edition, the list of quotations is omitted. Instead, available references are given where the quotations occur.]

An astrological chart of the planetary position at the moment of his birth is attached at the beginning of the life sketch. I believe the few readers who have an astrological insight will have much to read from it regarding the journey of his body and mind. The predictions of Indian astrologers upon this chart had been more or less correct regarding his life's experiences. [The astrological chart is omitted, in this 2nd edition.]

Nitya Tṛipta

My indebtedness

I may be permitted to avail of this opportunity to record my deep indebtedness to Mrs. Kamal Wood, M.A. (Nagpur), B.Lit. (Oxon.), Professor of English, Elphinstone College, Bombay, who had so graciously scrutinized most of these pages, patiently correcting the language mistakes, punctuation, syntax etc.

Mahōpaddhyāya Shrī Ravivarma Tampān, Professor of Sanskrit College, Trivandrum (long retired) has kindly verified and approved the Sanskrit quotations and the technical and shāstraic portions of the glossary.

Messrs. P.K. Sreedhar and M.P.B. Nair at Bombay have been of invaluable help and service to me in this work, particularly in their undertaking all responsibility regarding the photographs and photostats in the volume and executing them beautifully and in time.

I wish to express my sincere gratefulness to the many other co-disciples of mine who have helped me in editing and verifying the texts at different stages, and also to the proof readers, the printing staff of the Reddiar Press and many others for their hearty co-operation in bringing out this volume within reasonable time and so nicely. More than all, my heart goes to the handful of my dear co-disciples – both foreign and Indian – whose unstinted and voluntary financial help has enabled me to preserve in form for posterity this invaluable spiritual heritage from our revered Guru Shrī Ātmānanda.

Nitya Tṛipta

Introduction

It will be helpful to define beforehand the subject, the approach, the field of enquiry and the stand taken in these notes. The subject discussed is the ultimate Truth or Peace. The approach is the direct perception method of Advaita (the strict Vicāra-mārga). The field of enquiry is the totality of human experience, comprised of the experiences of the three states and the awareness still beyond. The stand taken is strictly in the absolute Truth, and reference made only to the being inside. All this is discussed in detail in the ensuing pages. The readers also would do well to adopt the same standard and perspective, at least hypothetically, for the time being. The large majority of friends who cannot cease to think in relative terms, even for a short while, are earnestly requested not to dabble with spiritual pursuits. That will spoil even their enjoyment in the phenomenal world.

Great advancement has been made in all human walks of life. Methods of transport in space have progressed from walking to flying. The achievements of science and technology have almost annihilated space. Vēdānta, which is a deep and relentless enquiry into the nature of Truth, has also not lagged behind in improving its methods. Thus, what real aspirants experienced after a whole life's intense effort in the vēdic age, is made attainable in the present age in a comparatively short period of time by a more direct application of the higher reason in man. Such was the method adopted by Shrī Ātmānanda.

He had a two-fold mission in life. The first part of it – in his own words – was to expound the highest Truth, the ultimate Reality , in a manner and language understandable even to the kitchen maid. It is the belief of most men and pundits that a high proficiency in Sanskrit is the first prerequisite of knowing the Truth. They believe also that Truth can be expounded only in high-sounding and abstruse philosophical terms, technicalities and terminologies. The numerous vēdāntic shāstras of a cosmological type (of course with rare exceptions) have contributed much to the growth of this pernicious superstition.

Shrī Ātmānanda, who was not a Sanskrit scholar himself, has successfully dispelled this wrong notion, both by his writings and by his discourses. His two books, *Ātma-darshan* and *Ātma-nirvṛiti* – written originally in Malayalam verse and which expound the ultimate Truth from various standpoints – are limpidly clear and simple. Most of the verses are written in the briefest and the simplest rhythm. They are so natural that they read like poetic prose. The English rendering of the two books by the author himself, though not in verse form, is equally simple and clear. Abstruse Sanskrit terminology has been avoided. He expounded the ultimate Truth even to illiterate women and children in simple Malayalam language, and to great lawyers, scientists and philosophers from home and abroad in simple and elegant English.

Some of the disciples who came from distant continents did not possess even a working knowledge of the English language, and even then they were able to grasp the Truth quite well. Therefore it is evident that no language is the language of Truth. All language is the language of untruth alone. Language is made use of to reach the very brink of untruth, beyond which the Guru – representing the languageless Truth – stands revealed in all his glory. The Truth is also revealed as the real nature of the aspirant himself.

The second part of his mission was to re-establish the dignity of the householder and his birthright to strive and to be liberated, while still remaining a householder. Since the time of Shrī Shankara, the fold of sannyāsa began to be looked upon with particular respect and regard by the people. Inflated by this undeserved title for reverence, some of these sannyāsins began to assert and proclaim that liberation is the monopoly of sannyāsins alone and that the householder is not even eligible for it. In their wild fury they even forgot the undeniable fact that the founders of the spiritual heritage of India were most of them householders (Shrī Janaka, Shrī Vasiṣhṭha, Shrī Vyāsa, Shrī Rāma, Shrī Kṛiṣhṇa, and the authors of many of the Upaniṣhads). The aphorism 'Tat tvam asi', which is meditated upon by every sannyāsin, was first composed and expounded by the householder sage, Uddālaka, to his son and disciple, Shvētakētu. There is no data for any argument in favour of the sannyāsin's stand; but their capacity for mischief cannot be gainsaid. Therefore a solitary yet glowing example in the course of several centuries often becomes necessary to blot out such superstitions. Such was the life of Shrī Ātmānanda, the Sage. He was an ideal householder, an ideal police officer (upright and fearless, who ruled his subordinates as well as the criminals under his charge by love and love alone) and an ideal Guru to his disciples in all the continents of the world.

He used to meet a general gathering of the disciples and visitors usually at 5.30 p.m. at his residence. After preliminary enquiries and introductions, he would call for questions, to 'set the ball rolling' as he would often say. Then somebody would ask a question – whether pertinent or not was immaterial. That would be enough for the day. He would immediately take up that question, analyse it exhaustively and answer it from different standpoints one after the other, never stopping half way but pursuing the problem relentlessly to its very foundation, the ultimate background.

He would never approach a problem from a perspective short of the ultimate Truth, and would always make the listening disciple contact his own real nature many times in the course of each talk. The visitor, besides, would experience an uncaused Peace and solace several times in the course of the talk, and this naturally increased his earnestness to know the Truth more intimately.

Shrī Ātmānanda's approach to every problem was direct and logical. He did not quote texts to establish his position. After establishing his own position by using deep discrimination and direct reason alone, he would sometimes, for the mere pleasure of it, cite parallels from texts of undisputed authority by great Sages. He never discouraged or discredited any particular path or religion; so much so that he had disciples from all castes and creeds: Christians, Muslims, Jews, Parsis and Hindus – brahmin as well as non-brahmin. They all continued quite smoothly in their superficial allegiance to their old religion, society and customs, even after visualizing the Truth through Vēdānta.

Shrī Ātmānanda held emphatically that the basic error in man was his wrong identification with body, senses and mind. When this was replaced by the right identification with Ātmā, the real 'I'-principle, everything would be found to be perfectly in order and no change or correction in any walk of life whatsoever would be called for.

He asserted that one's own perspective alone had to be set right. He always stressed the point that the answer to any question of an objective nature was never complete until it was ultimately applied to the subject; and the question had to be disposed of in the light of the ultimate Reality – the Self.

The evening discourse was a formal one, when all his disciples and strangers who had obtained previous permission were welcome. But he used to talk on spiritual problems for several more hours every day to the few disciples around him, who always waited upon him – eager to render any personal service needed. He expounded the Truth more unreservedly and informally during these unprovoked talks.

Questions were asked from different levels by different persons, and answers were always given in tune with the level and standard of the questioner himself. Therefore answers to the same question at different times might often seem varied, even contradictory, but they ultimately converge upon the same centre. Thus even repetitions have been really enriching and also entertaining.

Nitya Tṛipta

Why such open talk?

Shrī Ātmānanda expounded the ultimate Truth in the most direct and uncompromising manner, and he gives his reasons here below for adopting this drastic method.

13th January 1951

A disciple asked: Why was secrecy so strictly observed in expounding the Truth in the old shāstras?

Gurunāthan: Evidently, for fear of jeopardizing established religion and society. Religion had no place except in duality and social life. It was the prime moving force of social life in ancient times. But the concept of religion could not stand the strict logic of vēdāntic Truth.

The sages of old, who recognized the great need of religion in phenomenal life, expounded the ultimate Truth under a strict cover of secrecy, thus enabling religion to play its role in lower human society. But religion in the present day world has been dethroned in many ways, and ungodly cults have come into existence in large numbers.

Therefore it is high time now to throw off the veil of secrecy, and broadcast the whole Truth in the face of the world which has already advanced much, intellectually.

[This is the text of note 51, which may also be found in the main body of notes below.]

On the life sketch of the Sage, Shrī Ātmānanda

Its meaning, purpose and scope:

The life story of a Sage is a paradox. This is because life is only an appearance and therefore an untruth, while the Sage is the ultimate Truth itself – the impersonal. Shrī Kṛiṣhṇa Mēnōn (Shrī Ātmānanda) held that one should be known only for the principle one stands for. Therefore he would not agree to the writing of his life story, while he lived.

Nevertheless, modern practice obliges the author to write a brief life sketch of the person who shines through this book. A record of the phenomenal facts and aspects of his life is needed, in order to avoid wrong and exaggerated versions of his life gaining currency when genuine facts are no longer available. I make no attempt to point out anything extraordinary or miraculous in his life. My object is quite the contrary. Of course there was one thing quite extraordinary in him. He visualized the ultimate Truth and stood established in it. Therefore the so-called 'life story' of his, so far as he is concerned, is a misrepresentation of himself.

It is the transcendental essence, which the Sage is and knows he is, that makes him great in the spiritual realm. Therefore the so called 'life story' of a Sage cannot make anyone understand anything about the Sage. The Sage is impersonal. He has outgrown the shell of his own life, the shell called personality. The personality and the Sage are in two distinct and separate planes. Therefore it is quite futile to scan the life story of a Sage to measure his real worth.

This might seem quite an unusual warning. His life-sketch has very little direct bearing upon the body and theme of this book. Therefore I have incorporated at the end of this book [just before the glossary and index] a short life sketch of Shrī Kṛiṣhṇa Mēnōn, the 'man'.

Nitya Tṛipta

On devotion to a living Guru

ācāryavān puruṣō vēda

Chāndogya Upaniṣhad, 6.14.2

This means: 'He who is blessed with a Kāraṇa-guru alone knows the Truth.'

The following Malayalam verse is the instruction of Shrī Ātmānanda to the few earnest aspirants of Truth, as to how and when they should direct and express their sense of deep devotion.

bōdhaṁ yātorupādhimūlam udayaṁ ceytō, bhajikkēṇṭatuṁ
pūjikkēṇṭatum uḷḷaliññatineyāṁ śrīdēśikōpādhiyāy˘,
ellāṁ satguruvām upādhi maṟayunnērattatallāte
kaṇṭānyōpādhiyil āvidhaṁ bhramam udiccīḍāt irunnīṭaṇaṁ .

Shrī Ātmānanda, Ātmārāmam, 1.34

'That particular person through whom one had the proud privilege of being enlightened, that is the *only* form which one may adore and do pūja to, to one's heart's content, as the person of one's Guru. It is true that all is the Sat-guru, but *only* when the name and form disappear and not otherwise. Therefore, the true aspirant should beware of being deluded into any similar devotional advances towards any other form, be it of God or of man.'

This is confirmed by Shrī Ātmānanda's letter on the subject, as translated in volume 3, on pages 215-6.

And it is further confirmed by Shrī Shankara's bold proclamation, often quoted in this volume.

jīvō nā 'haṁ dēśikō 'ktyā śivō 'ham ..

Shrī Shankara, Advaita-pancaratnam, 1.2

'By the word of my Guru, I am not jīva (the personal life principle). But I am Peace-ultimate.' (God being comprehended as 'samaṣṭi-jīva' – the aggregate of all jīvas – and as the highest concept of the human mind.)

Nitya Tṛipta

Notes on discourses

20th November 1950

1. HOW IS DEEP SLEEP A KEY TO THE ULTIMATE?

Deep mental activity generates heat, which keeps off deep sleep. Cold in its intensity wakes you up. Deep sleep brings on a sense of happiness and peace with it. This experience we get only in the absence of all mental activity. When we direct our mind to this happiness aspect of deep sleep, we feel a sensation of gentle coolness, which wards off all sense of negation in sleep. So we get to our real nature by relaxing our mind from all forms of activity, and at the same time not losing sight of the happiness and peace experienced in deep sleep.

This positive aspect saves us from the probable shroud of negation and slumber. We should not allow the mind to be active and at the same time we should see that it does not become inactive. In other words: '*Sleep knowingly.*'

Thus, deep sleep can be utilized directly for establishing oneself in the real centre.

2. HOW CAN REMEMBRANCE BE FORGETTING?

Every thought merges into Consciousness and remains not as thought, but as Consciousness, pure. So your searching in that Consciousness for the resurrection of any thought, merged therein, is in vain. It can only result in your first forgetting your real nature of pure Consciousness, and in the subsequent creation of an entirely new thought, as though experienced some time earlier.

3. WHERE, WHEN AND HOW DO I SEE ME?

1. I see Me where the 'where' is not.
2. I see Me when the 'when' is not.
3. I see Me when 'I see me not.'

Explanation:

1. I shall see Me only when I transcend the gross body idea, which is governed by space as well as by time.
2. I shall see Me only when I transcend the subtle body or the mind, which is governed by time alone.
3. I shall see Me only on leaving both the gross and the subtle bodies – when I stop my objective search and turn inward to find myself as one with that which I was searching for; in other words only when the subject-object relationship vanishes.

23rd November 1950

4. WHAT IS THE NATURE AND OBJECT OF PERCEPTION?

A Jnyānin perceives the Absolute, diversified as objects. Ignorant men, identifying themselves with the gross body, perceive gross objects. Others, standing as mind, perceive only subtle objects.

Jnyānins, standing as Consciousness, perceive only Consciousness.

5. WHAT IS THE CONTENT OF THE INTERVAL BETWEEN MENTATIONS?

Let us examine our own casual statements regarding our daily experiences. For example, we say: 'He comes', 'He sits', 'He goes', and so on. In these statements, 'coming', 'sitting' and 'going' are somehow extraneous to 'him'. As such, they do not at all go into the make of 'him'.

'He' alone stands unqualified through all time, continuing without a break. So it is this pure 'he' or 'I' (or Consciousness) which shines through and in between all thoughts, feelings, perceptions and states. During this interval [between mentations], one has no thought of the state in which one happens to be. So here, one is *Peace* itself; and that is the 'I', in its pure state.

Suppose you see a beautiful picture, painted on white paper. On closely examining the picture, you will be able to discover some parts of it where the original colour of the paper appears, unaffected by the shades of the picture. This proves to you the existence of the paper behind the picture, as its background. On further examination, you will see that the picture is nothing but the paper.

So also, if you succeed in discovering yourself *between* two mentations, you easily come to the conclusion that you are *in* the mentations as well.

6. WHAT IS THE MEANING OF 'I'?

The same word, used in similar contexts, cannot carry different meanings with different persons. When I say 'I' meaning 'my body', another understands it in the same sense, meaning 'my body'. But when the other person uses the same word 'I', he means 'his body', which is entirely different from 'my body'.

Thus, in the case of everyone, the bodies meant are different; but the word used is the same 'I', always. So the 'I' must mean: *either* the individual bodies of all men – which is ludicrous – *or* it must evidently mean no body at all.

The latter being the only possible alternative, the 'I' must necessarily mean that changeless principle in which every body appears and disappears. This is the real meaning of 'I', even in our daily traffic with the world.

7. WHAT IS IT THAT APPEARS AS WORLD?

As soon as we wake up from deep sleep, the existence of a ready-made world – including our own bodies – confronts us. To examine it closely, we utilize our sense organs straightaway – one by one, relying on their superficial evidence without a thought.

The organ of sight asserts that the world is only form and nothing else; the organ of hearing that the world is only sound and nothing else; and so on. Each organ thus asserts the world as *its* sole and particular object. In effect, each sense organ contradicts the evidence of the other four organs, with equal force. This hopeless mess of contradictory evidence, and the stubborn denial by each of the sense organs of the others' evidence, form positive proof of the falsity of this world – as it appears.

But all the while, the existence of a positive something is experienced without a break, beyond the shadow of a doubt. This, on closer analysis, is found to be that changeless, subjective 'I'-principle or Consciousness itself.

8. Is there ajnyāna [ignorance] in deep sleep?

No. The absence of any objective perception, thought or feeling – which is wrongly called 'nothingness' – is the svarūpa [true nature] of real, unconditioned happiness. Here, happiness alone is the positive experience in deep sleep, and the sense of nothingness is a relative inference when out of it.

Thus, there is in fact no ajnyāna in deep sleep. The ajnyāna of Truth is the jnyāna [knowledge] of objects, gross or subtle. To know any object means not to know the Truth. From the knowledge of an object, if the object part is discarded, what remains is pure knowledge alone, which is the essence and the background of all objects as well as of myself.

The jnyāna of any one object may also be said to be the ajnyāna of all other objects. In that sense, the jnyāna of Truth and Happiness in deep sleep can also be said to be the ajnyāna of all objects. Thus happiness alone is the experience in deep sleep.

9th December 1950

9. How is deep sleep the touchstone of one's real nature?

The knowledge of one object implies the ignorance of all objects other than that particular object. The ignorance of all objects in deep sleep means really the positive knowledge of the self, which shines as happiness there. Consequently, the ignorance of the ordinary man in deep sleep is really the knowledge of his own self, which is happiness and Consciousness.

Our deep sleep experience, according to the lower shāstras, is ignorance coupled with the sense of subjective happiness. We have already proved that the so called ignorance of the world in deep sleep is nothing but the knowledge of the self, which is happiness itself. Thus the experience in deep sleep, if properly understood, is only *one*; and that is our own self, which is *Happiness* and *Peace*. The rest of the statement is but a commentary upon this.

There is only *one* there; and hence the ignorance of the many is no experience at all.

10. 'MIND AS MIND KNOWS NO PEACE, AND MIND AT PEACE IS NO MIND AT ALL.'

The most universal of all desires in man is unequivocally expressed in the spontaneous statement made by all alike: 'I want peace of mind'. It means that the activity of the mind is never our ultimate goal. Examining this statement closely and impartially, we find that *Peace* is the real goal of man's desire. But in his utter inability to extricate himself from the clutches of the mind, he links the mind also to that desire for absolute Peace, and claims himself to be the enjoyer. But alas, when the mind, freed from all its activities, comes into contact with the Peace it desired, it finds itself merged and lost in that peace, thus returning to its real nature.

Therefore, it is one's own real nature that everybody seeks, knowingly or unknowingly.

11. HOW TO ESTABLISH ADVAITA IN THE KNOWLEDGE OF AN OBJECT?

When I say 'I know an object', the knower and the object known both disappear; and the knowledge alone remains. Thus separated from the knower and the known, the knowledge can no longer be called limited. It is pure. It is absolute. So, during every perception, I remain in my real centre, as pure Consciousness.

It has already been proved that just before and after every perception, I am in my own real nature. The knower, knowledge and the known are themselves three distinct and separate perceptions, each appearing in a particular sequence corresponding to that in the expression 'I know it.'

Thus, it stands established that nobody is ever shaken from his own centre of consciousness and peace.

12. HOW CAN THE PHENOMENAL LEAD ONE TO THE ABSOLUTE?

Conceding that God created this universe, you have to admit that God existed even before creation. Man, with his created sense organs and mind, is capable of visualizing only the objects of creation, gross or subtle. So, in order to visualize God as he existed all alone, even before creation, we have to utilize some faculty which is present in us all and which transcends creation. This can be nothing other than the changeless 'I'-principle or Consciousness.

Reaching that, one is divested of all sense of duality. Even the conception of God does not arise there; and everything appears – if it ever does – as Consciousness alone. It follows therefore that the God that was there before creation was nothing other than the real 'I'-principle.

24th December 1950

13. HOW AM I THE WITNESS?

Every perception, thought or feeling is known by you. You are the knower of the world through the sense organs; of the sense organs through the generic mind; and of the mind – with its activity or passivity – by your self alone.

In all these different activities, you stand out as the one knower. Actions, perceptions, thoughts and feelings all come and go. But knowingness does not part with you, even for a moment. You are therefore always the knower. How then can you ever be the doer or the enjoyer?

After understanding the 'I'-principle as pure Consciousness and happiness, always use the word 'I' or 'knower' to denote the goal of your retreat. The 'I' always brings subjectivity with it. It is this ultimate, subjective principle 'I' – divested of even that subjectivity – that is the goal.

Consciousness and happiness may possibly have a taint of objectivity in their conception, since they always express themselves in the realm of the mind. When one is deeply convinced that one's self is consciousness and happiness, one finds it as the nameless.

Whereupon, even this namelessness seems a limitation. Giving up that as well, one remains as the 'I'-principle, the 'Absolute'.

When you try to visualize the Absolute in you, nothing can possibly disturb you, because every thought or perception points to yourself and only helps you to stand established as the Absolute.

To become a Jnyānin [Sage] means to become aware of *what you are already*. In this connection, it has to be proved that 'knowing' is not a function. In all your life, you feel you have not changed; and of all your manifold activities, from your birth onwards, the only activity that has never changed is 'knowing'. So both these must necessarily be one and the same; and therefore knowingness is your real nature.

Thus, knowing is never an activity in the worldly sense, since this knowing has neither a beginning nor an end. And because it is never separated from you, it is your *svarūpa* (real nature) – just as 'shining' is the svarūpa of the sun and not its function. Understanding it in this way, and realizing it as one's svarūpa, brings about liberation from all bondage.

When you reach consciousness or happiness, you lose all sense of objectivity or duality and stand identified with the ultimate, subjective 'I'-principle, or the Absolute. Then the subjectivity also vanishes. When the word '*pure*' is added on to consciousness, happiness or 'I', even the least taint of relativity is removed. There, all opposites are reconciled, all paradoxes stand self-explained; and everything, or nothing, can be said about it.

14. How to be alive and at home always?

While thus talking of the Absolute at a high level, Gurunāthan noticed a disciple withdrawing himself into samādhi and asked him suddenly how many months his wife had advanced in her pregnancy. It took the disciple a few minutes to come down even to understand the question. The object of this question was just to show that one should be equally alive in samādhi as well as in worldly activity. To be thus 'at home' always, shows one's stand in the natural state.

15. IS ANY EFFORT NEEDED AFTER REALIZATION?

Yes. You realize the moment you hear the Truth direct from the Guru. All subsequent effort is only to remove every obstacle that might come in the way of establishing oneself in the Truth.

25th December 1950

16. WHAT IS THE 'THING IN ITSELF'?

The fundamental worldly experience of man is that something which was unknown subsequently becomes known. This statement clearly shows that the 'thing in itself' was the background of both the unknown and the known, and as such could not exactly be either the one or the other. Looking at the background closely, you find that some sort of a limitation was put upon the 'thing in itself' by the mind, to which it therefore appeared as the 'known' or the 'unknown'. Take away that mental limitation from the experience, and immediately it becomes the Reality itself; because it goes beyond the known and the unknown.

That which was called unknown is in the known as well, and is still unknown. It is the Reality itself. Take for example the 'I' in I think and I feel. The 'I'-principle can never be the thinking or the feeling principle, but is beyond both, and is present equally in the thinking as well as in the feeling.

Examining this from another angle, the 'unknown' means that which is not grasped by the sense organs or the mind. That which is not comprehended by these two, but which transcends them both, cannot be anything but the Reality. Therefore, what is called the 'unknown' is the Reality. And now coming to the 'known', when correctly examined, a sense object merges into Consciousness. Therefore, what is known is also nothing but Consciousness.

When an ordinary man – who believes himself to be the body – sees an object, he sees and emphasizes the object part of it and ignores completely the most important factor – consciousness. But when a Jnyānin sees the same object, he sees it not as object but as consciousness itself. He emphasizes only the consciousness part of it, and feels that it is the Self. Thus to him, every perception doubly reaffirms his knowledge that he is Consciousness. It is experience of the Truth itself, repeated as often as there are thoughts or perceptions.

17. WHAT IS THE NATURE OF THE WORLDLY ACTIVITY OF A SAGE?

A subjective transformation alone is needed for 'realization'. When one who has realized the Truth looks at the world, conceding the existence of the world, he finds that every object asserts one's own self or consciousness, without which the object could never appear.

Perceptions are liable to mistakes regarding the object perceived; for example the stump of a tree is mistaken for a man. But regarding yourself, the 'I', there can never be any mistaking whatsoever.

18. THE ENJOYMENT OF PLEASURE BY AN ORDINARY MAN AND THE SAGE?

To the ordinary man, pleasure is an end in itself and he attributes it all to objects. But to the Sage, who apparently enjoys the same pleasure, it is all the expression of the happiness aspect of the Absolute or the Self, *purely uncaused.*

During the sādhana period of a disciple, experiences of pleasure sometimes occur, as a result of particular states of mind attained through discipline and practice. Because of their great similarity to the experiences of intense pleasure he may have had in worldly life, the disciple is likely to desire a repetition of these, as an end in itself. This worldly interpretation of spiritual experiences is likely to entangle him there, impeding his spiritual progress.

But, under the guidance of a Kāraṇa-guru, the disciple understands such experiences to be expressions of the Absolute in him; and he is enabled to proceed further in order to reach 'what is expressed', regardless of the pleasure experienced on the way.

To the Sage, every experience of happiness is only an expression – in the realm of the mind – of the happiness aspect of the absolute 'Self'; and as such he never attributes it to external objects. To the Sage, all the activities of the mind and body are but expressions of the Absolute, and as such *purposeless* in themselves.

But the worldly man takes to activities with a definite purpose, as a means of enjoyment.

26th December 1950

19. WHAT CONSTITUTES A SAGE? AND HOW DOES HE CONDUCT HIMSELF?

Mere realization, as is usually understood, does not make one a Sage in the full sense of the term.

A Sage should be a yōgin to a yōgin, a bhakta to a bhakta, and a householder in every detail to his own family and to the other householders. In all his relations – with society, state etc. – he behaves exactly as any ordinary citizen. But, in reality, he is always a Jnyānin [knower] and is none of these.

You cannot express the Truth by word of mouth, by thought, or by feeling. But the Truth expresses itself, in all these varied activities.

20. HOW ARE OBJECTS RELATED TO ME?

All this world is my object, and I am the changeless subject. Each one of my objects serves only to point to me and to prove me. I need only make my stand there firmer and establish myself at the real centre, as the ultimate subject 'I'.

27th December 1950

21. HOW TO RETREAT INTO THE REAL 'I'-PRINCIPLE?

What do you mean when you say 'I'? It does not at all mean the body, senses or mind. It is pure experience itself – in other words, the end of all knowledge or feeling.

First of all, see that the body, senses and mind are your objects and that you are always the changeless subject, distinct and separate from the objects. The objects are present only when they are perceived. But I exist, always changeless, whether perceptions occur or not, extending through and beyond all states. Thus you see that you are never the body, senses or mind. Make this thought as deep and intense as possible, until you are doubly sure that the wrong identification will never recur.

Next, examine if there is anything else that does not part with the 'I'-principle, even for a moment. *Yes*. There is Consciousness. It never parts with the 'I'-principle, and can never be an object either. So both must mean one and the same thing. Or, in other words, 'I' is Consciousness itself. Similarly, wherever there is the 'I'-principle left alone, there is also the idea of deep peace or happiness, existing along with it.

It is universally admitted that one loves only that which gives one happiness, or that a thing is loved only for its happiness value. Evidently, happiness itself is loved more than that which is supposed to give happiness. It is also admitted that one loves one's self more than anything else. So it is clear that you must be one with happiness or that you are happiness itself. All your activities are only attempts to experience that happiness or self in every experience.

The ordinary man fixes a certain standard for all his worldly activities and tries to attain it to his satisfaction. Thereby, he is only trying to experience the self in the form of happiness, as a result of the satisfaction obtained on reaching the standard already accepted by him.

For every perception, thought or feeling, you require the services of an instrument suited to each activity. But to love your own self, you require no instrument at all. Since you experience happiness by retreating into that 'I'-principle, that 'I' must be either an object to give you happiness, which is impossible; or it must be happiness itself. So the 'I'-principle, Peace and Consciousness are all one and the same. It is in Peace that thoughts and feelings rise and set. This peace is very clearly expressed in deep sleep, when the mind is not there and you are one with Consciousness and Peace.

Pure consciousness and deep peace are your real nature. Having understood this in the right manner, you can well give up the use of the words 'Consciousness' and 'Happiness' and invariably use 'I' to denote the Reality.

Don't be satisfied with only reducing objects into Consciousness. Don't stop there. Reduce them further into the 'I'-principle. So also, reduce all feelings into pure Happiness and then reduce them into the 'I'-principle. When you are sure that you will not return to identification with the body any longer, you can very well leave off the intermediaries of Consciousness and Happiness, and directly take the thought 'I, I, I', subjectively.

Diversity is only in objects. Consciousness, which perceives them all, is one and the same.

22. WHAT IS MY REAL GOAL? THE 'I'-PRINCIPLE.

The word 'I' has the advantage of taking you direct to the core of your self. But you must be doubly sure that you will no longer return to identification with the body.

By reducing objects into Consciousness or happiness, you come only to the brink of experience. Reduce them further into the 'I'-principle; and then 'it', the object, and 'you', the subject, both merge into experience itself. Thus, when you find that what you see is only yourself, the 'seeing' and 'objects' become mere empty words.

When you say the object cannot be the subject, you should take your stand not in any of the lower planes, but in the ultimate subject 'I' itself.

In making the gross world mental, the advaitin is an idealist. But he does not stop there. He goes further, examining the 'idea' also and proves it to be nothing but Consciousness. Thus he goes beyond even the idealist's stand.

The realist holds that matter is real and mind is unreal, but the idealist says that mind is real and matter is unreal. Of the two, the idealist's position is better; for when the mind is taken away from the world, the world is not. Therefore, it can easily be seen that the world is a thought form. It is difficult to prove the truth of the realist's stand; for dead matter cannot decide anything.

The advaitin goes even further. Though he takes up the stand of the idealist when examining the world, he goes beyond the idealist's position and proves that the world and the mind, as such, are nothing but appearances and the Reality is Consciousness.

Perception proves only the existence of knowledge and not the existence of the object. Thus the gross object is proved to be non-existent. Therefore, it is meaningless to explain subtle perceptions as a reflection of gross perceptions. Thus all perceptions are reduced to the ultimate 'I'-principle, through knowledge.

When a Jnyānin takes to activities of life, he 'comes out' with body, sense organs or mind whenever he needs them; and he acts, to all appearances, like an ordinary man, but knowing full well, all the while, that he is the Reality itself. This is not said from the level of the Absolute.

23. WHAT IS MEANT BY 'NATURAL STATE'?

Without a thought or a feeling, the ordinary man knows himself to be the body and claims all its activities. In the same way, a Jnyānin, without a thought or a feeling, knows that he is the Reality – expressing itself in all perceptions, thoughts and feelings, without a change.

What you call *experience* is the real 'I'-principle, shining in its own glory, beyond the realm of the mind. The use of the word 'realization' as an action is wrong, since it brings with it a sense of limitation by time.

You can never become conscious of an object unless you are 'self-conscious', beyond the realm of the mind. So even when you say you are conscious of an object, you mean you are conscious of the knowledge of the object, further reduced into knowledge alone, and again reduced into the subjective 'I'-principle or Experience itself.

This means that you are always in your real centre.

28th December 1950

24. WHAT IS MEANT BY 'SVABHĀVA'?

'Svabhāva' means one's own real nature. All activities, like perceiving, doing etc., are 'asvabhāva' – the opposite of one's real nature.

Svabhāva is knowledge without object, or happiness without object. For you are knowledge itself, or happiness itself, and cannot know anything else.

25. WHAT HAPPENS WHEN I SAY 'I KNOW' A THING?

You actually transform the thing into knowledge. At the moment of knowing, you realize yourself in fact. Knowing a thing means you absorb it into you.

Similarly, loving a thing also means you absorb it into yourself. Hence, knowing and loving actually destroy all illusion, all separateness.

26. WHAT IS THE END OF AN IGNORANT MAN'S ACTIVITY OF KNOWING?

The end of all knowing is pure knowing itself, or 'vēdānta' (the end of knowledge), or the 'I'-principle. Knowing proves only knowledge, and not the object as is ordinarily understood.

In every perception, you are there as that and that alone. All the mischief of wrong identification is done only after the event.

27. I CANNOT BE LIBERATED BY KNOWING MY EXISTENCE ASPECT ALONE. WHY?

Both the *cit* [consciousness] and *ānanda* [happiness] aspects have also to be known. You must also know that all these three are one and the same, and that it is your real self. Thus transcending the three aspects, you reach the Reality beyond.

According to Vēdānta, the Reality can be expressed only by negative imports; because it is nameless and attributeless. But it expresses itself in all names and forms.

29th December 1950

28. HOW TO RECONCILE THE SPIRITUAL AND WORLDLY ASPECTS OF ONE'S LIFE?

The world is examined and proved to be non-existent, through your own experiences:

1. By comparing impartially the dream and waking state experiences, and finding them to be exactly similar.

2. By proving that the objective world has no existence, independently of the subject 'I' or Consciousness.

You understand this fact, and accept it completely and unreservedly. Think about it more intensely, until it descends into your heart, becoming experience itself. Then you become what you mean by 'jīvan-mukta', and all your problems automatically cease.

To an ordinary man, life constitutes actions, perceptions, thoughts and feelings – one of these alone being experienced at any given time. In other words, you stand detached from all activities, excepting the one in which you seem engaged at the given time.

To this list of four categories [actions, perceptions, thoughts and feelings], the spiritual man adds just one more, which indeed is the most important one: 'Consciousness'. This last one is doubly important; because, over and above its importance as a separate entity, it shines in and through the four categories already mentioned. You are simply asked to direct to the consciousness aspect the attention legitimately due to it. This is all.

When you are engaged in thought, you are not engaged in action, perception or feeling. When engaged in action, you are not engaged in thought, feeling or perception. So also, when you are engaged in knowing, you cannot be engaged in any other kind of activity.

The presence and recognition of subjective Consciousness, your real centre, is the one thing needed to make your life possible and connected. Make it so, by knowing that knowing principle to be your real centre. You never go outside it, and you can never leave it, even if you will. This does not deny or negate your worldly life, as is ordinarily supposed, but makes it richer, firmer, truer and more successful.

To have deep peace and not to be disturbed from it, even for a moment, is the ardent desire of everyone. For this, you have necessarily to be at a centre which does not change. That is the real 'I'-principle or Consciousness. To *be* it and to establish oneself there is the end and aim of life. This alone makes real life possible.

30th December 1950

29. HOW CAN AN ORDINARY MAN ATTAIN RENUNCIATION?

When you are engaged in any action, thought or other activity, all the world except for that one activity is dead, so far as you are concerned. This can really be called vairāgya or detachment. Therefore, you are always in perfect dispassion, and that again in the most natural and effortless manner.

30. HOW TO ATTAIN ĀTMA-TATTVA?

Ātma-tattva [the truth of self] is not something to be imported or acquired; but it already *is*, as the real 'I'-principle. If you once recognize it and turn to it earnestly, it begins to enlighten you and does not stop till you are led on to the very core of your being and are established there.

31. HOW IS THE SPIRITUAL LIFE OF A LIBERATED SOUL RECONCILED WITH HIS PHENOMENAL LIFE?

The spiritual life of a liberated soul is part and parcel of his life here, and not something separate from it. That oneness alone makes his life meaningful and an integral whole.

In the Rāmāyaṇa epic, the monkey king Bāli possessed a boon by whose power he took over to himself half the strength of every adversary he met. So also when *Ātma-tattva* [the truth of self] is once recognized and accepted, it begins to gain additional strength from every experience, worldly or unworldly, viewed and analysed in the light of the Truth. It comes into every thought and takes possession of it unnoticed (without a thought).

32. HOW TO BECOME DISPASSIONATE?

Dispassion is not only possible, but is present in all your states. You can see it, if you direct your attention that way.

You say you are attached to objects in the waking state. But what happens to that attachment, when you go into the dream state? Likewise, what happens to the objects of the dream state, when you come back to the waking state? Leaving these two states, you go into the deep sleep state, where there are no objects at all.

So there is dispassion throughout; and there is no necessity to cultivate it. Even in the waking state, when you are thinking of one object, are you not dispassionate as far as the rest of the world is concerned?

33. HOW CAN OUR EVERYDAY CONDUCT ITSELF BE OUR TEACHER?

We have only to get our everyday conduct properly examined and explained, in the light of the Truth. For this we need a Guru. By hearing our own daily experiences correctly, logically and clearly explained by the Guru himself, we immediately visualize our real centre, the 'I'-principle.

This is found to be present in feelings, thoughts, perceptions and actions. So the 'I' can certainly be none of these, 'as they are'. Ātma-tattva is neither attached nor detached, because there can be nothing beside it.

Any object, once known, remains only as Knowledge. It gets immediately transformed into pure Knowledge. If afterwards you begin to think of it as an object again, with some kind of interest in it, and come down and explain it in its own plane, you certainly go out of your real centre and require immediate correction.

31st December 1950

34. IS THERE CONSCIOUSNESS IN DEAD MATTER?

The question is absurd. Dead matter or body does not exist in its own right, but exists only as the object of the perceiver. It is the perceiver who lights up the object with his consciousness. In other words, his consciousness appears limited in the form of the body, or the body is his consciousness itself. But Consciousness cannot be divided. So it is the whole Consciousness itself. Therefore the question is absurd, on the face of it.

Yōgins, while reading the thoughts of others, read only the gross part of the mind concerned. They give their own interpretations of what they perceive, since the knowledge part of the thoughts can never be objectified or read.

When you know any object, you stand as Consciousness; and the object also cannot help appearing as Consciousness, since Consciousness cannot perceive anything but Consciousness. Or, in other words, when you rise to the level of Consciousness to examine the object, it is also transformed into Consciousness and its objectivity disappears.

So objects cannot exist as such, when you stand as Consciousness. While everything shines by the light of Consciousness, Consciousness does not require any other light, because it is self-luminous.

The term 'ghaṭākāsha' [the limited space in a pot] is wrong; since ghaṭākāsha can never be separated from 'mahākāsha' [the unlimited totality of space and time], excepting by words. But at a lower level, it can be said that bodies abide in mind and mind in Consciousness.

Nothing can limit Consciousness. A beginner in the spiritual path can, as a preliminary course, conceive that Consciousness is in him first. But when he becomes centred in Consciousness, the inside and outside vanish, so far as he is concerned; and he is lifted up to Consciousness pure.

Look at your image in a mirror. What is inside or outside your image, and all through it? Nothing but the mirror. So also, there is nothing but Consciousness in the object.

It is in *me* that thoughts arise, and in thoughts that bodies arise. So, compared to the 'I'-principle, the gross world is evidently very, very small; and can never exist as such, along with the 'I'.

It is wrong to say that the world exists in thoughts, or that thoughts exist in the 'I'; because gross forms as such vanish when thoughts appear, and thoughts become Consciousness when they touch it. Nothing is inert or jaḍa; but all is Consciousness appearing as limited, and even that apparent limitation is Consciousness itself.

Thus Reality is seen existing here and now – in you, in and beyond all states. It only *appears* as if it is tagged on to something else like body, senses or mind. Eliminate that 'tagged-on' part and you remain in your self, the real centre. But when you try to eliminate the apparently unreal parts from Consciousness, you find that each of them is mysteriously transformed into that Consciousness itself, leaving nothing to be eliminated. This method takes you direct to the natural state.

35. One of the shāstraic methods to reach the Reality

Certain shāstras hold that everything – from intellect down to the gross body – is dead, inert matter, as it is. They ask you to get away from all that matter and get to Ātmā in its pure form, in a state called the *nirvikalpa* state (samādhi).

In that state, there is no sense of bondage, it is true. But, coming out of that state, you find the same world. To find a solution to this, you have to examine the world again, in the light of the experiences you had in samādhi. Then you find that the same Reality that was discovered in samādhi is found expressed in the objects also, as name and form. And that name and form, which the shāstras also call māyā, are nothing but the Reality itself. Thus you find yourself to be one with the world, and all doubts cease.

Before beginning to examine this world, you must necessarily take your stand on some changeless ground which is best known to you. The best known of all things to you is Consciousness, which is also self-luminous. It is your real self, and never something possessed by you. Things known by the mind are liable to be mistaken. But as regards the fact of your being conscious, there can never be any mistake.

What we ordinarily call the 'consciousness of an object' is only mind-consciousness. This, when further examined, gives up that limitation also and becomes pure Consciousness. The Consciousness of an object is itself part of the object experienced. Try to reject all but Consciousness from that experience. Then you find that whatever you turn to is immediately transformed into Consciousness, leaving nothing at all to be rejected.

36. Realization is only here and now.

Only know it and hold on to it, till it becomes your natural state.

37. HOW CAN SOUND BE UTILIZED AS A MEDIUM OF ENQUIRY TO REACH THE ABSOLUTE?

It has four distinct stages:

1. *Vaikharī* or gross sound. Here consciousness appears limited by the audible word. It is practised by repetition of a mantra by word of mouth, audible to one's own ears.
2. *Madhyamā:* Here consciousness appears limited by the inaudible word. It is practised by mental repetition of a mantra, inaudibly, in contemplation of an idea.
3. *Pashyantī* represents that pure idea which is capable of being expressed in different languages, but which remains languageless all along. This limitation is binding only when viewed from the mental plane; and it really takes one to the very brink of the Absolute, or to the Absolute itself when correctly understood.
4. *Parā* is pure Consciousness itself, or myself. Every sound or word, when traced in the above sequence, leads to the Reality, or the 'I'-principle.

An elephant is the best object for concentration for those who find it difficult to fix their mind on the form of their iṣhṭa-dēva. This is why meditation on Gaṇapati (the elephant god) brings one to siddhi easily.

5th January 1951

38. WHO EXISTS? I ALONE.

Actions, perceptions, thoughts and feelings cannot be independent. The 'I'-principle alone stands independent of everything else; and present in all these, unattached.

It is the mind that is said to be the knower or witness of gross objects. But the mind cannot come down to the gross to bear witness to it or to know it. The gross has to be transformed into the subtle, if it has to be witnessed by the mind. Or in other words, the mind can never witness the gross, but only the subtle. That is, the gross exists only in mere words, because the mind's knowledge is the only evidence of its existence as gross. Therefore the gross, as gross, has no existence at all.

Similarly, the 'I'-principle is said to be the witness of thoughts. The 'I' cannot come down to the mind's plane to witness the thoughts. But thoughts get transformed into pure Consciousness in order to be witnessed by the 'I'-principle; and Consciousness is the real nature of the 'I'-principle. Therefore it means: 'I know myself.' If one applies the same argument here also, it is evident that thought is nothing but Consciousness or the 'I'.

Therefore, all that appears – gross or subtle – is nothing but myself alone. Or in other words, in all activity or inactivity, it is 'I' alone that shine.

6th January 1951

39. POET TENNYSON ON KNOWLEDGE

The poet Tennyson says: Pursue 'knowledge, like a sinking star, beyond the utmost bound of human thought'. It will take you a long way if you think deeply about what Tennyson meant by this statement.

'Sinking star' may mean this. Sinking implies relaxation. You have only to retreat and retreat into the 'I'-principle, and rest there. Allow yourself therefore to be led on. Sink, sink, sink… Sink from the body, sink from the senses, and sink from the mind…

Aṣhṭāvakra says, in a similar context:

> yadi dēhaṁ pṛthak-kṛtya citi viśrāmya tiṣṭhasi .
> adhunai 'va sukhī śāntō bandha-muktō bhaviṣyasi ..

Aṣhṭāvakra-samhitā, 1.4

This means: 'Separating body from you, if you take rest in Consciousness, you stand liberated here and now.'

7th January 1951

40. WHAT IS THE TEST OF EXPERIENCE?

Examine your experience always, and ask yourself whether it changes in time or space. If it is found to change, advance further till you come to that experience from which you can never change, even for a moment, even if you try. That is then no experience either, but your real nature itself.

8th January 1951

41. WHAT IS THE RELATIONSHIP BETWEEN GOD AND MYSELF?

God, you say, is omnipresent, omnipotent, omniscient, and so on. This clearly means he cannot be confined to a body. Because he has these attributes, he has to possess a cosmic mind; and there must be a cosmic world also, for the cosmic mind to function in.

But the real 'I'-principle goes beyond body and mind, and therefore beyond everything objective; and so beyond God also. Nothing else exists beside it. It is therefore attributeless brahman.

For God to become brahman, he has to give up all the attributes mentioned above; and then he stands as one with the 'I'-principle.

9th January 1951

42. WHAT IS AN EXPERIENCE?

An experience is composed of two parts:

1. the background, which is the Reality itself; and
2. the expression, which is only a superimposition of the mind and senses upon the background Reality.

In examining any experience to see what it is, we must give up the expression part of it as belonging entirely to the mind and senses, and take only the background which alone is permanent and real. Thus examined, every experience reduces itself to the ultimate Reality.

In any experience, the expression is the objective part and the background is the subjective part or the Reality behind it.

The test of every experience is to see whether it is strictly *subjective* or *objective*. The subjective alone is real and the objective all illusion.

Ākāsha, though not perceptible to the senses, is certainly conceivable by the mind. So it is really objective in nature. If we take out of ākāsha this last taint of objectivity, it ceases to be dead and inert, becomes self-luminous, and it immediately shines as its background – the Reality.

43. WHO LIVES REALLY?

We generally say that every man lives. If the term 'man' refers to the changeless 'I'-principle (and it cannot refer to anything else), we are guilty of a contradiction in terms. The changeless 'I'-principle can never undergo such changes as birth and death.

Don't we speak of 'my past life' and 'my future life'? It is clear from these that the 'I'-principle is beyond birth and death. For in these statements, we imply that the 'I'-principle is present before birth and after death. How then can birth and death pertain to the 'I'-principle?

Therefore, the real 'I'-principle alone lives. The ignorant man believes that either the body or the mind lives, while in fact each of them dies at the end of every perception or thought. But the 'I'-principle continues unchanged through all thoughts and perceptions, lighting them up as well.

Therefore, the ignorant man who identifies himself with body and mind is dying every moment, along with every perception or thought. And the Jnyānin, who identifies himself with the changeless 'I'-principle, alone really lives and knows no death.

The body idea or the ego has to die, in order that *you* may really live. In this sense, it is the Jnyānin alone that really lives, and knows he lives. His advice to every man is: 'Die, in order to live.' In other words, annihilate the personal element, or ego, in order that the impersonal element may not appear shrouded. This is realization – establishing oneself in the Reality.

44. WHY DID THE SHĀSTRAS PREFER METRICAL FORM AS THE MEDIUM FOR DISCUSSION OF THE TRUTH?

Truth is not expressible in words; it can only be hinted at. Prose is generally suited for precise and definite expositions within the realm of the intellect.

In the shāstras which deal with the Truth, the reader is only to be helped to separate himself from all that is not the Reality; and his attention is drawn to the inconceivable Reality by mere suggestions, leaving much of the Truth unsaid.

In this process of drawing attention to the Reality, the Ācārya is in a plane beyond the reach of the intellect; and the expositions also come as spontaneous inspiration from the Absolute, against a background of simple harmony far beyond intellectual grasp.

Under these conditions, the verse form is naturally preferred for exposition of the Truth in the shāstras; because the metrical harmony gradually leads the way to the divine harmony, to which attention is being drawn. And that is the Reality itself.

10th January 1951

45. How is the subject and the object one and the same Reality?

I act, I perceive, I think, I feel; and I also remain all alone in my own glory. It is this unattached 'I'-principle itself that appears in the acting, perceiving, thinking and feeling – while still remaining unattached and unchanged.

But the ignorant man wrongly attributes all these activities to this 'I'-principle', and at the same time admits without hesitation that the 'I' is never-changing.

I am unaffected by any of these apparent activities. So I appear in my own glory, without a change, even in all apparent activities. This shows that all these activities are unreal. And this unreality can be seen if we look at these apparent activities from a subjective standpoint.

Now looking at objects, we find that the ordinary man's experience is that the unknown subsequently becomes known. Examining this statement more closely, we find that the 'unknown as unknown' is certainly not the 'known as known'. Because, in what we call the 'known', there is so much of our own superimposition – such as name, form, dimensions and numerous other attributes – heaped upon the 'unknown'. But the 'unknown', on the other hand, has only one general superimposition – namely the characteristic of being unknown – made upon the 'thing in itself'.

So the 'thing in itself', or the Reality, was called unknown when viewed from the sphere of the known object. Or in other words, it was the Reality itself that appeared as the unknown and as the known, without undergoing any change in itself. That is, the Reality is neither the unknown nor the known, but is the background of both.

Thus, the subjective 'I'-principle and the 'objective Reality' are one and the same. In other words, the ultimate subject devoid of its sense of subjectivity and the object devoid of its objectivity are one and the same Reality itself.

46. WHAT IS MEANT BY 'WATER DOES NOT FLOW'?

Water as water, or as the element water, is both in the flowing water as well as in the stagnant water. So the flowing-ness or the stagnancy does not go into the make of water. Therefore, water does not flow, nor does it stagnate.

Similarly, the 'I'-principle is both in activity and in inactivity. Therefore it is neither active nor inactive. The 'I'-principle shines unchanged: before, during and after every activity or inactivity.

This method, of understanding the objective world and the 'I', not only establishes one's self in the right centre, but also destroys the samskāras relating to them.

11th January 1951

47. THE 'THING IN ITSELF' IS BEYOND THE KNOWN AND THE UNKNOWN.

When the unknown is sensed, something objective comes in. When you try to objectify the Reality, you first superimpose form upon it; and upon this most general form, innumerable other details are superimposed, by one or more of the sense organs. This is how an object is visualized.

The form never exists independently of the sense organ, and so it can never exist outside the sense organ which perceives it. What we know in a perception is only our own superimposition, including our own samskāras; and it is not the Reality at all, which of course is not perceivable. The thing in itself – the Reality – transcends both the known and the unknown.

All objects, thoughts and feelings are known through the senses or the mind. But I always know that 'I am'. This knowledge is not obtained through any sensory organ or agent, and so it is called *direct knowledge*.

Looking more closely, we find that even in sensory perception, it is only direct knowledge that is experienced. When I say I know an object, the object is reduced in terms of knowledge to knowledge itself, and can no longer be called an object. As knowledge, it can have no limitation either, there being nothing other than knowledge existing beside it.

So, what actually happens, even in sensory perceptions, is that the self (Consciousness) knows the self (Consciousness). Every sensory perception is in fact direct knowledge. Thus, when you come to knowledge, no object can exist as such. The object is only an object of the sense organs, and never the object of knowing. *Knowledge can know only knowledge*.

When a disciple retreats consciously from his body, senses and mind to his innermost self – pure Consciousness – knowledge dawns; and he is said to have realized. When knowledge dawns, objects and senses vanish. The same process also repeats itself during every sensory perception; and you always know nothing but the Reality.

> viṣayaṅṅaḷkk˘ aṙiyappeṭuṁpōṟuṁ sattayilla .
> [Objects have no existence, even when known.]
>
> jñāta sattayuṁ illa .
> [Even what is known does not as such exist.]

Objects have no existence even when known; since every perception brings only direct knowledge of the self, proving only the Reality behind all. So you stand self-realized.

48. *BHAGAVAD-GĪTĀ*, 2.16

> nā ’satō vidyatē bhāvō nā ’bhāvō vidyatē sataḥ …

The existent can never go out of existence, and the non-existent can never come into existence. This is the meaning of the verse. The test of the Reality is whether it disappears or not. According to this test, the only thing that never disappears is the ‘I’-principle or ‘Consciousness’.

Perceptions can exist only if there are external objects. But it has been proved already that objects as such have no existence. The Reality can never be an object. So it follows that even perceptions are not perceptions at all.

Similarly examining the subject, we find that the body, senses and mind are also mere empty words, having no independent existence. Each in turn gets reduced into the ultimate 'I'-principle or 'Consciousness', which alone is real.

Therefore, I alone am shining in my own glory at all times, without change.

13th January 1951

49. THE REALITY IS BEYOND THE KNOWN AND THE UNKNOWN.

The unknown is nowhere in existence. At a higher level, it has to be said that nothing is known either. So everything is beyond the known and the unknown and therefore is the Reality.

50. WHY SUCH OPEN TALK?

A disciple asked: Why was secrecy so strictly observed in expounding the Truth in the old shāstras?

Gurunāthan: Evidently, for fear of jeopardizing established religion and society. Religion had no place except in duality and social life. It was the prime moving force of social life in ancient times. But the concept of religion could not stand the strict logic of vēdāntic Truth.

The sages of old, who recognized the great need of religion in phenomenal life, expounded the ultimate Truth under a strict cover of secrecy, thus enabling religion to play its role in lower human society. But religion in the present day world has been dethroned in many ways, and ungodly cults have come into existence in large numbers.

Therefore it is high time now to throw off the veil of secrecy, and broadcast the whole Truth in the face of the world which has already advanced much, intellectually.

51. WHAT IS THE OBJECT OF KNOWLEDGE?

Nothing. Because, when the so called object comes into the plane of knowledge, it loses its objectivity and becomes knowledge itself, or one with the knower. Just as, in the plane of the senses, the form which is supposed to have been perceived loses its form and becomes seeing itself. Form is nothing but seeing.

Knowing is always directed to the Reality. The object of knowledge is always the Reality – if the Reality can ever be an object. Therefore, it is only the Reality that is known, in every case.

52. WHAT ARE NAME AND FORM? AND HOW TO TRANSCEND THEM?

Being attracted by the existence aspect of the Absolute everywhere, we start to examine what it is and immediately utilize our senses to do the job. The senses at once project their own respective objects, and superimpose their own particular form upon the existence 'sensed', attributing the permanence of the Absolute to the forms thus superimposed. In this way, we are deluded into the thought that the forms thus created are permanent, and we lose sight of the Absolute.

In order to get beyond this delusion, we must go beyond these forms, as well as the mind. Then we will see the Reality as one with our Consciousness.

On the subjective side, there is Consciousness; and on the objective side, there is existence alone. Existence and Consciousness being two aspects of the same Reality, the subject-object relationship vanishes. Existence may be said to be objective, but really is not. Because that which exists is really neither inside nor outside.

Names can be given only to objects. Objects have been proved to be nothing but Consciousness. Therefore the name also vanishes completely, or all names are the names of Consciousness.

53. WHAT IS THE RIGHT APPROACH TO THE SOLUTION OF ANY SPIRITUAL QUESTION?

The answer can never be found in the same plane as the question itself. When you look from the next higher plane, the question as such disappears altogether.

The mind is incapable of explaining itself in its own plane. So, in order to explain it, you must rise to the background – the plane of Consciousness. Looking from there, you see the mind with all its doubts and difficulties transformed into Consciousness; and nothing ever remains over which needs to be explained.

The mind is fitful or changing. Nothing but a permanent something can venture to examine anything changing. The same rule applies to the relative plane also. Relatively speaking, seeing is more permanent than form, and knowledge is more permanent than the senses. So the senses can well be utilized for a preliminary examination of the variety in objects. Similarly, knowledge can be utilized to examine the various perceptions, thoughts and feelings.

A Jnyānin's apparent talking is no talking and his apparent silence is no silence, from his own permanent stand. He is always at the changeless, beyond all sense of relativity.

54. WHO IS A JĪVAN-MUKTA?

Every man is a jīvan-mukta [free within, while living as a person in the world]; but he has only to know it.

The spontaneous and unaffected conduct of every man proves beyond the shadow of a doubt that he is always a jīvan-mukta. He has only to know it. And that is called realization. His conduct and words show that the 'I'-principle is not at all affected by actions, perceptions, thoughts and feelings – all of which he is called upon to witness and apparently participate in, from time to time.

Yōga does not destroy the false identification with the body. It takes into account only the waking state experiences for its consideration. So its conclusions can never be complete or unassailable.

15th January 1951

55. HOW SHALL ONE ACT AFTER REALIZATION?

The correct answer to the question is that there is no action after realization. Therefore the question does not arise.

But the question can be taken up at a lower level and answered differently. The world and its activities – including that of the body which you call yours – may continue in the usual manner, apparently as though nothing has happened.

By being established in the Truth, you are not going to get any definite advice about your future activities. But the light from the centre will so react on your mind that eventually it will run only in the proper groove. The world of your perceptions will henceforward be illuminated by an entirely new light and significance. Your way of life will definitely improve and will shine on a clear and new basis – being absolutely purposeless and goalless – because you have become impersonal, and your activities can be assigned to no criterion whatsoever.

The world and Ātmā are only apparent contradictions. Whatever you assume yourself to be, so you will see outside you.

> If you stand as the body, you see only gross objects.
> If you stand as the mind, you see only subtle objects.
> If you stand as the self, you see only Consciousness.
>
> A bhakta sees all as bhaktas, everywhere outside.
> A yōgin sees all as yōgins, everywhere outside.
> A jnyānin sees all as jnyānins, everywhere.

56. IS THERE ANY RELATIONSHIP BETWEEN WEALTH AND LIBERATION?

Shāstras and teachers of old say, with one voice: 'If anyone, at the height of worldly happiness or at the depth of desperation, is able to direct his mind with one pointed attention to the right Absolute, he may very well be said to have gone a long way towards the establishment of his own right centre.'

Wealth, unless one possesses discrimination, is often supposed to be an obstacle to spiritual progress. But if a wealthy man has the good fortune to take to the spiritual quest earnestly, he is blessed indeed. He easily rises to the very top and becomes a beacon light of spirituality. Such are the great seers like *Shrī Janaka*, *Shrī Rāma*, *Shrī Kṛiṣhṇa* etc., who were all jīvan-muktas as well as virtual rulers of great kingdoms. Innumerable sannyāsins were instructed and initiated by them into the Truth.

When a wealthy man gets to the Truth, he has transcended much of what may possibly tie him down. Though still in possession of all the worldly objects of pleasure, he has found them to be non-existent and meaningless, in the light of the absolute Truth.

Thus, anything that inflates the ego can also be used to attenuate it as well. When a wealthy man finds that what is sought by wealth, namely happiness, is not to be gained by wealth, he turns his attention away from wealth, though he may still continue to possess it. So, in order to gain that happiness, he seeks other means; and having gained it, he finds that it is not 'wealth' that is an obstacle to spiritual progress but our sense of possession of it.

For a spiritual aspirant, there can never be an obstacle.

57. WHAT IS THE PLACE OF WOMEN IN SPIRITUALITY?

It is said that women cannot rise to the Absolute as easily as men. But we find that in ancient times many men reached the highest by following the instructions given by women like Cūḍālā [in the *Yōga-vāsiṣhṭha*] or Gārgī [in the Upaniṣhads]. And there are many other such examples.

58. LORD KṚIṢHṆA'S WAYS OF RAISING HIS DEVOTEES TO THE HIGHEST TRUTH WERE PECULIAR AND EXCEPTIONAL.

His method was aimed at capturing the hearts of his devotees by intelligent and skilful means; and thus purifying their hearts, as a result of the reaction from him as self-luminous Truth or *prēma* (objectless love). No other example of a teacher of Kṛiṣhṇa's type is known in the past.

1. Lord Kṛiṣhṇa's stealing butter and curds from the houses of the Gopīs was not done for greed or self-enjoyment. He was the son of the king of the cowherds and had plenty at home. His object

was evidently to keep the Gopīs incessantly thinking of him in some form or other.

The reaction to those thoughts – since it came from him, the impersonal – was so pure and elevating that the Gopīs were lifted from level to level, gradually, without any effort on their own part.

2. There is the story of Kṛiṣhṇa's pretended headache… the refusal of the devoted wives of Kṛiṣhṇa to give him some dust from under their feet to be applied to Kṛiṣhṇa's forehead, as prescribed by the disguised physician (Nārada)… the subsequent transportation of cartloads of earth trampled under the feet of the Gopīs of Vṛindāvana for their Lord Kṛiṣhṇa, for the same purpose, without a remorseful thought… Kṛiṣhṇa's recovery… the chiding of the Gopīs at first by the wives of Kṛiṣhṇa… the subsequent humiliation and enlightenment of the wives… and their acceptance of the Gopīs as the real devotees of their Lord.

   The refusal of the wives of Kṛiṣhṇa was dictated by their ego, and the ready compliance of the Gopīs was due to the absence of the ego in them.

3. And then again there is the story of Arjuna… the story of Arjuna's Gāṇḍīva being snatched away by a small monkey when Arjuna's thoughts were inflated by the ego, which amounted to an insult to Shrī Rāma and his army of monkeys… Arjuna's recovering the Gāṇḍīva when he was made to admit his egotistic thoughts and to make amends for them, by bowing and praying for pardon before the apparently insignificant monkey, who was but a representative of the invincible army of monkeys that went with Shrī Rāma to kill Rāvaṇa and conquer Lanka.

   The appearance of the monkey, his snatching away the Gāṇḍīva from the hands of Arjuna and the latter's subsequent humiliation were all the tricks of Kṛiṣhṇa meant for killing the egoism in Arjuna. Here also, Arjuna's ego was annihilated in a most ingenious manner.

Though the devotees' thoughts and actions would appear to have been tainted, the reaction from Kṛiṣhṇa, the impersonal, was so pure and forceful that it had the instantaneous and most mysterious effect of lifting them from level to level to the right Absolute.

59. WHAT IS RENUNCIATION?

'Renunciation' or 'sannyāsa' is not likely to annihilate one's samskāras, even after the attainment of nirvikalpa samādhi in the yōgic fashion.

The tendency for renunciation shows a diffidence, or unwillingness, or fear, to look straight at the apparent world and analyse it to its very source. So the sannyāsin sometimes chooses to get away from the apparently more dangerous parts of the world, relying upon his own mind and intellect which are themselves parts of the world and which he must ultimately renounce.

Thus, as the field of his enquiry is incomplete, his renunciation is also incomplete. The result of such an enquiry can never be satisfying. The enquiry can be complete only when he is able to visualize the Reality of his own self, even in the apparent variety.

To achieve this, the sannyāsin, even after attaining the nirvikalpa samādhi of the yōgin, has to labour afresh on the path of direct knowledge.

60. WHAT IS THE FITTEST OF ALL INSTRUMENTS?

Consciousness is the fittest of all your instruments for examining the world – if it may be called an 'instrument'.

The sense organs sense the object and Consciousness knows it, immediately transforming it into Consciousness itself.

You are the perpetual knower; and the known can never tempt the knower, which is yourself. See yourself as such and the whole trouble disappears.

61. WHAT HAPPENS TO OBJECTS WHEN KNOWN?

In order to perceive anything, we must use any one of the five senses. Each sense returns the verdict that the thing is its particular object. That is to say that after the sense organ has sensed it as its own object, Consciousness faces the object and knows it. At the end of every function, knowledge dawns.

Just as each sense organ is capable of sensing only its own particular object, Consciousness also can know only Consciousness.

Thus, knowing the object means that the object is transformed into knowledge; and the object is no longer the object as before.

The objective counterpart of knowledge can only be knowledge. After every activity, knowledge dawns. This means that knowledge is the background of activity as well as of inactivity, just as it is in the interval between two perceptions when you stand all alone in your own glory.

When looked at through the eyes, the object appears as form (the counterpart of that sense organ); and when looked at through knowledge, the object appears as knowledge itself, since knowledge can have no other counterpart.

I know it = I know myself = I know the Truth = I am the Truth.

The background of objects and sense organs is the same. Similarly, the background of senses is also the same Consciousness or 'I'. Knowledge has nothing for its object except knowledge. With the seeing, form appears. But when you know the seeing subsequently, it becomes knowledge itself. So everything is transformed in terms of the instrument used.

Thus using Consciousness, everything is reduced or transformed into Consciousness. Even the statement 'I know' is wrong, because 'I' and knowledge are one. In experience or knowledge, both subject and object merge.

62. Progress on the path of devotion to a personal God

You approach God to get your desires fulfilled, one after another. This cuts at the root of your self-dependence and self-confidence, and makes you weaker and weaker day by day; till at last you become quite helpless and passive, without any power of initiative.

Seeing that most of your desires are not fulfilled, you are slowly disillusioned and finally dare even to dethrone the personal God. Then you begin to depend upon yourself and, looking back from that standpoint, continue to rise slowly and steadily.

When your earnestness is deep enough, you get a real teacher and you are gradually taken to the right Absolute.

20th January 1951

63. THE LIMITATIONS OF THE ACCEPTED PATHS

In our search for Truth, beginning with an examination of the world before us, we use as our instrument the faculty of reason. This reason can well be divided into two. One is lower reason, which is exercised by the mind in examining the mutual relationship of objects, from intellect down to the gross world. The other is higher reason or transcendental reason, which is exercised in examining the mind and its objects – gross or subtle – with a view to discover their real content.

There are usually three accepted paths to the Truth. They are the paths of *devotion*, *yōga* and *jnyāna*. Of these three, devotion and yōga deal only with relative things falling within the sphere of the mind and sense organs, taking into consideration only experiences in the waking state. Their findings, therefore, can only be partial and incomplete.

The jnyāna path looks from a broader perspective and comprehends within its scope both yōga and devotion. It takes into consideration the whole of life's experiences – comprised in the three states – viewed impartially. It demands a high degree of real devotion, in the sense that the aspirant has to have a high degree of earnestness and sincerity to get to the Truth. This is *real devotion, to Truth*; and it is infinitely superior to devotion to anything else, which can only be less than the Truth.

The yōgin controls, sharpens and expands the mind to its maximum possibilities, attaining samādhi and powers (or siddhis) on the way. But in the case of those who follow the jnyāna path, the mind is analysed impartially and minutely; and proved to be nothing other than pure Consciousness itself, beyond which there is no further power or possibility of development.

So it is through jnyāna alone that Truth can be visualized, while yōga and devotion only prepare the ground for it.

64. THE CONTENT OF DEEP SLEEP

Are you not annoyed when you are suddenly woken up from deep sleep? That is because you love deep sleep more than you love activity. Deep sleep is complete rest.

Egoism is the wrong identification of one's self with the body, senses and mind. To get to the Truth, one has to get the body, senses and mind separated from the 'I'-principle. This elimination, coupled with your finding your real centre, and establishing yourself there, is called 'realization'.

Consciousness never parts with you, in any of the three states. In deep sleep, you are conscious of deep rest or peace. Inference is possible only of those things which have not been experienced. The fact that you had a deep sleep or profound rest is your direct experience, and you only remember it when you come to the waking state. It can never be an inference. Experience alone can be remembered. The fact that you were present throughout the deep sleep can also never be denied.

The only three factors thus found present in deep sleep are Consciousness, peace and yourself. All these are objectless and can never be objectified. In other words they are all subjective. But there can be only one subject; and that is the 'I'-principle. So none of these three can be the result of inference; since they are all experience itself.

Prakṛiti in the guise of an old woman says to an earnest aspirant: 'Poor fool, thou diest!' Immediately, the spiritual aspirant retorts: 'Hush hag. Thou liest!' And in he walks to peace. A real aspirant should be bold and firm as the aspirant mentioned above in facing the ego at every step, to be assured of a steady progress to the right Absolute.

65. THE SPIRITUAL SIGNIFICANCE OF AN OIL LAMP BEING LIGHTED AT SUNSET AND SUNRISE IN HINDU HOMES

It has been shown that the Reality shines by itself in between two thoughts, two feelings, actions, perceptions, states, etc. So, symbolically speaking, there is the Reality, shining between day and night. It is that Reality that is symbolized by the light. The oil lamp is lighted to symbolize that Reality, shining between the two states. This objective light is meant to put you in mind of the subjective light of the Reality in you.

66. SIGNIFICANCE OF FAMILY POLLUTIONS (PULAVĀLĀYMAKAḶ)

The family pollutions of the Hindus have a similar significance. After the birth or death of an individual in a Hindu home, the inmates observe pollution rites for some days. This shows that these two occurrences are unwelcome, since they obscure the Reality. The 'I', which is beyond birth and death, is really degraded when supposed to be born or dead. It is for the atonement of this sin, and in order to remember the changeless Reality of the 'I'-principle, that one observes the pollution.

Going beyond the existence and non-existence of anātmā [objects], one reaches the Absolute. It is not enough if the world (both gross and subtle) is found to be unreal. The unreality or non-existence of the world, which remains as a samskāra, must also vanish, leaving you as absolute Truth alone.

But for a general shroud of ignorance, babies and children are very much akin to the Absolute, in their conduct and expressions. They speak of themselves in the third person; as if they are the subject, distinct and separate from their body. This is an apparent expression of the Absolute. To a child, everything is nameless as the Reality. But parents begin to bind them, by thrusting into their minds names, one after another, calling them knowledge.

The conduct of children is superficially almost similar to that of a jīvan-mukta; and is similar to wakefulness in deep sleep. For, though the jīvan-mukta appears to function just as an ignorant man does in the waking state, he does not get away from his centre of Consciousness, even for a moment, as in his deep sleep.

67. KARMA-SANNYĀSA AND KARMA-YŌGA

Karma-sannyāsa is the perfection of the supposed passive principle in man; and *karma-yōga* (the path of the house-holder) is the perfection of the active principle in man.

But realization is beyond both passivity and activity.

68. THE THREE STATES OF MAN EACH INDEPENDENT OF ONE ANOTHER

Deep sleep is usually said to be the cause of the dream and waking states. This is dependent upon the law of causality, which is misapplied here. A law obtains only in that particular state in which it operates, and it operates only between objects existing in that particular state. But if a law is to affect all three states, it must obtain in a common state, of which these three states are but parts.

The only thing common to these three states is the 'I'-principle, which permeates all of them and lights them up. This is no state at all and is beyond all laws and limitations. The 'I'-principle cannot be the cause of the three states; and much less can the deep sleep state be the cause of the other two states. Therefore, among the three states, there can never exist any causal relationship. Hence each state is independent in itself, and bears no relation whatsoever with the other two.

To examine the three states impartially, one has necessarily to take up a position not in any one of the three states, but as a witness to all the three, i.e. as the witnessing principle standing out of the three states. When you take your stand in the 'I'-principle and try to examine the three states, the states will not remain as such, but will be transformed into Consciousness. This proves all three states to be only illusion.

24th January 1951

69. WHY IS NOT DEEP SLEEP A CAUSE OF THE OTHER TWO STATES?

In the waking state, you can decide whether there is any connection between three objects A, B and C, *if* they are things perceived in the waking state itself. In the same state, these three objects are governed by the same order of time and the same law of causality.

Take the deep sleep state, dream state and waking state as three objects between which you want to know whether there is any connection or not. To do so, you have to see whether these three states are governed by the same order of time and by the same law of causality. But we find that it is not so. The time which exists in the waking state is different from the time which exists in the dream state. In deep sleep, there is no time. Therefore, there is no common order of time governing the three states. Time is the parent of the law of causality, and therefore there can never be a causal relationship existing between the three states.

Therefore, the deep sleep state can never be a cause of the other two states.

70. HOW DOES MEMORY FUNCTION?

Memory is an undeniable experience to the ordinary man. Unless there is a permanent principle equally connected with the past, the present and the future, the functions of memory, recognition and hope are impossible. So memory helps us to prove the existence of such a permanent principle behind our mental activities. Therefore let us discuss memory here, conceding the existence of the world, gross as well as subtle.

Memory functions by way of remembering past thoughts, activities and events. It is clearly a function of the mind. To justify its reality, it must satisfy two conditions. It must first be proved to have been present at the time of the thought referred to and must have known or witnessed it. And secondly, it must also be present at the time of the act of remembrance.

That memory is present when it appears is admitted. Memory, which is itself a thought form, cannot exist along with another thought; since you can never have two thoughts simultaneously. Therefore, memory by itself cannot recall a past thought.

A thought can be recalled only by that principle which perceived it at the time of its occurrence. Therefore, the 'I'-principle alone can recall a thought at any point of time. That principle – because it always knows the mental activities – is the changeless witness. It can never cease to be a witness at any time.

Recalling a past thought is a function different from the act of witnessing. That activity can never be attributed to the 'I'-principle. Then the question arises: how is a past thought remembered?

Well, there is an usurper in the picture. Just as he usurps the existence aspect, consciousness aspect and happiness aspect of the real 'I'-principle, and claims them to himself in his own activities in the relative sphere, he also claims the witnessing function to be his. Does he not say 'I think', 'I feel', 'I perceive', 'I do', and along with these functions does he not also say 'I know'? The usurper is the ego.

Because of the identification of the real 'I'-principle with body, senses and mind, he can very well play the role of the real 'I'-principle in his daily activities. Further the ego itself is a compound of Consciousness and body – gross or subtle. That makes it possible for the ego to steal the characteristics of the real 'I'-principle to some extent. Thus the ego remembers a past thought. When he so remembers, the real 'I'-principle stands behind, witnessing that mentation of memory also.

One thing has to be particularly borne in mind in this context. Memory helps us to see the witnessing principle. But we have no right now to go into a discussion relating to memory, the thought recollected and other things relevant to that thought, because we concede the existence of all things in the relative world.

The point at issue is how is it possible for the memory to recall past thoughts. Leave other things out of consideration for the present. The point is only to prove that there is a certain permanent principle standing behind every mental activity, witnessing it.

Because there is the possibility of confusion arising out of the function of memory, its function was taken up and discussed at this length; so that he who wishes to get established as the witness may not have any difficulty.

71. THE DIRECT METHOD EXPLAINED

1. By examination of the subjective element in man, from the body backwards to the 'I'-principle, it is proved to be pure Knowledge or Consciousness itself.
2. Similarly examining the gross objective world, it is found that since the gross object cannot exist even for a moment apart from the perception concerned, the object is clearly the perception itself.

> Similarly, taking one's stand in the mind and examining perceptions, it is found that perceptions are nothing but thoughts.
>
> Lastly, examining thoughts and feelings, by the use of vidyā-vṛitti or the 'functioning Consciousness', it is found that they are Consciousness itself, the ultimate subject.

Thus both subjective and objective worlds, when properly analysed, are reduced into the Ultimate – which is neither subject nor object. To know this beyond all doubt, and to establish oneself there, is the direct method.

72. What is a Sage?

A *Sage* is one who has experienced that the 'I'-principle, or Consciousness, is the only subjective and objective reality. In all apparent activities, he is concerned with Consciousness alone.

When one's attention is directed to Consciousness, the material part of perception drops away as unreal. It is *after* every perception that we are to emphasize the consciousness aspect of our activities. I know my actions, perceptions, thoughts, feelings; and I know myself also. So I am the ultimate knower always. But when I look from my own level of the 'I'-principle, the known disappears altogether and the knowership also ceases.

When the Sage takes to any activity, that activity is seldom preceded by a volition of the will, all his real interest being in Consciousness alone, which is involved in it. His deep conviction that Consciousness has not undergone any change by all these apparent manifestations keeps him at his centre and never disturbs him, as it does a sādhaka.

Just as the gold you purchase does not undergo any change in itself by being worked into a ring, so also Consciousness does not undergo any change by merely appearing as objects.

To a Sage, it might sometimes happen that from the first formless manifestation of Consciousness, he might go back to the unmanifested Consciousness itself, without coming to object perception at all.

Manifestation (or being known) implies Consciousness. When you say 'Consciousness manifests itself', immediately your attention is drawn to the Consciousness part of it. So also in the manifestation of objects. All manifestation proves the Consciousness aspect beyond doubt.

73. How is the unknown behind everything proved to be only one?

Whatever is perceived can be explained only in terms of the instruments used for the purpose of that perception. So their findings cannot be final. When, however, you withdraw to the 'I'-principle, or Consciousness, and examine the thing through it, the thing is found to be Consciousness or the 'I'-principle.

An instrument as such can never be the Absolute. The 'I'-principle is taken as an instrument only conventionally but is really no instrument at all. It can neither be a functioning principle.

To a Sage, the manifestation of Consciousness with or without form has the same significance, and both are immaterial so far as he is concerned, since he is always at his real centre.

26th January 1951

I perceive objects through the senses.

I perceive the senses through the mind
(taking mind and buddhi as one generic mind).

I perceive the mind by myself.

I am therefore the ultimate perceiver in all cases. When I stand as that and look back, the perceived disappears and is transformed into myself or Consciousness. When the perceived disappears, my perceivership also ceases and I remain as pure Consciousness.

Witnesshood or knowership is only in the relative sphere. But when the objective world is explained as Consciousness itself, I also get to pure Consciousness and the witnesshood then vanishes.

74. What is anubhava or experience?

Experience is the Absolute. Everybody has anubhava every moment of his daily life. At the end of every action, perception, thought or feeling, there is experience. But as it is beyond even the mind, we do not usually note it or understand it as it really is.

We wrongly attribute experience to the lower field of expression, namely feeling, which is the highest standard of worldly experience in our traffic with relative things. One has only to understand it correctly, and see it as the only Reality in this world.

Experience is that state (which is no state at all) where even feeling expires. In all experiences, there is nothing other than yourself, the real 'I'-principle. The ignorant man takes his feeling alone to be his anubhava or highest experience; since it is the highest in the scale of his relative experiences, in which alone he moves.

75. What is jnyānin?

Jnyānin [the one who knows] is anubhava [experience], or Truth, or the 'I'-principle. Thought must have an object, but Consciousness has none. Feeling must have an object, but anubhava has none.

The 'I'-principle is experience itself, and is the end of all the so-called worldly experiences. It is beyond subject-object relationship. It can never be brought down to the level of the mind, where only relative things can appear. So to experience Truth by feeling is impossible.

If you want misery, be a worldly man; and if you want happiness, be a spiritual man understanding that Happiness is in misery as well. You are really helpless in Happiness, because there is none other than Happiness at that moment either to give or to take. You are helped in misery, because the objects help you to prolong the misery.

'I am Happiness' is my real nature, at the impersonal level. But viewed from the relative sphere, the same thing appears as 'I am happy'.

31st January 1951

76. What are unity and diversity?

Unity is the cause of diversity and not the other way about. The 'thing in itself', the Reality, is beyond both diversity and unity.

1. Unity (of the subject) is the connecting link between everything in diversity.

2. It is only by standing in this unity that diversity is perceived. This means that it is the unity that lights up the diversity.
3. Unity is the deciding principle regarding the existence, qualities, properties etc. of any object in the diversity.
4. From a higher level, it is the background of all.

In this sense, the unity stands as the Reality. But when the unity is taken to be the opposite of diversity, as it is usually understood, the Reality must be said to be beyond both diversity and unity.

77. What is the 'thing' in the unknown and in the known?

1. (a) Before seeing, the thing could not have had form, since seeing was not there.

   (b) When seeing is completed, knowledge dawns and the form vanishes.

   (c) It is admitted that the thing, which was without form both before and after the seeing, could not have undergone any change during the seeing. During the seeing, there was neither the see-er nor the seen.

   So it was unknown during the seeing also. Thus the thing remains unknown in the past, present and future, when knowing is understood to mean sensory knowledge. Therefore it can never be the seen or known, as distinct from the unknown.

   Thus the unknown alone existing always cannot be called the unknown, without reference to the known, which is proved to be non-existent as such. Therefore the thing is beyond even the unknown and is the Reality itself.
2. The doer, the doing and the deed cannot exist simultaneously. When you take up any one of these positions you become that at once. So it is evident that you were really none of these, but only the background of all and changeless.
3. The past and future are produced by and dependent upon the present. When we examine more closely what we call the present, it vanishes into the past or future, leaving only an impercep-

tible point of time, which also flits into the past before you even perceive it.

So it comes to mean that the present remains only as a mere word: representing an agreement – so to say – between the past and the future, to provide a common meeting ground for them. So the '*now*' is nowhere to be seen, nor is the past nor the future.

Without the past, present and future, time cannot exist. If time is conceived as the background of the past, present and future, it is the Absolute itself.

78. How am I to order my life after realization?

Answer: After realization, you may live exactly as before. The answer is only in terms of how another man sees your activities of life, in both cases.

Subjectively, you have undergone a definite change, from your identification with the unreal to the identification with Reality. So you can no longer lose your equanimity and become desperate; because you know you are perfect and changeless.

After establishing yourself at that centre firmly, you will be able to engage in the usual activities of life even with interest, as an ordinary man does; leaving all interest and activities to the mind, senses and body, but never losing your centre in the least.

1st February 1951

79. How can the apparent 'I' progress to pure Consciousness?

To the ordinary man, the apparent 'I' is a compound of Consciousness and body – gross or subtle. Conceding for the time being the existence of the lower self, let us proceed to examine its composition, to eliminate from the 'I'-principle all the rest.

We see that the body acts, the senses perceive, and the mind thinks and feels. But the 'I' is found to be present in all these activities, knowing every one of them. So the first stage is that *I am the knower* of the body, senses and mind. I am standing separate from them: as the functioning witness or functioning Consciousness, in all activities.

Examining this witness, we find that occasionally we experience a state where all objects disappear, and Consciousness alone remains. That is to say, the functioning part vanishes and the second stage, *functionless Consciousness*, alone remains.

(For example, the sun shines. The ordinary man takes it to be a function. But so far as the sun is concerned, it is never a function but its very nature; because it can never remain even for a moment without shining. A function should necessarily have a beginning and an end.)

Thus taking our position in functionless Consciousness, the world as such disappears altogether, being transformed into Consciousness itself; proving thereby that even the manifested is Consciousness alone. Thus, the third stage is that knowing is not a function, but the nature of Consciousness.

Therefore, it is clear that the 'I'-principle has never been the perceiving Consciousness, but is pure Consciousness.

Through the path of devotion alone, it is possible to rise to the highest plane of objectless love, without adopting any separate jnyāna sādhana. But as far as the devotee is concerned, the object world and problems relating to it still remain to be solved or explained, to make his experience complete. He only forgets it completely in the flush of his deep devotion. Formerly, he used to perceive the world with its usual sense of reality. Until it is proved to be what it really is, there is always the danger of the object world being an impediment to his ultimate perception and establishment in his real centre.

Even after reaching the stage of objectless love through devotion, corresponding to pure Consciousness through jnyāna, one has yet to understand that this objectless love is but the expression of that which can never be expressed.

This light can be obtained only from the real Jnyānin, and so even at this late stage the devotee has to take direct instruction from the Kāraṇa-guru and go beyond. In this new light, all doubts about the world stand automatically solved; and he sees the world as nothing other than his subjective self.

In this connection, it is said that Shrī Caitanya, after long years of experience of so-called objectless love, had to take instruction about the Truth from one of the sages of Shrī Shankara's order, in order to get to the Absolute.

tanne maṟannōraṟivu tōnnīṭilō
pinne maṟaviyoru kālavuṁ varā .

Eṟuttacchan, Bhāgavatam, Tīrttha-yātra

Means: Knowledge that dawns on the subsidence of the ego can never cease to be.

80. YOU ARE KNOWLEDGE AND LOVE.

1. You do not know anything but yourself.
2. You do not love anything but yourself.

So both knowledge and love have yourself as their object. Therefore, you are pure Knowledge and Love.

81. I AS EXPERIENCE CAN HAVE NO OBJECT.

You are the background of all your emotions and passions. Feeling is the one word to denote all these. It means that feeling is their general background; and so it must be the Absolute, called '*rasa*'. Likewise, knowing is the background of all thoughts.

A man's thirst to know and to be happy proceeds from his real nature. He is happiness and knowledge. Knowing and feeling in their secondary senses may have an object; but in their correct sense, they can have no object at all.

Because that which goes into the make of all feelings, and always remains as their background, is what is called 'rasa'. We use the word 'feeling' to denote particular feelings such as anger, pride, etc. We use the one word 'feeling' to denote all feelings. So, feeling is the common background of all feelings. This pure feeling is called 'rasa'. It is the right Absolute.

Likewise, thoughts and perceptions are one when viewed as knowing, because knowing has to be present in all thoughts and perceptions. That again is the 'I'-principle, and that is pure Consciousness.

Similarly, all objects are one when viewed as existence.

2nd February 1951

82. KNOWING IS KNOWLEDGE ITSELF.

Take knowing as a function for the time being; and examine it along with the other four functions of doing, perceiving, thinking and feeling. We find that of all these, knowing is comparatively the most natural and effortless function. For the performance of the other four functions, different conditions and degrees of effort are essential.

The natural effortlessness of knowing, and the fact that it is always present, clearly prove it to be really the nature of the self; because this knowingness does not come and go like the other functions and does not part with the 'I'-principle, even for a moment. The 'I'-principle has always to be the knower; and since the same principle cannot be engaged in more than one function simultaneously, it stands as the Knower alone.

That thought which goes into the make of all thoughts is no thought. It transcends time. That which transcends space or time can be nothing other than the absolute Reality. Therefore all objects, thoughts and feelings are the Reality itself.

To think deeply means to bring in the higher reason.

3rd February 1951

83. IS THERE ANY RELATIONSHIP BETWEEN BODY AND CONSCIOUSNESS?

Actually there is no such relation to be established between them; since the body, when examined in the right perspective, is found to be Consciousness itself. Knowing a thing means transforming it into knowledge. And then you will have to say you know knowledge. That is absurd. Therefore it means that you are yourself alone.

84. REALIZATION

Realization consists in becoming deeply aware of the fact that you have never been in bondage. Because realization can never happen: it can never occur in time. To the question: 'When shall one realize?', the answer can only be: 'When the "*when*" dies.'

In your perceptions, you only see form, hear sound, and so on. Form, sound etc. by themselves do not prove or belong to any object. Each only proves and belongs to the particular sense organ concerned.

You can never have more than one perception at a time. Therefore, the projection of an object as a result of one perception – together with the innumerable other concepts which are joined on to it – is indeed a real impossibility.

So every perception, concept etc. proves and belongs to only that thing in itself which is beyond the senses and mind. That is to say it is the only Reality, behind all manifestation.

4th February 1951

85. DUALITY AND ADVAITIC EXPERIENCE

Question: Is it not in duality that the advaitic Truth is experienced? When the teacher expounds the advaitic Truth to the disciple, and when the disciple understands it, is there not duality? How then can it be said that the advaitic Truth transcends all duality?

Answer: When the teacher is talking with the intention of conveying an idea to you, if you direct attention to the language part – namely the pronunciation, intonation, words used, their arrangement, grammar, the structure of sentences etc. – the idea meant to be conveyed will certainly be missed. Therefore, in order to understand the idea, you have to direct attention to the idea and not to the language used.

Likewise with other ideas, also. If several ideas go conjointly to prove a central idea, you have to direct attention to the central idea. If you direct attention to the several ideas, the central idea is missed. Whenever the central idea is understood, you stand as the central idea.

When the Truth – which transcends the realm of ideas and mind – is expounded, you have to direct attention to the Truth, leaving aside also the central idea. When you understand the Truth, you stand as the Truth.

Here, you have been following in the footsteps of the teacher, who was rising from the language to ideas, from several ideas to the central idea, and from the central idea to the Truth. The Truth, as is shown above, transcends the realm of ideas and mind. The personal element ceases here, and does not exist in the beyond. So when the teacher was standing as the Truth and the disciple was also standing as the Truth, only the impersonal was there, as Truth is impersonal. There is no duality there.

But when you come out of it, you use the language of the ego and say you understood it. It was not a case of understanding at all, but of being one with it.

Here, possibly, you may raise a question. It was said that when the idea was understood by the disciple, the disciple was standing as idea and the teacher was also standing as idea. Then, is there not non-duality there? Why should you go beyond, to find the Truth?

This question can never be there. Ideas are many, and there is diversity in the conception of ideas. The word 'idea' brings in personalities also. Two personalities can never become one. But beyond the realm of ideas, there is only the impersonal. The impersonal can never be many. Therefore, non-duality is only in the impersonal, and it is wrong to assume that the advaitic Truth was expounded in duality.

The ordinary man believes that he is the body, senses or mind. By a careful examination of the three states, you can know beyond doubt that the 'I' is a permanent, changeless principle. This is the *sat* or existence aspect of the 'I'.

But this knowledge by itself does not complete your liberation. Take for example the illusion of a serpent in a rope. Here, 'This is a serpent' is illusion, and 'This is a rope' is the Reality. If nothing of the rope is seen, no superimposition is possible. It is only on a partial knowledge of the rope that the superimposition takes place. It is the 'this'-ness or the existence aspect of the rope that is common to both the Reality and the illusion. It is upon this that the serpent is superimposed.

So, if by some process you understand that it is not a serpent, the serpent illusion vanishes and the 'this'-ness alone remains. But the likelihood of your superimposing other things upon this – like a stick or a crack or a shadow – still remains. If you want to avoid every possibility of any further superimposition you must necessarily bring in clear light and see the rope in its real nature.

Now, applying this analogy to your own subjective self, you see that the 'I' stands for the 'this' and the body, senses and mind for the serpent. Even if you understand that you are not the body, senses or mind and that you are the changeless principle 'I', any other illusion is liable to be superimposed again upon that same 'I', without prejudice to its existence aspect.

To avoid this possibility, you must also understand the other positive characteristics of the 'I', namely Consciousness and Happiness. The knowledge 'I am Consciousness and I am Happiness' stands parallel to the knowledge 'This is a rope' in the illustration.

12th February 1951

86. KNOWING THE *SAT* ASPECT ALONE DOES NOT MAKE LIBERATION COMPLETE.

Going subjectively beyond the body and mind, you know you are the unqualified 'I'. But this knowledge of the *sat* aspect alone does not make your experience complete. So long as you do not understand the other two positive characteristics, viz. Consciousness and Peace, there is every possibility of your superimposing something else upon this unknown.

For example, if you only know that what you mistook to be a serpent is not a serpent and you do not know what it is exactly, there is every likelihood of your mistaking it the next moment for a stick, or a shadow, or anything else. But if you definitely know – in clear light – that it is only a rope, there is no possibility of your mistaking it any further.

Therefore, to make your liberation complete and unmistakable, you must understand the 'I' to be pure Consciousness, the object being only its expression and both of them being absolute Peace.

13th February 1951

87. HOW CAN PRAYER TO A PERSONAL GOD LEAD TO FULFILMENT?

Man ordinarily takes himself to be very, very insignificant, compared to the vast universe. He finds his mind, with all its limitations, is unable to explain many things in this vast universe. It is also unable to achieve many of its desires.

He conceives God as the Lord of all the universe, all-powerful. So, naturally, he prays to God to get his desires fulfilled. Though ignorant of the immense powers and potentialities of his own mind, he unconsciously releases in this way all the powers that lie dormant in him, towards the creation of the Godhead he has conceived. Thus the very powers of the devotee himself, in the name and form of the God he has conceived, come back and take effect, in the fulfilment of his own prayers. But the devotee takes it all meekly, attributing it to the grace of the God, taking God as something entirely different from himself.

In getting his prayers thus fulfilled, he attaches more importance to the fulfilment of his desires than to knowing the nature of the Godhead called to his help. He relinquishes thereby all the spiritual values involved in that communion with God.

He who wants to get to the Truth does not crave for the fulfilment of individual desires, for he is concerned with spiritual values alone. Proceeding that way, he ultimately comes back to his own self and realizes God as his own Self.

14th February 1951

88. GOD IS ETERNAL.

Some of the shāstras admit also of many eternals other than God. It is absurd, because plurality is possible only under the limitations of time, space and causality. Eternal means transcending time and space. There can never be other eternals, because there is no agency to distinguish them. Hence there can be only one eternal and that is God.

Conceding God as eternal, it has to be admitted that God created this universe, including time and space. How and from what? Taking God as the creator, there must be two causes for creation: (a) the *efficient cause* and (b) the *material cause*, distinct and separate from each other.

But there is nothing other than God to afford material for these two causes. Still conceding that God created the world out of himself, it has to be admitted that he has further to divide himself into two distinct and separate parts to provide two causes for creation. Such a division makes him finite and he at once loses his Godhood and infinitude. Hence, God remaining as God, creation as ordinarily conceived is impossible. So the world has never been created, in fact.

18th February 1951

89. REPENTANCE IS NO ROAD TO PROGRESS.

An evil deed is very often committed not because one does not know it to be evil, but because one is not able to resist the cravings of the heart. One's reason gives the right advice, but the heart is not able to follow it. Repentance is usually suggested as an atonement and as a means to prevent the repetition of the deed. But experience and logic are against this.

When we begin to repent a past evil deed, we are bringing in the past deed and that makes the heart crave for it again. So, whenever you bring in the picture of the evil action, the heart welcomes it; because it gives the heart some pleasure, even to think of it. Thus repentance means the constant repetition of the evil.

So if you want to transcend the evil permanently, you have scrupulously to forget it for ever, until you are able to realize that you are neither the doer nor the enjoyer, but the eternal knower.

If it is a feeling-repentance and not a thinking-repentance, there is no objection to it. But that is very rare. In the majority of cases, it is the other way about; and it is that kind of repentance that is dangerous.

20th February 1951

90. ONLY HE REALIZES WHOM ĀTMĀ CHOOSES.

> Nā 'yam ātmā pravacanēna labhyō
> na mēdhayā na bahunā śrutēna .
> yam ēvai 'ṣa vṛṇutē tēna labhyas
> tasyai 'ṣa ātmā vivṛṇutē tanūṁ svām ..

Kaṭha Upaniṣhad, 2.23

This is a statement in the Upaniṣhads. It means: 'He who is chosen by the Ātmā itself is alone eligible for realization of the Truth.'

It is ordinarily said that a thing attracts one. It is not on account of anything done by that particular thing that it is said to attract, but one gets attracted to it of himself. It is in this way that Ātmā's 'choosing' has to be understood. It means that he who is earnest about getting to Ātmā – the ultimate Truth – gets attracted to it without anything being done by Ātmā itself. That is the 'choosing'.

Not only is the direct perception path the easiest and the shortest of all the paths to Truth, but it also gives the most satisfactory explanation of all the problems that arise for those who follow other paths.

21st February 1951

91. STANDARD OF MORALITY

Current standards of morality are purely relative and differ vastly with time, place and various other factors. But man being essentially one all the world over, a common and absolute standard of morality is necessary. But this, however, is rarely thought of. Such an absolute standard becomes necessary only for those who are on the path to the absolute Reality. These are incredibly few, and hence the absence of any satisfactory definition of a single standard of morality in the shāstras.

The following can be such an absolute standard of morality.

- *Vice* is that particular act or thought or feeling that tends to inflate the ego.
- *Virtue* is that act, thought or feeling that tends to attenuate the ego.

All acts, thoughts and feelings directed towards the 'I'-principle or to its nature are virtuous. Virtue and vice have a place only in the relative sphere. In the relative sphere, that which tends towards selflessness is virtue and that which tends towards selfishness is vice.

Love itself can be both selfish and selfless, according to its goal or motive. Objectless love is virtue.

When you understand from your Guru 'who you are' and 'what you are', you transcend both virtue and vice.

92. How and why do I live?

'Do you live at all?' is my question. It has been proved that the thing that lives from birth till death is the same, changeless 'I'-principle. The 'I' is the centre of life. That alone lives.

The 'how' and the 'why' of life are sought in the manifestations outside. When you turn to the manifestation, you lose sight of your centre and cease to live really. So the best way, for the best living, is to cling on to the living alone, forgetting the 'how' and the 'why' of it completely.

93. What is an object?

One perception, as we generally call it, is really the resultant of ever so many distinct and separate perceptions. We see only one point at a time. It is only after this point has disappeared that the next point can be seen. It is only thousands of such points that seem to make up a so called object.

A point that has disappeared does not remain as such. It is foolish to try to collect and join them together, to make up the object or perception in question. Even the point itself, when examined, is reduced to a geometrical point – a mere idea.

So, looked at in the right perspective, an object and its perception are non-existent.

94. I and object are one.

1. Objects are nothing but form, sound, touch, taste or smell. It is evident that any one of these can never be separated from its respective sense organ, even in thought. So objects and sense perceptions are one.

   Similarly, seeing, hearing etc. can never shine independently of Consciousness. So, by the same logic, they are Consciousness itself.

   Thus objects are only Consciousness; and that is the 'I'-principle.

2. One directs attention to *something*. But is it that something that we perceive by the senses? No. We perceive only the superimpo-

sitions of the senses upon that something. This vague something remains as the substratum of form, sound etc.; and always remains unknown to the senses or the mind.

But it is that unknown something that we want to know, without any superimposition. So, no agent like the senses or the generic mind can be utilized, for they can only superimpose their own objects. The mind always functions conjointly with the sense organs. In the absence of these agents, neither forms nor thoughts appear. But using Consciousness to know it, we see it as Consciousness alone, that is to say as one with the 'I'-principle.

There is a fundamental difference between the functionings of the agents and of Consciousness. When the senses and mind function, they have separate objects and they superimpose these objects upon that something. In the case of Consciousness strictly viewed, Consciousness has no object of its own. Therefore, when anything is viewed from the standpoint of Consciousness, superimposition is impossible.

25th February 1951

95. SEVERAL WAYS OF CONSOLING PEOPLE IN MISERY

Examine what misery is and rise above it. That is the advice from the highest level.

But, from a lower level, one can say that real life is the result of the harmonious functioning of the head and the heart. Excessive misery or joy is caused by the intense working of the heart divorced from the head; and callousness is the result of the head working divorced from the heart. In both these cases, each should correct the excesses of the other and bring it to normality. In the case of the man groaning under misery, his faculty of reason should be aroused. He should be made to feel that his misery is beyond the control of human effort and that no amount of grief will mend matters; indeed it can only make him more miserable.

96. IN EVERY QUESTION, YOU FORGET YOUR REAL SELF.

Every question arises only in the relative sphere and is concerned only with the manifestation. When you turn to manifestation, you forget or get away from the 'I'-principle.

So the correct method of solving every question is to turn to the centre and then look back at the question. Then the question will stand revealed as absurd. Sometimes, you get the correct answer at once.

It may also be said that every question brings its own answer with it.

97. HOW CAN I BE WORTHY OF MY GURU?

Immediately came the answer: 'Only by your death' – meaning thereby the death of the ego.

As long as there is that sense of separateness of Guru and disciple in one's mind, one's worthiness is not complete. It can only become complete when that sense of separateness vanishes – either by the annihilation of the ego completely, or by the disciple merging in the Guru and becoming inseparably one for ever – that is when he is established in his natural state.

98. LOVE AND SACRIFICE

You love your Guru for your true death.

Even ordinary, mundane love involves a certain amount of sacrifice of the lower self or the ego. When love becomes more and more sublime, the degree of sacrifice involved also increases proportionately. Ultimately, when you want to love the Truth, Guru or the Self – the Absolute – the sacrifice required is also not partial. It demands the whole of the lower self or the death of the ego itself. Thus, in all cases of pure love, there is no trace of the lower self to be found. So love is said to be *only giving and never taking.*

Love of objects is really love of the happiness supposed to be derived from objects. Happiness is your real nature. Therefore, you are loving your real nature. You cannot split yourself into two – the subject 'loving' and the object 'loved'. So it is yourself or Happiness that is loved. Therefore love and self are one. It is the Ultimate.

But to reach it, you must begin to cultivate that love even here, by sacrificing the interests of the lower self, little by little. Because the love of objects is limited, the sacrifice of the ego involved is only partial. But the love of Truth is unlimited and the sacrifice involved is also complete. It is the death of the ego.

99. WHY IS SHIVA CALLED THE DESTROYER?

Shiva is absolute love or the 'I'-principle in man. Directing one's attention to him wholeheartedly brings about the total annihilation of both the ego and the world of its creation. This is a necessary corollary when Shiva is visualized as the Ultimate. This destructive aspect of establishing oneself in the Absolute is attributed by the ignorant man to the personal god Shiva; and thus he has come to be called the destroyer.

100. WHAT DO YOU SEE?

I see the 'seeing' – or 'form', which is only a synonym for seeing. Likewise, sound is only a synonym for hearing. I hear the hearing or sound. But these – seeing, hearing, touching, tasting and smelling – can never become the objects of seeing, hearing etc. Therefore, you do not see anything, you do not hear anything, you do not touch anything, you do not taste anything, you do not smell anything.

Form can never exist independently of seeing – even in thought, for thought is only subtle perception. Form is seeing itself and never outside it. This means not only not outside the body, but also not outside the seeing or not separate from seeing. When understood as such, perception ceases to have any meaning whatsoever.

The realist philosophy built upon the reality of gross objects and the idealist philosophy built upon the reality of mind (thoughts or ideas) both crumble before this argument. So there is only perception, without its corresponding object. But a perception, thought or feeling without the taint of any object is pure knowledge or the Reality itself. Therefore, even when you see an object, you really see only yourself.

Abstract thinking is impossible without bringing in some concrete object or other, in order to support it. But this rule has two exceptions, when abstract thinking is possible – i.e. when you take the thoughts:

1. 'I am pure Consciousness.'
2. 'I exist.'

If you try to concentrate upon either of these two, you will find that before long your thought itself expires, leaving you at your real centre in Consciousness pure. Even in the case of these two thoughts, you should never allow the thought to become concretized in any form. You should only transcend all limitations by allowing that thought-form to expire. This leads you on to the 'I', which is always *anubhava-sphuraṇa*.

101. KNOWLEDGE AND HAPPINESS ARE ONE.

Where knowledge is complete, happiness is also complete.

With the object of driving this truth home in the Gopīs, Lord Kṛiṣhṇa once asked them each to narrate truthfully the uppermost desire in her heart at that moment, and asked them if their happiness was ever complete or permanent.

They said 'no' and began to narrate their desires, each Gopī differing in her desires from the other. This showed that their desires were so vast and varied; and out of these each one could choose only one object in fulfilment of her desire at a time; and again, this one object could satisfy her only for a short while. As long as there was such a vast number of desires always eluding their grasp, they could never be completely and permanently happy.

It was evidently the knowledge of the limitation of their chosen object of enjoyment that was the cause of the apparent limitation of their happiness as well. Thus the only means to make their happiness complete was to bring the whole field of their objects simultaneously under enjoyment. This was impossible. Therefore the only alternative was to make the knowledge of the object complete or infinite.

This proves that infinite Knowledge alone can give infinite Happiness. But two infinites cannot exist simultaneously, since there is nothing else to distinguish them. So knowledge and happiness must be one and devoid of objects. This infinite Happiness can also be attained by the reverse process, namely by knowing it to be objectless and independent of objects. It is only when the knowledge of the object gives up the limitation of the object, and becomes pure knowledge that you enjoy happiness. Thus again we see that happiness and knowledge are one, when devoid of objects.

By an examination of deep sleep, you see that there are consciousness and happiness alone there. And they are not objective, there being only the 'I'-principle there. But the 'I'-principle cannot be split into two. So Consciousness and Happiness are one, and are intrinsic in the 'I'-principle.

26th March 1951

102. EVERY NAME POINTS TO THE ABSOLUTE.

Soon after your birth, your parents give you a particular name. You continue to be known by that name alone till your death. So we see that the name is changeless. Changeless means beyond time and space. That which is changeless in you is the real 'I'-principle. Therefore the name can pertain only to that 'I'-principle, and the 'I'-principle is the right Absolute. Therefore, every name is the name of the Absolute.

Now coming to such names as 'man', 'chair', 'water' etc., all these are generic names and we have already proved that there are no objects corresponding to these names. You may then think that they are mere ideas. But there can never be ideas conceiving gross objects, without the gross objects themselves being there. Therefore these names transcend both the physical and mental realms.

That which transcends the mental and physical is the right Absolute. Therefore, all these names denote the right Absolute.

103. HOW CAN ONENESS BE ESTABLISHED?

Science wants to establish oneness outside, in objects perceived. But Vēdānta wants to establish oneness inside and outside and everywhere.

Science starts on the basic error that you are the body, senses and mind and that the object-world is real.

But the vēdāntin starts from the Truth that the 'I'-principle transcending body, senses and mind is the only Reality, and that it is indeed the Absolute.

Beyond the mind, there is something present. It is evident only in deep sleep, as Happiness and Consciousness.

104. WHAT ARE THOUGHTS AND FEELINGS?

In order to understand this, the mind must first be defined. The mind is not a substance in itself. It is nothing but the name of a function. So the mind is thought or feeling itself. When these are absent, the mind cannot be said to exist. Beyond the mind, there is only Consciousness or the 'I'-principle.

If a thought occurs, to whom does it occur? Is it to the body? No. Because body is by itself dead and inert matter. Then is it to the mind? No. Because the mind is itself a thought, and one thought cannot occur to another thought. Therefore, it must certainly be to 'Me', who am beyond the mind as Consciousness, that every thought occurs.

The thought rises in Consciousness, exists in Consciousness and vanishes into Consciousness. So, of what stuff can the thought possibly be made? Of pure Consciousness alone, just as waves are made of water. When Consciousness is limited or objectified – so to say – it is called thought. So *the content of thought is only Consciousness.*

Similarly, examining all feelings – like the feeling of anger, feeling of fear, feeling of lust etc. – we find that they all manifest themselves on a common background or factor called feeling, which is divested of all difference. This feeling by itself is pure Peace or Happiness. Thus all these so-called different forms of feeling rise in Peace, exist in Peace and vanish into Peace – which is my real nature.

105. HOW DO YOU THINK ABOUT OR REMEMBER A PAST ENJOYMENT?

You can only try to recapitulate, beginning with the time and place, the details of the setting and other attendant circumstances or things, including your own personality there. Thinking over them or perceiving them in the subtle, following the sequence of the incident, you come to the very climax, to the point where you had the previous experience of happiness. At that point your body becomes relaxed, mind refuses to function, you forget the long cherished object you had just acquired, and you forget even yourself. Here you are again thrown into that state of happiness you enjoyed before.

Thus, in remembering a past enjoyment, you are actually enjoying it afresh, once again. But some people stop short at the point where the body begins to relax, and they miss the enjoyment proper.

Similarly, when you begin to think about your experience of happiness in deep sleep, you begin with your bedroom, bed, cushions … and pressing on to the very end you come to the Peace you enjoyed there. You enjoy the peace of deep sleep; that is to say you find that the peace of deep sleep is the background of the variety in wakefulness, and that it is your real nature.

2nd April 1951

106. WHEN ARE YOU FREE?

When the thought that you are Ātmā, the Reality, becomes as strong as your present thought that you are the body, then alone are you free.

107. WORLDLY KNOWLEDGE

Worldly knowledge is nothing but giving the unknown a name and dismissing it immediately from your mind.

3rd April 1951

108. SIGNIFICANCE OF YŌGA AND SOCIAL SERVICE

All practices of haṭha-yōga or any other yōga – based upon the body idea in some form – were compared to the strivings of a man bitten by a mad dog, and acting under the effect of the toxin which makes him believe that he is a dog. He tries to straighten his tail which is non-existent and which he feels curling behind him, like a dog's. This seems foolish to all sober men.

Similarly, the yōgin is trying to perfect his body and mind by yōgic practices. This is laughed at by the Jnyānin, who sees clearly that the body and mind are mere illusions, like the tail of the man bitten by the mad dog.

It is just in this manner that persons try to improve the world, without carefully examining what the world is.

4th April 1951

When time is proved to be non-existent, one third of the world disappears. And the other two thirds also disappear when space and causality are similarly proved to be non-existent.

6th April 1951

109. WILL, EGO, SVARŪPA ETC. DEFINED

A disciple asked: 'What is will?'

Answer: 'Will' is that volition appearing just before every activity. It is in essence desire itself. It is one of the manifested forms of the mind itself, forming the lowest link between the subtle and the gross spheres. It is thinking in terms of the needs of the lower self. The different manifestations of mind, according to the western system, are called mind, reason, will and egoism. But according to the eastern system, they are manas, buddhi, citta and ahankāra. [See note 152.]

Ego is a spurious entity apparently personating the 'I'-principle, always after the activity.

Svarūpa of anything is the highest generalization of that thing and is the Reality itself.

Svarūpa of a thing (looked at from a relatively high plane):

1. Svarūpa is that which maintains or keeps the identity of the thing.
2. It is that upon which the identity of a thing essentially depends.
3. It is the essence of a thing or the thing in itself, which underlies all phenomenal attributes.

That general background is one and indivisible, and so it cannot have parts. It is that which remains, even after the removal of all the attributes heaped upon it by your mind and senses. This is pure Consciousness.

Relatively, it can also be said that the svarūpa of a thing is the same as its immediate material cause. For example, the svarūpa of the table may be said to be wood, and that of wood may be said to be panca-bhūta: the five elements. Thus tracing it to its irreducible source, we reach the same ultimate svarūpa of man, viz. Consciousness pure.

So body does not go into the svarūpa of a man, senses do not go into the svarūpa of man. Therefore, when all that do not go into his svarūpa are taken away, what still remains is the svarūpa of man. Thus man is svarūpa, tree is svarūpa...; and that is pure Consciousness.

110. THE STAGES OF THE PROGRESS OF ONE'S LOVE

Lower stage	*Second stage*	*Highest stage*
Love for objects (kāma).	Love for self (snēha).	Love pure or objectless (prēma).
Ego is predominant.	Ego much attenuated by equal consideration for the object also.	No ego, but selfless love alone.
Consideration only for yourself.	Consideration both for yourself and for the object of your love.	No consideration for yourself at all, but only for what is loved.
Activity of taking only.	Activity of both taking and giving.	Activity of giving only.

All these are expressions of the impersonal 'I', ranging from the gross to the Absolute.

Love has three distinct and separate stages in the course of its progress from the mundane to the Ultimate. They may be classified as follows:

1. In the lowest stage of love, you love another only for your own sake. That is only for something that the other does to make you happy and for nothing else. That other is discarded, if the desired pleasure is not forthcoming. This sort of love is called *kāma*, and

the ego is most predominant in this. The only activity here on your part is taking and not giving.

2. The second stage is a little more elevated, less selfish, and demanding mutual consideration. Here you expect something from the other to make you happy, and at the same time you do not like the other to suffer on that account. But in return you are also prepared to do something to make the other happy. This sort of love is called *snēha*. It is not directed to the lower self alone, and therefore the ego by its operation gets much attenuated. Here, the activity is both that of taking and giving.
3. The third stage is the highest, and the ideal of love. Here you do not want any return from your partner in love and you do not love your partner any the less for this. You are prepared to do everything possible to make the other happy and your partner's happiness is your happiness. Here, the love is selfless. This is called *prēma*, and it is the Ultimate. Here, there is only giving and no taking. The ego is virtually dead.

Thus, it can be seen that it is the same love – which is the right Absolute – that expresses itself as these three and that it is your real nature. If you take away the limitations from the first and the second, the love stands as pure selfless love: as represented in the third stage – prēma.

111. THE CONTROLLING PRINCIPLE

Every perception by itself is invariably governed and corrected by the relatively higher faculty called buddhi (lower reason). This buddhi is in its turn controlled and corrected by another faculty called higher reason (or vidyā-vṛitti) , which is well beyond the mind. This is Consciousness itself, appearing to be functioning.

We are usually slow to accept the existence of this faculty, as it is usually confounded with the lower reason itself, their workings being apparently similar.

112. SELF-LUMINOSITY

Self-luminosity is the particular prerogative of Consciousness alone. Consciousness is the light of lights, because it does not require any other light for its manifestation. Therefore Consciousness is self-luminous.

Examination of things nearest to you, like 'memory', can easily lead you to the real 'I'; since you have only to advance just a little from there. If memory leaves you, you become an idiot in ignorance. But become an idiot in the beyond, and you are blessed.

'Sleep away the whole world, clinging on to Consciousness,' said the Sage.

The use of the word 'sleep' in the transitive form, though peculiar, is specially meaningful. It means give up name and form, and rest in the background.

	To be more exact
Senses perceive objects.	I perceive objects through the senses.
Mind perceives the senses.	I perceive the senses through the mind.
I perceive the mind.	I perceive the mind by myself.

113. YOU ALONE LIGHT UP OBJECTS.

If objects are lit up, your real nature alone shines there. When the emphasis is on the objects lit up, Consciousness appears limited. But from the standpoint of Consciousness itself, it is never limited, there being nothing else beside it to limit it.

114. THE SAME WORLD VIEWED BY SCIENCE AND BY VĒDĀNTA

Scientists, depending upon the *lower reason* alone, examined the world and came to the great objective generalization 'matter', and enunciated the law of the indestructibility of matter. There they were stranded, finding no means to transcend it; for the instrument utilized was itself only part of the generic mind. Sometime later, science went a step further and admitted that matter was composed of atoms. The nucleus of this atom, scientists admit now, is energy which is the source of matter. But here again they are stuck in the mind's realm of relativity.

It is at this point that Vēdānta comes to their rescue and takes them higher still. Vēdānta first proves to them that the world and its objects – both gross and subtle, including the instrument they have so far been using, viz. the 'lower reason', for examining the world – are all objective, and that they have to be examined again exhaustively. For this they are shown a new organon or faculty in themselves, called *higher reason* or vidyā-vṛitti, which though beyond the mind has sway over the whole world of the mind and the senses.

From this new stand, they are shown that matter and energy cannot be manifested or exist even for a moment without the help of Consciousness, and that Consciousness is the background of both matter and energy. These are only two different states, so far as objects are concerned. They are the manifestations of the same reality: 'Consciousness'. Thus Vēdānta establishes the Truth that the whole objective world is nothing but Consciousness.

115. HOW TO BRIDGE THE GULF BETWEEN THE RELATIVE AND THE ABSOLUTE?

There is absolutely no bridge which can take you from the relative to the Absolute. The only bridge existing is Consciousness. But here, there is only the bridge and no one to cross over. So a jump alone is possible, to take you across.

The Absolute ceases to be the Absolute if it stoops to give directions in worldly matters. But the disciple is corrected by his Guru, even in the relative sphere. Thus you are led on to the Absolute.

116. DEEP SLEEP

There is proof to show that even the lower shāstras admit that you are in your real nature in deep sleep. The names given to the individual soul in deep sleep, even by the lower shāstras, are 'paramārthika' or 'prajnya' – meaning Truth or Consciousness. That proves that there was no ego present and that you were there as Consciousness and Peace.

It is only when you consider things just as they appear that any problem arises.

117. SELF-CLARIFICATION

A disciple asked Gurunāthan: 'You have told me that I am not the body, senses or mind, that thought is pure Consciousness alone, and I am the witness always. How to reconcile all these?'

Answer: The difficulty arises out of your reluctance to accept that thought is made up of Consciousness alone. But instead, you take thought to refer directly to objects.

It has been proved to you that you are pure Consciousness, the ultimate witness to all your activities. This thought you are *not to take during any activity*, but only after it. A thought after the incident, that you had been the knower all along, relieves you of even the least taint of an attachment – as doer or enjoyer – that might have crept in unawares during the incident. During the activity, if you take the thought of the witness, the mind engaged in the activity gets diverted, and the activity suffers to that extent. This is neither desired nor advised.

By a subjective transformation alone can realization be complete. Then you have only to make it natural. For that, you must outwardly allow the body, senses and mind to continue their activities as before; but inwardly, after every activity, emphasize the Consciousness or witness aspect, so as not to allow those activities to form new samskāras.

You must understand that these statements were made from different levels. When I say that the 'I' in you is the witness, there thoughts, feelings, perceptions and doings are conceded. But when I say that thought is Consciousness, I do not stand out as the witness of thought, but I go into the make of thought. Then the thought as such vanishes. Body, senses and mind also vanish likewise.

When they are conceded, I am the witness. But when they are severally examined and proved to be Consciousness, I cease to be the witness.

It is he who has the ego present in him that does or does not do. He who has destroyed the ego in him knows neither doing nor non-doing.

118. JĪVA

A jīva [personal ego] comes into being as a result of the false identification of the Ātmā [Self] with body, senses and mind; or as a result of the superimpositions of doership or enjoyership upon the Ātmā (Ātmā + doership = jīva).

'Who superimposes doership upon Ātmā?' is the question usually asked at this stage. Is not he who superimposes himself a doer? The question is absurd on the face of it. The question arises upon the false presupposition that a doership exists even before doership comes into being.

119. 'WHO?'

'Who' is the law obtaining only in the realm of the jīva or mind. From there, usually, it is bodily lifted and applied in the realm of Ātmā, where there is no duality or relativity. So that question, in the present context, becomes meaningless.

In every activity, the 'I'-principle is the witness. The activity is in the mind's plane, or lower still. But the witnessing, conceding that it is a function, is taking place in the plane of Consciousness, without an agent, instrument, or object.

You can never bring the Ātmā – as such – down to the realm of the mind, nor take the mind – as such – up to the realm of Ātmā, to effect a contact.

Though the 'I' is always present in thought to help it to function in my light or presence, higher up I am witnessing it in my own plane, where I am all alone and unattached.

120. 'TO KNOW THAT YOU ARE THE WITNESS' AND 'TO BE A WITNESS'

These are entirely different things. But you should not try to know that you are the knower. Both together are impossible. Your knowership is objectless and can never be objectified.

You are always the witness. But you need not attempt deliberately to take the role of a witness. Only take note of the fact that you are always the witness.

You are asked to strengthen the conviction that you are the knower, in order to counteract the old samskāras that you are the doer, enjoyer etc. Though the substance of doership and enjoyership is effaced, the samskāras might still remain as shadows.

You are only to argue in your mind how you are always the real knower, and repeat the arguments over and over again. The time will come when the arguments will become unnecessary, and a mere thought will take you to the conclusion. Gradually, you will find that even when you do not think about the Truth, and whether you are engaged or not engaged in activities, you will feel without feeling that you are always the witness and that you are not affected by any activity or inactivity of the mind and senses in the relative sphere.

Witnessing is silent awareness. Do not try to make it active in any way. Consciousness never takes any responsibility for proving the existence or the non-existence of an object.

121. TIME AND SPACE

Space begets objects and objects beget space. Space must come in to make objects and objects must come in to make space. Therefore, they are both non-existent as such. But it has been proved in other ways also that objects are non-existent. Thus space is an illusion.

Time is conceived as past, present and future. These, when closely examined, cease to exist. The past and future have existence only in relation to the present. The present, when analysed, splits up into the past and future, leaving only an imperceptible point of time as the 'present'. This is but a fancy. The present being a fancy, the past and the future are equally fanciful. Therefore time does not really exist. Here, it is proved objectively.

It can easily be proved subjectively also. Time is only a thought form. Thought arises, abides and subsides in consciousness. Therefore, time as such is non-existent and is in essence pure Consciousness.

122. SOME SAY VĒDĀNTA IS NOT PRACTICAL. WHY?

To them 'practical' means subject to the senses or mind. They forget that even the senses and mind shine only in the presence of the 'I', and the 'I' shines all alone as in deep sleep. So the I is more practical than senses or mind. Here, Vēdānta whose subject matter is this 'I'-principle, is the most practical of all practical things. It is the most concrete of all things.

123. SOME SAY THEY ARE ABLE TO GRASP THE TRUTH INTELLECTUALLY, BUT ARE NOT ABLE TO FEEL IT.

This only means they have been attempting the impossible and have naturally failed. Because Truth transcends the senses, mind and intellect. It can never be brought down to the level of the mind, to be thought, felt or grasped by the intellect. If it were grasped at all, it would never be by the intellect, but by the higher reason alone.

124. APPARENT ACTIVITIES THAT ARE REALLY EXPRESSIONS OF THE ABSOLUTE

Sometimes when you see a sprightly baby, you feel an instantaneous pleasure. Immediately you take it in your hands, throw it into the air, catch it, embrace it, kiss it and fondle it, even to the extent of irritating it and making it cry by the pricks of your sharp beard. All this is not to enjoy pleasure. You had that pleasure even at the first sight of the baby. Then what was all this for?

The lower reason can never explain it. Here, the higher reason comes to your help and says that the gush of pleasure you first had was your real nature of happiness itself, and that the rest of the activities were only expressions of the same – sometimes not exactly in tune with the lower logic and reason.

This is an instance of action without any incentive behind it. These activities are activities of Happiness itself.

125. WHO REALLY ENJOYS THE PICTURE EXHIBITED FOR SALE?

The witness alone enjoys it. Neither the vendor, nor the vendee enjoys it really. The shopkeeper always wants to exact the maximum price for it, and the purchaser wants to get it for the minimum. So both of them do not really enjoy the picture. But the stray onlooker or witness – who does not want either to buy it or sell it – really enjoys the picture, since he has no other motive.

So also, you would be able to enjoy the world disinterestedly, only if you stand as the witness of it all.

126. 'WHO TAKES THE THOUGHT THAT HE IS CONSCIOUSNESS?'

It is the ego that takes this thought. The ego is a crude mixture of Consciousness and the material part. When this ego takes this particular thought that it is Consciousness, the material part drops away and Consciousness shines alone, in its own glory.

Thus the ego itself gets transformed into pure Consciousness, in course of time.

9th April 1951

127. CONSCIOUSNESS AND ACTIVITY

Consciousness is always your centre, in all your activities.

This fact is only to be understood, and not to be thought of, during the activity itself. It will hamper your activity, and sometimes even stop it, if you think of Consciousness during the activity. So think about the Consciousness part therein, which is your own nature, only after the activity is over and when you are free.

But before the activity, you can take the vague thought, avoiding all details, that Consciousness is the general background of all activity.

128. 'WORK FOR WORK'S SAKE'

This should be our real goal. Work will be more successful in the absence of the ego than when it is guided by it, because in the absence of the ego all your energy is available for the work alone. When the ego is present, part of this energy is usurped by it, for its own maintenance.

129. Why did Shrī Shankara expound the māyā theory?

The world was first being examined by him only from the level of the generic mind, and brought into line with subtle experiences. He was attempting to prove only the unreality of the gross world. How? He first divided unreality into two classes:

1. Never existing at all, like the horns of a hare or the son of a barren woman.
2. Appearing and disappearing, subject to conditions and depending upon something else even for that apparent existence.

Shrī Shankara classes the world in the second group, since it exists not in its own right, but depending upon the mind and senses for its manifestation, and appearing only in one state and disappearing in the other states. Thus it is said to be not completely unreal like the horns of a hare, but unreal in the sense that it appears sometimes and then disappears. This is called māyā, which is said to be neither fully real nor fully unreal.

This view of Shrī Shankara has not been rightly understood by many. Except in this context, Shrī Shankara does not speak of māyā at all. His way of approach here is peculiar, being concerned only with the gross world which he tries to explain relatively in terms of the subtle, or the mind. This is not intended for the uttamādhikāris, who approach the Absolute directly. This was intended only for the lower adhikāris, who could not – even in idea – transcend the mind's realm.

Examining the objective world from a purely subjective standpoint, one finds that the objective world as such is non-existent, like the horns of a hare. In that examination, one does not require any explanation of the world in the dualistic plane.

But when one comes a step down from the subjective standpoint, some sort of an explanation may be needed for the world that appears there. It is in this way that the māyā theory has come in.

In this approach through māyā, the gross world alone is taken up for examination. But it is never the gross that binds you down. It is only your thoughts and feelings that actually bind you. So you must examine the whole world exhaustively, or at least the vital part of it –

namely the subtle, which is comprised of thoughts and feelings – in order to get to a satisfactory solution.

130. EXISTENCE AND NON-EXISTENCE

Existence can never be destroyed, nor non-existence ever made to exist.

The usual way of expressing the relationship between pure existence, which is permanent, and the object, which is fitful or changing, is itself unnatural and misleading. This method of approach emphasizes the fitful part of the object more than the permanent part of it.

For example, we say: 'This chair exists'; as if existence comes in and goes out of the chair. It would be more correct to say existence objectifies itself or manifests itself – meaning thereby that existence remains over, even when not objectified or manifested.

Existence is the possessor, 'dharmi'; and objects are the possessed, 'dharma'.

131. PAIN AND PLEASURE

Pain and pleasure are the obverse and the reverse of the same coin, and they actually beget each other. The more you suffer, the more you enjoy afterwards; and vice versa. If your hunger or thirst has been very sharp, which is unmixed pain, your subsequent enjoyment of pleasure at a sumptuous meal will also be proportionately intense. You can never accept or reject any one phase of it alone.

But the moment you understand the source of it all to be your own self or real nature, every pleasure or pain you feel becomes yourself, losing the characteristic of pleasure or pain. And then eternal peace prevails.

11th April 1951

132. VIDYĀ-VṚITTI AND MIND

Vidyā-vṛitti, functioning consciousness, higher reason, higher logic and shuddha-sattva all denote the same faculty (if faculty it may be called).

Even in worldly enjoyment, it is your own real nature of peace that you experience as Happiness. For example, you enjoy Happiness listening to sweet music. Here music helps you only to empty your mind of all thoughts other than music, and finally it is emptied of the thought of music also. Thus the mind ceases to be and you come to Happiness, and that is your real nature.

It is wrong to believe that the happiness came from the hearing of music, because music was not there when the happiness was enjoyed.

133. MIND

Some shāstras hold that the mind functions in the waking and dreaming states, and remains functionless in deep sleep. This position is quite untenable. If mind should remain functioning in one state and functionless in another, mind should be the background of both function and functionlessness, having nothing to do with either. In this sense, mind is Ātmā itself.

> guṇakāmaṅṅaḷ nīṅṅīṭil mānasaṁ tanneyātmā …
>
> [Where qualities and fancies are removed,
> mind is Ātmā itself …]

Eṟuttacchan

Mind is not a substance in itself, nor a container of thoughts and feelings.

You cannot simultaneously have a thought and a feeling. So it shows that when you have a thought, no part of the mind remains over to take a feeling. Therefore mind is thought itself or feeling itself. So when there is no thought or feeling, one cannot say that mind as such exists.

If mind is taken to be the container of thoughts and feelings, it has to be changeless. If it is changeless, it transcends time. Then it must be Truth itself.

The word 'mind' ought to be correctly understood as the name of a function. Thought is a function – mind is thought. Feeling is a function – mind is feeling. So when there is neither thought nor feeling, there is no mind at all.

134. SPIRITUALITY REPLACES THE OBJECT BY THE SUBJECT.

The worldly way of life is to emphasize the object alone in every activity, ignoring the subject altogether. Spirituality comes in when you begin to bring in and emphasize the subject also, alongside of the object. Ultimately, when spirituality leads you to realization, the object as such vanishes and the real subject, the 'I'-principle alone shines. Then all activity points to you, or all activities vanish.

Mind has usually three stages of expression.

1. *Instinct:* With the body as its instrument.
2. *Reason:* With the particular mind and senses as instruments.
3. *Intuition:* The word 'intuition' is used in different senses in different texts. What is taken up here is yōgic intuition. With intuition, time and space are curtailed to a very great extent. But still, they are there, to enable the intuition to function. The mind is much expanded in intuition. Still, it does not cease to be mind.

Complete annihilation of time and space can never be accomplished by the mind. The background is in an entirely different plane.

135. SPIRITUALITY REVERSES THE IGNORANT MAN'S OUTLOOK.

To an ignorant man, the objective world is an obstacle to spiritual progress; because objects always draw him away from his real centre, which has not yet been shown to him.

But to one who has heard the Truth from his Guru, the same world serves as a help to his spiritual progress, since each one of its objects points to his real centre.

136. WHAT IS THE MEANING OF 'GRACE'?

Really it is a meaningless word. But shāstras endorse it in a certain way, explaining this with the words:

> durlabhaṁ trayam ēvai 'tad dēvānugraha-hētukam .
> manuṣyatvaṁ mumukṣutvaṁ mahāpuruṣa-saṁśrayaḥ ..

Shrī Shankara, Vivēka-cūḍāmaṇi, 3

It means:

1. To be born as a human being,
2. To have a keen desire for liberation, and
3. To come into contact with a Sage

are the three rare possibilities attained by divine grace alone. Animals exist, and man also exists. But man exists and knows he exists. This differentiates man from animals, and it is this which is meant by the 'man-ness' (manuṣhyatva) referred to above. (The word 'manhood' is weak and does not convey the sense implied, so a new word 'man-ness' is coined for the purpose.)

137. HOW TO MAKE THE BEST USE OF 'MAN-NESS' (MANUṢHYATVA)

Some men make good use of this higher quality they possess, even from their birth. They begin to think what they are, and strive on. All this being within the mind's realm, they begin to look beyond, for the ultimate Truth.

Finding this not attainable by self-effort alone, they search for long, far and wide, for a real Guru. At last, the fortunate one gets a Guru, under whose guidance he rises from level to level to the right Absolute.

Some others ignore this higher quality, and sink into samsāra ('worldliness') again.

12th April 1951

Consciousness alone is *alive*. Everything objective is dead and inert.

sakalaṁ dṛśyaṁ jaḍam

Upaniṣhad

14th April 1951

138. PHILOSOPHY OF THE WEST AND THE EAST (Reply to some American journalists and philosophers)

According to the West, philosophy is a string of assumptions, speculations and inferences. But Vēdānta philosophy is based on incontrovertible direct perceptions or experiences. Knowing the Truth thereby, and establishing your real centre there, you can take to your life's activities with even more energy, ease and confidence.

139. WHAT AM I?

I can perceive and know my body, sense-organs and mind. Therefore I am evidently the subject, distinct and separate from all of them.

140. WHY IS THE KNOWER NOT THE DOER OR THE ENJOYER?

Because you never cease to be the knower. Doership and enjoyership come and go. Knowing takes place in a different plane.

The doing, perceiving and thinking take place either in the realm of the body or of the mind. When these activities are taking place, they are simultaneously perceived by the 'I'-principle, from a higher plane.

The doer and the enjoyer always change. The knower is beyond all changes. It is evidently Knowledge or Consciousness itself. And it is no function, since it is changeless.

16th April 1951

141. MIND'S ROLE IN THE EXPERIENCE OF HAPPINESS

A disciple asked: 'You say I get happiness when the mind comes to rest, as soon as I get the object desired. But if the desire is for happiness itself, how can the mind come to rest before happiness is attained?'

Answer: The mind may be said to desire happiness, but not directly. The object of its desire is always that from which it supposes it can derive happiness. Happiness can never be the object of desire. For Happiness can never be objectified. Therefore it is only when the desired object is gained that the mind comes to rest and Happiness is experienced.

142. 'HOW TO EXPERIENCE THE TRUTH?'

This is the question usually asked from the relative plane. Truth is uncaused, and can never be experienced by effort of any kind. All efforts to that end amount only to thinking and feeling. This is clearly within the mind's realm, and Truth is well beyond it. So no amount of effort can ever take you to the Truth.

Hence a Guru may probably bless you like this: 'May you never experience the Truth.' Because Truth is experience itself. So *be* the Truth and do not desire to experience it. *The Guru is always impersonal.*

143. FROM QUALITIES TO THE ABSOLUTE

Qualities cannot subsist independent of a permanent background. In the subjective realm, there is such a changeless, deathless, permanent principle as the background; and that is the 'I'-principle.

It is the presence of this permanent subjective background that prompts you to search for a corresponding permanent background behind the objects as well. Examining the objective world from the standpoint of this 'I'-principle, you come to such a permanent background behind objects also.

These two backgrounds meet, and are one in Reality.

144. THE BASIC ERROR

The basic error is the false identification of the 'I'-principle with the body, senses or mind – each at a different time. This is the pivot round which our worldly life revolves.

145. 'KNOWING', AND FUNCTIONS OF SENSE ORGANS AND MIND

The functions of the sense organs and mind take place only one at a time, and have always a beginning and an end.

But there is always knowing, and it has neither a beginning nor an end. So knowing is no function at all. You can attribute beginning and end to it only when you look at it from the standpoint of the objects of knowledge which have a beginning and an end.

But knowledge exists without objects. Therefore, it has neither a beginning nor an end.

146. How to get over attachment?

Even when you say you are attached, you are really detached. From the height of happiness or misery in one state, you pass into its opposite in another state in the course of a few moments; and vice versa. And soon after, you pass into deep sleep, divorced of all ideas of body, senses and mind.

This shows beyond doubt that you are really unattached to anything, in any state. If you are really attached to anything, that attachment should continue with you, in all the states in which you happen to be. But that is not the case. Therefore, that proves that in your real nature, you are not attached.

Know it and take note of it. That is all that is needed. Take that line of thinking, and you will find that this mistaken notion of attachment will leave you very soon.

147. Truth is always new.

The method of direct approach to the Truth (vicāra-mārga or the path of discrimination) is found only very rarely, even in the higher Indian scriptures; and that again as mere assertions only, and seldom elaborated upon. Hence, it has always its virgin novelty.

148. Man's hunt after happiness – an analogy

Man hunting for happiness is just like a beetle with a drop of butter on its head. Getting scent of the butter, the beetle hovers around, knocking about everywhere for the source of the scent, but is ignorant of the fact that the butter is on its own head.

Likewise, man hunts for happiness because it is in himself and he is not able to see it there. But the urge which makes him hunt comes from that happiness itself.

18th April 1951

149. 'I AM' TO THE IGNORANT MAN AND THE SAGE

We all say 'I am clever', 'I am happy', and so on. In this, the layman ignores the vital part 'I am', and emphasizes the rest. But the 'I am' alone is important for the Sage, and he ignores the rest.

150. ĀTMĀ IS BEYOND BOTH THE PRESENCE AND THE ABSENCE OF OBJECTS.

Thoughts, feelings etc. are like pictures on the wall of Ātmā. Their presence and absence must both vanish, if you want to see the background Ātmā in its Reality.

There is no container in you to hold a series of past thoughts or subtle objects, in readiness for any future remembrance. Thought can have neither a gross object nor a subtle object. So it is objectless, and hence pure Consciousness itself.

Vēdānta wants to go into the heart of everything, and is never satisfied with mere names.

151. HOW YOU SHOULD EXAMINE YOURSELF

Exactly in the way that the ego would examine other persons or activities outside you, standing separate from and unattached to the person or thing examined. Here, you should stand separate from the body, senses and mind; and dispassionately examine them.

Any attempt to adjust the object-world to suit your goal of enjoying permanent Happiness is doomed to failure, like the attempt to spread a sheet of leather all over the world to afford smooth walking. A pair of leather shoes applied to the soles of your feet is an infinitely easier, cheaper and more effective solution.

So also, in the quest after Truth, a subjective correction and establishment in your real centre as the ultimate 'I'-principle will remove all your doubts, difficulties and troubles. The other way is endless and impracticable.

20th April 1951

152. WHAT IS THE DIFFERENCE BETWEEN MIND AND EGO?

The inner organ loosely called 'mind' is divided into four categories, according to its different functions. The ego is one such.

1. *Mind* (particular) is that which gathers impressions from the outside world.
2. *Reason* (intellect) discriminates and selects from the impressions thus gathered.
3. *Will* is that which precedes and directs action. It may be loosely called 'desire' (svārthā-'nusandhāna-vaśēna cittam).
4. *Ego* is that which claims all activities of the mind.

[This note and its quotation seem to have come from Shrī Shankara's *Vivēka-cūḍāmaṇi*, 93-4:

> nigadyatē 'ntaḥ-karaṇaṁ manō dhīr
> ahaṁ-kṛtiś cittam iti sva-vṛttibhiḥ .
> manas tu saṁkalpa-vikalpanādibhir
> buddhiḥ padārthā-'dhyavasāya-dharmataḥ ..
>
> atrā 'bhimānād aham ity ahaṁkṛtiḥ .
> svārthā-'nusandhāna-vaśēna cittam ..
>
> The inner faculty is spoken
> of as 'mind' or 'reason' or
> as doing 'ego' or as 'will'.
> It gets these names according to
> its various modes of functioning.
>
> *Mind* is the function that conceives
> of things together and apart.
> Next, *reason* is the function that
> determines what is meant thereby.
>
> The *ego* is an acting 'I'
> that claims to be this body here.
> And *will* is that desire which seeks
> out what it wishes for itself.]

153. WHAT IS IGNORANCE?

It is said to be the source of the world. The usual example taken to illustrate this is the illusion of the serpent in the rope. Here the ignorance of the rope, coming just between the rope and the serpent, is said to be the cause of the serpent. So when the serpent disappears, it is the ignorance that should naturally remain over.

But when you bring in a light and examine the serpent, it disappears altogether; and in its place, instead of the ignorance supposed to be its cause, you see only the rope in its nakedness, beyond all doubt.

So this ignorance, which never had any existence independently of the serpent, is also non-existent. Hence the ignorance is the object perceived itself, or ignorance means only *wrong notion*. The world is only a distorted vision: 'of the Self, by the self'.

We should accept only that which agrees with our higher reason and reject all the rest. In the illustration, we do not first see the rope in its entirety, but only its existence. That is to say the 'this' alone of the rope is seen. So in the two experiences – 'This is a rope' and 'This is a serpent' – it is upon the 'this' that the serpent is superimposed. So when the serpent disappears, naturally the 'this' alone, which is the real part of the perception, remains over.

Assuming that the 'this' remains, you must not leave the 'this' vague, as it is likely to give rise to other superimpositions. It should be made clear, beyond any possibility of a mistake, and seen as Consciousness itself.

The serpent of superimposition is not likely to be removed until you get a clear perception of the rope. When the serpent is removed, the rope alone shines.

154. VISION OF A PERSONAL GOD

Vision of a personal God is quite possible. It would seem even more real than any experience in the waking state, because that vision takes place in an intenser light.

155. Pūja done to the idol is also pūja done to the self. How?

The first item of a shāstraic pūja is sitting erect before the idol, and transferring by thought the ātmic principle in you to the idol in front of you. This is called 'āvāhana'. Then, after going through all the different items of the pūja, again the final act is restoring it (or taking it back) by thought to its original centre. This is called 'udvāhana', and this finishes the pūja.

This shows most clearly that you had actually been doing pūja only to the Ātmā in you. Moreover, if you happen to forget often the last part, namely the udvāhana, you will find in course of time your energy being slowly reduced and your mind getting weaker.

156. Hṛidaya-granthi

Hṛidaya-granthi is the knot of the ego or false identification, which apparently binds the Ātmā to the body.

29th April 1951

157. How do I get entangled?

When I rest in myself alone, in my own glory, there is no manifestation and no question either. I am the only Reality, and this Reality is my own birthright.

Very often, I slip down to the mind and begin to perceive thoughts and feelings. Immediately, I begin to attribute my own Reality to the mind; and even to its objects, namely, thoughts and feelings.

Sometimes, I slip further down to the body and perceive gross objects. Here again I attribute my own Reality to these, the body and objects. Thus I apparently entangle myself in the web of this universe.

It may further be explained as follows.

In the waking and dream experiences, all perceptions are understood only in relation to their opposites. For example, talk is understood in relation to silence, running in relation to stillness, and so on. This practice has created in man a very strong tendency to superimpose the imaginary opposite of any perception whenever that particular perception vanishes.

It is as a result of this tendency that he ordinarily superimposes ignorance in deep sleep when all activities cease. This vicious practice must be given up.

You must understand that all perceptions arise in Consciousness, abide in Consciousness and merge into consciousness. So, whenever a perception vanishes, it is Consciousness or Myself alone that remains over, as the background of it all.

You must steadily cultivate this habit of perceiving the Reality as the background of all activity.

158. REALITY INDIVISIBLE?

Reality is only one and cannot be affected by quality or degree in any way. Reality is purely subjective. I am the only subject, and all the rest are objects.

Diversity can be diversity only through me, the 'One'.

159. RELATIVE (SĀPĒKṢHYA)

'Relative' means in relation to Me; and not in relation to other objects, as is ordinarily understood. Everything is connected with Me first, and only through Me to something else.

7th June 1951

160. CREATION

Creation is described in the shāstras in two ways: (1) Creation in a regular order (krama-sṛiṣhṭi), and (2) Simultaneous creation (yugapat-sṛiṣhṭi)

1. The *creation happening in a regular order* (krama-sṛiṣhṭi) represents the cosmological view through ajnyāna, māyā, the five subtle elements (panca-mahābhūtas) etc., down to the gross world.

   This is intended for all aspirants who are not uttamādhikāris (ripe souls).

2. By *simultaneous creation* (yugapat-sṛiṣhṭi) is meant the creation of the perceiver, perception and perceived at the same instant the perception takes place. And they also cease simultaneously, all being transformed into pure Knowledge.

   Therefore it is said that objects do not exist except when known (viṣayaṅṅaḷkkˇ ajñāta sattayilla). This method is intended for higher adhikāris alone. Here, no faith of any kind is called for, and you rely on your direct experiences alone.

   The 'form' is disposed of as nothing different from 'seeing'. Thus I transcend the form as seen by me, and my 'seeing' immediately becomes pure seeing without a personal see-er. Thus I become one with Consciousness or the Reality.

161. Jnyāna

Jnyāna [knowledge] is attained as a result of relaxation of the mind and the giving up of all that is foreign to the real Self, leaving you as the Absolute, in your own glory.

All sādhanas in the jnyāna path have no purpose other than the elimination of the anātmā elements from the Ātmā, and so they are nivṛittis in themselves. When the last trace of anātmā is also eliminated, the effort ceases and you rise to the Absolute.

But, to stand permanently established in the Absolute, the world gross as well as subtle – from which you eliminated yourself – has to be examined again and seen to be nothing but the Reality.

162. Yōga and devotion

These are both processes of intense activity, always upholding the doer and enjoyer – even at the highest state, though in a highly general form.

As long as this taint of duality lasts, you do not shine as the Absolute.

163. Form and seeing –a controversy

It has been proved that form has no existence independent of seeing, and that form is therefore seeing itself. Then why can it not be said that the seeing is form alone and that form is more permanent than seeing itself?

Answer: In order to answer that question, you must understand the whole process. I said that form is one with seeing and merges into seeing. Next, I said that seeing is one with Consciousness and merges in Consciousness, which is the 'I'-principle.

So, in order to answer the question you put to me, you must direct your attention to this whole process. It then comes to this: Consciousness or the 'I'-principle merges into seeing and seeing merges into form. Therefore form alone exists, dead inert matter.

But who can say this? Form cannot say it. Who can think this? Form cannot think it. Thus you have to go to knowledge, beyond seeing, thoughts, feelings, perceptions and form.

You have to stand in knowledge to examine anything, and not the other way round. Therefore, the form which is examined will merge into seeing, and seeing into Consciousness. Then the questioner dies and is no longer there to receive the answer. Who then is to judge when the questioner is no more? I believe that the absurdity of the question is now very clear to you.

Now coming back, who is to judge this controversy? 'Form', which is inert, or 'seeing' which is illumined by Consciousness? Certainly the latter. Seeing is more permanent and comprehends all forms. Further, in the order of proximity to the ultimate 'I'-principle, seeing – which is much more subtle than form – stands much closer to the 'I'-principle; and it is the 'I'-principle that examines it.

So seeing is always much better known than form. This 'I'-principle is the knower of all.

164. 'HERE' AND 'THERE' ARE ALSO MENTAL.

Once a great pandit asked Gurunāthan: 'If you say everything objective is mental, why does not the Shrī Padmanābha Temple gōpura (steeple) *there* appear before you *here* now?

Gurunāthan asked: 'And what about the "here" and "there", please! Are they not also mental?'

This silenced the questioner, and he did obtain some light from the answer.

17th June 1951

165. VICĀRA-MĀRGA (THE DIRECT PERCEPTION METHOD)

Of the different Upaniṣhads, dealing with the different paths to attain the Absolute, the *Aitarēya Upaniṣhad* deals with the vicāra-mārga or direct perception method in detail.

This path takes you straight to the Truth. Looking from there, you see the world of mind and senses to be non-existent as such. One who has taken to this path and reached the goal does not stand in need of any independent explanation of ordinary worldly problems like desire, feelings, etc. They are all solved.

But for those who take to other paths, like yōga or devotion, the world of thoughts, feelings and perceptions – as also the gross world – have to be explained.

166. DESIRE

Desire always shows want, and this again shows your imperfection. So, until you become perfect, desire is sure to torment you. Then examine more clearly what desire points to.

It always points to Happiness; and it has been proved to you that when a desired object is gained, there is desirelessness for the time being. The mind comes to rest and Happiness dawns.

So, strictly speaking, desire is directed to desirelessness; because it is that desirelessness that brings in Happiness.

167. SUBJECTIVE TRANSFORMATION AND ADJUSTMENT OF PERSPECTIVE ALONE NEEDED

The worlds appearing in different states are different from one another. As you change, the worlds change also.

Standing limited by the body and mind, if you try to change the world so as to make it beautiful or enjoyable to your mental satisfaction, it will be all in vain. The world will remain only as it is.

But if you change your stand or perspective and identify yourself with the real 'I'-principle, the world also changes; not as beautiful or enjoyable, but as Beauty and Happiness themselves being one with the 'I'-principle.

So correct your inner perspective alone and you shall be free for ever and happy, in whatever world you are. This is possible only by realizing the Truth, in all its aspects.

168. RELATIVITY

Relativity, according to science and in ordinary parlance as well, is only between objects themselves.

But according to Vēdānta, relativity is only between the subject and the object. Without the subject's perception, there can never be any object.

Happiness is something that transcends the mind. It expresses itself in pleasure. If the mind part is taken away from pleasure, it becomes Happiness itself.

Pleasure is something that pertains to the realm of the mind.

Personality rests with body, senses and mind. If you think you are impersonal, if you feel you are impersonal and if you act knowing that you are impersonal, you *are* impersonal.

18th June 1951

169. LIFE COMPARED TO A GAME OF CHESS

You first make certain laws to guide your play, and then voluntarily submit yourself to the laws you have made. You are however, always confident that you can at any moment throw away the whole thing overboard and rise above all those laws, and then there ceases to be a game of chess. In the play, the pawns alone can be said to win or lose; and you, the player, go away as you came.

Live likewise in the world, knowing that you are the Absolute – the creator of all laws – and that you can transcend those laws whenever you want. Then you transcend the world.

170. WHY DID LORD KṚIṢHṆA ADVISE ARJUNA TO FIGHT AND KILL, WHICH IS CONSIDERED A SIN AND HIMSA?

Seeing the invincible army of the Kauravas before him, Arjuna became diffident and he was seized by cowardice. But to save his face and vanity, he fell back upon the two common dicta of morality and justice, and thus tried to evade the battle. Lord Kṛiṣhṇa knew this quite well; and wanted to help Arjuna to transcend this momentary weakness of cowardice, which appeared to have all the characteristics of shānti. This could be achieved only by persuading him to fight and win.

Tamas [reluctance] may often assume the form of *sattva* [resolution]. There is no direct jump from tamas to sattva. You must go through *rajas* [action]. It was tamas that was overpowering Arjuna in the form of cowardice, and he was speaking to Kṛiṣhṇa as though his problem arose in the plane of sattva. Kṛiṣhṇa saw through it and Arjuna was made to act (fight).

Rajas comes in here. Kṛiṣhṇa's idea was that he could then take Arjuna to sattva through this rajas. This accounts for Kṛiṣhṇa's advice to Arjuna to fight. His advice was that he should fight without caring for the results. So there is something put in to take him to sattva also.

171. SAMĀDHIS

According to some shāstras, a samādhi-minded person is asked to be incessantly in one or other of the following six kinds of samādhis throughout his life till death.

1. antar-dṛishyānuviddha [with sight inside]
2. antar-shabdānuviddha [with sound inside]
3. antar-nirvikalpa [with no diversity inside]
4. bahir-dṛishyānuviddha [with sight outside]
5. bahir-shabdānuviddha [with sound outside]
6. bahir-nirvikalpa [with no diversity outside]

According to certain shāstras, nirvikalpa samādhi is the ultimate goal. But according to still other shāstras there are three more other samādhis as yet to be experienced even beyond nirvikalpa samādhi. They are:

nissankalpa samādhi [without intention]
nirvṛittika samādhi [returned back]
nirvāsana samādhi [without residual conditioning]

It must always be borne in mind that samādhi, of whatever nature it may be, is only for the mind and not for the real 'I'-principle. Even when the mind gets absorbed as in the nirvikalpa state, the real 'I'-principle stands out as its witness, showing thereby that it has no connection with samādhi.

jāgratyudbhūtabāhyēndriyaviṣayasamudbhāsasākṣīśivōham .
*svapnēdṛṣṭaprapañcapratiphalanamanōvṛttisākṣīśivōham .
*svapnēsaṅkalpajātēndriyagataviśayābhāsasākṣīśivōham .
suptaucittēvilīnē prabalataramahāmōhasākṣīśivōham .
nityānandēturīyē vigatamatigatissarvasākṣīśivōham .

[Source of quotation uncertain]

(*The second line of the foregoing verse has two alternative texts, each marked with a preceding asterisk. The former speaks from the phenomenal level – vyavahāra-pakṣha – endorsing interdependence of states. But the latter is from a higher standpoint, denying the interdependence of states. The latter is preferable and more appropriate to the context.)

Here, turīya is also witnessed by the 'I'-principle. From this, it is clear that samādhi by itself cannot take you to the Reality.

Again, samādhi is a state, and being a state is limited by time. Reality is something transcending time. Therefore, until you come to the sahaja state (natural state), you cannot claim to be established in the ultimate Reality.

The samskāra that one goes into and comes out of samādhi has also to be clearly transcended, in order that you may reach the Absolute. Therefore, samādhis of any kind only pave the way for your establishing yourself in the ultimate Reality.

19th June 1951

172. How to justify the merging of Īshvara in brahman?

A mango, even if called by the name of 'coconut', does not change its nature at all. Similarly brahman, even if called by the artificial name 'Īshvara', does not change its real nature in any way. Therefore Īshvara can very well be merged in brahman.

(Īshvara is merged in brahman only when the cosmological path is followed.)

173. WHAT IS DESTRUCTION?

The word destruction can really have no meaning, because you cannot destroy anything in this world.

An ignorant man thinks that causing the disappearance of any particular thing is destruction. This is wrong. When you know things in the right perspective, you find that an object – even when it is perceived – is non-existent. Then what is the meaning of 'destruction', in reference to that object?

23rd June 1951

174. PLEASURE AND PAIN, THOUGH MY EXPERIENCES, DO NOT AFFECT ME. HOW?

I feel pleasure at one moment and pain at another. But I am changeless all along. Thus my pleasure and pain do not go into my real nature. So how can they affect me?

24th June 1951

175. KNOWLEDGE IS NOT A FUNCTION.

A function should necessarily have a beginning and an end. Knowledge has neither of these, and so it cannot be a function.

The mind works conjointly with the senses. So the workings of the senses and knowledge alone need be examined, to prove our position.

Taking the senses and their workings first, we find that each sense has a distinct object of its own to deal with. The sense of hearing has sound as its object, and so on. These objects are so exclusive that they never transgress into the sphere of any other sense or faculty.

Now, considering knowing to be also a function likewise, it has no separate and exclusive class of object to deal with. In place of the strict exclusiveness of the field and form of activity of the senses, knowledge penetrates into the spheres of all the sense perceptions, without claiming any as its exclusive object.

Therefore knowledge is not a function in itself. It serves as the background of all functions, lighting and co-ordinating all of them and their experiences.

25th June 1951

176. The 'thing' as seen by an ignorant man and a Sage

The Sage sees the 'thing in itself'. The ignorant man sees only the sense objects superimposed upon the thing in itself.

177. Guru and shāstras

The Upaniṣhads and higher shāstras on Advaita have all without exception made many bold assertions regarding Truth, based upon their authors' experiences alone. Gurunāthan is only explaining and proving these very assertions clearly, to the limit of our understanding, in the light of the higher logic or higher reason, till they sink into our experience.

178. Consciousness indispensable to any form of approach to the Reality

The Absolute can be attained through the happiness aspect of Reality – or love. But in order to analyse love and to prove its identity with Peace, the service of consciousness is indispensable. Thus, by following the path of Consciousness alone can you be established in Peace.

179. What is the relation of objects to thoughts and feelings?

The question arises on the assumption that objects exist independently of thoughts. That is never the case. Without thought, there is no object; and thought itself is nothing other than Consciousness.

180. Vēdānta and the cosmos

Much talk is heard in the relative world about government, organizations, human suffering and the like. Our ancestors faced exactly the same problems; and in their search for a solution, they approached them through the objective sphere at first. After hard and strenuous search, they found that a complete and satisfactory solution of the problem was impossible from the outside.

So they immediately beat a hasty retreat and directed their search afresh, turning inwards. Thus transcending body, senses and mind, they were able to reach their centre, the 'I'-principle, and to realize it to be nothing other than Consciousness and Happiness.

This subjective experience of the Ultimate Truth gave them immense strength. Thus reinforced, they came back and began to examine the world, which had puzzled and eluded them before. But now they easily found it to be nothing other than Consciousness, their own subjective self or 'I'-principle; and all their problems were automatically solved.

This is immortalized in the Upaniṣhad in the verse:

> parāñci khāni vyatṛṇat svayaṁ-bhūs
> tasmāt parāṅ paśyati nā 'ntarātman .
> kaścid dhīraḥ pratyag-ātmānam aikṣad
> āvṛtta-cakṣur amṛtatvam icchan ..

Kaṭha Upaniṣhad, 4.1

Our senses are created as outward-going. Therefore we see things in the outside. But one dhīra (a bold man, or one who withdrew his senses from objects), longing for deathlessness, turned his eyes (sense perceptions) inward and perceived the real 'I'-principle.

27th June 1951

181. IS A GURU NECESSARY?

If, on birth, you are guided by tendencies to enjoy good or bad, you are bound and cannot help yourself to rise beyond. If, on the other hand, you had no such tendencies, you would never have been born.

If you are in the former group and have reached a sāttvic level, even then your iṣhṭa-dēva remains only a thought form. As such, even your iṣhṭa-dēva is not likely to help you to go beyond body and mind.

It is here that a living Guru becomes absolutely necessary to take you to the Truth beyond body and mind. Such a Guru stands quite independent of you; and is capable of moving freely between the gross and the Absolute, or between the body and the 'I'-principle.

You find that in your life in the present world, you have a guru for every little thing. Why then do you raise this question in respect of spirituality alone?

> yasya sākṣādbhagavati jñānadīpapradē gurau
> martyāsaddhīḥ śrutaṁ tasya sarvaṁ kuñjaraśaucavat

> [The teacher who imparts true knowing
> is that light of truth itself,
> from which all help and guidance comes.
> Where someone thinks of such a teacher
> as a dying and unreal
> personality, there all
> that's heard is like the bathing of
> an elephant – which then goes on
> to dust its skin with dirt again.]

Bhāgavata Purāṇa, 7.15.26

182. CHARACTERISTIC OF ADVAITIC PHILOSOPHY

Advaitic philosophy does not talk in terms of opposites. It always means only what it says. When it says 'It is not active', that does not mean 'It is inactive.'

183. HOW CAN YOU SAY THAT ALL IS ĀTMĀ?

All shāstras of old have unanimously concluded that all is Ātmā. They did not explain it in detail, but left it to experience. Here let us prove it, without leaving it to experience alone.

The usual illustration of the wave and the ocean, to prove your identity with the Absolute, is not strictly correct; since the wave can never become the ocean by merging in the ocean and disappearing. The wave, when it loses its name and form, becomes water and not the ocean. The ocean is also similarly reduced to water. It is as this water alone that wave and ocean realize their common identity. So in Advaitic philosophy, the counterparts in the illustration should properly be wave and water.

The illustration of the wave and the ocean, however, is best suited to show the relationship between jīva and Īshvara, in the dualistic sphere.

For further elucidation of the illustration 'wave and water', refer to *Ātma-darshan*, chapter 14.

Gold and ornament, earth and pot, etc. are other usual illustrations. All these are apt illustrations to show the advaitin's position that all is Ātmā.

184. CAN A PERSONAL GOD BE A GURU?

Answer: 'I say *no.*'

Because a personal God is nothing but a concept. Truth is beyond all concepts. Truth by itself can never be your Guru; because, looked at from the standpoint of Truth, there is nothing else existing by its side. Truth knows no duality.

Therefore, only one who has realized the Truth can be a Guru and take you from the relative sphere to the Absolute. Hence the necessity of a *living Guru.*

A personal God cannot help you in the matter.

10th July 1951

185. THE SAGE, AS HE IS, IS NEVER UNDERSTOOD IN THE PHENOMENAL LEVEL.

There is an erroneous tendency, found in some yōgins who have not reached the highest, to assess the greatness of a Sage only from the extraordinary powers exhibited by him at some time before his death.

As a result of this vicious tendency, even Shrī Shankara is misrepresented as having bodily ascended to Kailāsa and attained sāyujya [union] with Shiva. Any Sage would protest against such an atrocious scandal. A Jnyānin is one who has transcended both the body and mind. His stand is not merely that he is not the body, but that he was never one, and that he is the absolute Truth itself. As such, it is nothing short of sacrilege to think that a real Sage would choose to demonstrate such physical wonders with a body which never was his and which has never even existed. Much less would he choose to take refuge in Shiva, who was after all nothing but a concept.

Such unbaked stories of mere fancy might tickle the ignorant mind. But the learned will only shun them. The bold assertions of Shrī Shankara, Shrī Vidyāraṇya, Shrī Aṣhṭavakra and innumerable other Sages, in their higher works of experience, disprove all such statements.

The illusion of the body in you is just like the illusion of the snake in the rope. The Jnyānin has seen his reality to be the Truth, just as the snake is discovered in clear light to be the rope alone. After that, it would be foolish to expect him to kill that illusory snake and to tan its skin to make a beautiful purse. Much less can you think of a Sage stooping to do wonders with a body which he never possessed, which he does not possess even now, and which has never existed.

It is the illusion alone that has to leave you, and not its objects – the snake or the body. When that illusion is transcended, as in the case of the Jnyānin, no problem of the disposal of those objects arises; because, on your transcending the illusion, the objects are proved never to have existed.

Therefore, the body of Shrī Shankara was only the creation of the onlookers' fancy, and they alone were responsible for its final disposal. They could very well plan to dispose of that body, which they called Shrī Shankara's, in any manner they liked, to the height of their ingenuity. But all these stories could never affect the sage Shankara, since he was Truth itself and had no body at all.

Thus we see that any talk about the apparent activities of a Sage – from a purely worldly or relative angle of vision, even though it may command the greatest admiration – is often erroneous and even suicidal. So it is always wise to leave the Jnyānin alone, beyond comment, till one is able to know him as he is. And to know the Jnyānin, one has to become a Jnyānin oneself; and thus both become one. Then all comments cease, and Truth alone shines in its own glory. In fact there are no two Jnyānins but only one; and, to be more precise, only Jnyāna or Truth itself.

From this level, we see that anyone who dares to view a Sage rather objectively stands only in the mind's realm, which is mere illusion so far as the Sage is concerned. So never ask questions about how a particular Sage lived or how he died. It is a matter for history alone, and does not belong to Vēdānta or to the Sage. A true life history of a Sage is impossible. Historians record the history of only the body they see. But the Sage is the changeless principle behind all bodies, and as such the Sage transcends all history.

186. THE MIND – ITS FIELD AND SCOPE

The mind has generally three distinct stages, in the course of its development.

The first is *instinct*: which comes into existence at the very inception of the mind, its main field of operation being the animal kingdom.

The second is *reason* (of course 'lower reason' as we call it): functioning mainly in the man kingdom.

And lastly *intuition*: functioning in the God-man kingdom alone. This shows the course of progress of the yōgin's mind.

One has to transcend even this yōgin's intuition, in order to reach the Absolute. Though, generally, the faculty of reason predominates in man, he has also occasional experiences of instinct as well as of intuition.

12th July 1951

187. HOW TO TRANSCEND THE VOID OR NOTHINGNESS?

In your attempt to reach the Absolute, you transcend the realm of objects and senses, and sometimes get stranded in a state of void or nothingness. This void or nothingness, though highly subtle, is still objective in character; and you remain as that positive principle which perceives that nothingness also.

The real nature of this 'I'-principle is Consciousness, or knowledge itself. Looking from this stand, as Consciousness, you see the void or nothingness transformed into Consciousness; and it becomes one with the 'I'-principle.

So, whenever the concept of nothingness confronts you, take the thought that nothingness is also your object, and that you are its perceiver, the ultimate subject, whose nature is Consciousness itself. Immediately, the shroud of nothingness disappears in the light of Consciousness, and it becomes one with the 'I'-principle.

This void is the last link in the chain which binds you to the objective world. Its appearance in the course of your spiritual sādhana is encouraging, since it forebodes the death-knell of the world of objects, of course in the light of knowledge.

(Refer *Ātma-nirvṛiti*, chapter 20, *The Natural State – Svarūpāvasthiti*, verse 5).

Even when you take this last 'I'-thought, people ask you what you are thinking about. They cannot understand that you are not thinking of any object at all, but that you are only trying to stand as that principle which is the background of all thoughts. The thought that you are Consciousness removes all sense of space limitation.

Shrī Buddha first analysed the external objective world in the right yōgic fashion, utilizing mind and intellect as instruments, and at the end reached what may from the phenomenal level be called void or nothingness. A negative can never subsist by itself. Much less can it be the source of positive things. That which was called void or nothingness has to be understood as Ātmā itself. Buddha must have gone beyond and reached that ātmic principle himself. But Shrī Buddha's followers seem to have stopped short and interpreted the Ultimate to be that void or nothingness.

The following verse, describing the last determination of Shrī Buddha, proves this:

> ihāsanē śuṣyatumē śarīraṁ
> tvagasthi māṁsaṁ pralayañ ca yātu .
> aprāpya bōdhaṁ bahu-kalpa durlabhaṁ
> nai 'vāsanāt kāyamataścaliṣyate ..

Lalita-vistāra, 19.57

This means: 'Unless I know the ultimate Truth, I am not going to stir from my seat, even if it be for several kalpas (for many thousands and thousands of years).' This proves that Shrī Buddha must have reached the ātmic principle which is the absolute Truth.

188. CONCEPTION OF GOD AS IṢHṬA-DĒVA [CHOSEN DEITY]

To say that you conceive of God as infinite, all-powerful, all-pervading etc. is all empty words. To conceive anything, your mind must be capable, at least for the time being, of becoming that particular thing in subtle form. So, if your conception of the attributes of God is to be an actuality, you should be able to stand during that period as those particular attributes.

Or in other words, you should become God himself for the time being, if you are really to conceive him. Then there is no need of any conception, since you have already become what you set out to conceive.

Thus, to conceive of God as all-knowing, you have to become pure Knowledge. To know that he is all-pervading, you have to become pure Existence. And to know that he is all-kindness or love, you have to become feeling-absolute or Peace.

Before reaching such a state of yōgic perfection, to say that you conceive of God is meaningless; since your conception would be of exactly the same standard as your own mind. A man cannot conceive of God except as a man, and an animal cannot conceive of God except as an animal (if it can conceive at all).

For example, a boy's iṣhṭa-dēva would be a skilful player, a musician's iṣhṭa-dēva would be a master musician, and a literary man's iṣhṭa-dēva would be a high literary principle – all of them being conceptions of their own ego. The mind is the architect of all conceptions of iṣhṭa-dēvas.

But when you become the disciple of a Sage, you go beyond all concepts, and the whole thing changes.

189. HOW DOES ONE REALIZE?

One realizes neither as a direct result of renunciation, nor as a direct result of action; but only through the deepest conviction that one is not a doer even when engaged in incessant activity, and that one is not a renouncer or non-doer even when one takes the role of a sannyāsin or in deep sleep.

So realization depends upon the perspective alone, and not upon any external manifestation.

19th July 1951

190. HAPPINESS AND MISERY COMPARED

Misery is caused and sustained only by the incessant remembrance of the objects connected with it. Happiness also may appear to have a sense object, at the beginning. But the sense object as well as the thought of it will both disappear entirely when happiness dawns; while the continuance of both these are necessary for misery.

Thus, when happiness dawns, you are drawn into your real nature, where sense objects and thoughts have no place. So, if you want misery, you must go out of your nature; and if you want happiness, come back to it.

191. *SAT* AND *CIT* ESSENTIAL FOR PERCEPTION

Perception is possible only through *sat* [existence] and *cit* [consciousness]. Because you can perceive only something existing. This brings in *sat*. Perception has necessarily to be illumined by knowledge, to enable it to function. This brings in *cit* also.

Sat is no *sat* until it shines, and Consciousness has necessarily to be there for *sat* to shine. Therefore, both aspects of *sat* and *cit* are essential for perception. The *sat* aspect of the Self or the Reality is not generally taken by itself and elaborated upon, because the elaboration of the Consciousness aspect brings in the *sat* aspect also.

Shrī Vidyāraṇya defines the *sat* aspect thus in the *Pancadashī*:

> palatil cērnnu nilkunna sattu tān dharmmiyāyvaruṁ .
> onnil tanneyirikkunna vyōmamō dharmmamātramāṁ .
>
> [Existence in itself is 'dharmi'
> (the 'support'), which stands united
> in the many things of world.
> On that same unity sits all
> extended space, which is just 'dharma'
> (the 'supported' world of change).]

Bhāṣha Pancadashi, Mahābhūta-vivēka, 79
(Malayalam translation)

The meaning is that *sat* – 'dharmi' or the 'qualified' – is the background of all objects. Dharmi exists in many 'dharmas' or 'qualities'. It is that which is limited to itself. Dharma can never exist in anything other than that dharma. Dharmi is subject and dharma is object.

For example, man may be said to be dharmi in relation to body, senses and mind, which are dharmas. Separated from the dharmas, the dharmi is only one – impersonal and ultimate. Thus man, tree, animal etc. as dharmi are the same – Reality itself.

We generally say '*its existence*'. This is not correct. For, this would mean that the 'it' would remain over, even after existence has disappeared. This could never be. Really, even after the disappearance of the 'it', existence pure would still continue. Therefore, we should really say '*existence's it*'. Here, existence would remain over, even after the 'it' has disappeared.

Existence never comes and goes. When all objects vanish, *sat* alone remains over. That which is incapable of being even thought of as non-existent can alone be existent. There is only one such thing that cannot be thought of as non-existent, and that is the real 'I'-principle.

If you make the attempt to think that you are non-existent, the principle that makes the attempt jumps over from the category of objects, and becomes the subject (principle) who attempts to think.

192. *SAT-CIT-ĀNANDA* – HOW TO EXPERIENCE IT?

Sat is the greatest generalization of the objects of the world, that is to say it is the existence aspect of it.

The individual 'Rāma' sheds off his limitations one by one and develops into *sat* or pure existence, in the following manner. He first transcends his name and possessions, then his community, his nationality, his manhood, his being a living being, then his being one whose only attribute is that he exists; and finally he becomes one with that very existence or *sat*, common to all objects of this world. All this is admitted by Rāma implicitly, at every stage. This is how your inmost principle is traced out, beginning with your body.

To have this experience, you have to employ your own knowledge or Consciousness. But the method of tracing the real Self through the medium of Consciousness establishes simultaneously both your nature of Consciousness and Existence (*cit* and *sat*). Hence, usually the *sat* aspect of one's self is not sought to be established separately. Consciousness keeps company with existence till it is established.

Sat-cit-ānanda, though positive in form, is negative in meaning. Viewed objectively, the Reality beyond body and mind could be described only as nothingness. But viewed subjectively, from the position of the 'I'-principle, it could never be termed as nothingness. It is Peace. Nothingness in deep sleep is the svarūpa of Peace, or yourself; because you are there beyond all doubt. Nothingness in the objective world is Peace in the subjective world; and that is *ānanda*.

In order to experience *sat-cit-ānanda*, you must transcend body, senses and mind and the objective world. He who experiences *sat-cit-ānanda* must himself be *sat-cit-ānanda*. But this is not possible, since the subject and the object can never be one.

So *sat-cit-ānanda* is experience itself, or the 'I'-principle. The stand from which you called it nothingness was not itself nothingness, but your svarūpa of peace.

193. Qualification and degree of renunciation required for initiation into the Truth

Earnestness and sincerity to know the ultimate Truth is the only qualification required to receive initiation into the Truth. These bring in all that is needed.

194. Sincerity and earnestness

Sincerity and earnestness in themselves represent an insatiable thirst for Truth. They never belie your self. They come from the deepest level, without any desire for conspicuousness or ostentation.

195. Truth about visions

All visions are only projections of your own mind. But you do not know or feel this to be so, during the vision itself. It is only when you rise to the higher plane that you realize the previous visions to be only projections of your mind.

196. ULTIMATE REALIZATION

Nirvikalpa samādhi is not the ultimate state of realization. You have reached the highest only if you have established identity with the real 'I'-principle. The sahaja state alone may be said to be the highest.

We are trained in a wrong groove of thinking, from our very birth. We have only to give up this wrong groove and take to the right groove of thinking.

25th July 1951

197. NEGATIVES

Negatives can never subsist independently, by themselves. They want a positive something, as their background.

Some people consider the mind as a container of thoughts and feelings. If so, it should be a permanent container. When permanency is attributed to mind, its material part – which can never be permanent – drops away, and the Consciousness part – which is permanent – continues as the Reality itself.

Changelessness, Awareness and Peace are the nature of the 'I'-principle. This is found by examining the three states impartially.

By the examination of the waking-state experiences, we find that I am in action, perception, thought and feeling. But I can never be any of these as such, but only the background of all these – upon which all these come and go.

Mind, as thought, can well be split up into its material and Consciousness parts. But the Consciousness part can never be further split up into the doer and the observer.

198. ASAMPRAJNYĀTA-SAMĀDHI

Rāja-yōgins, after going through concentration of the mind in different planes, come at last to mind itself and make the mind react upon the mind itself. As a result thereof, the mind comes to a standstill. And that state is called 'asamprajnyāta-samādhi'. Duality is still there.

26th July 1951

199. REALITY TO THE SAGE AND THE IGNORANT MAN

To the Sage, Reality exists at all times (transcending time). In other words, it exists in its own right.

If a thing does not exist in its own right, it is said to have only 'derived existence'. Relatively, between the pot and the earth, the existence of the pot can be said to be only derived from the earth, and that of the earth to be more real.

> nā 'satō vidyatē bhāvō nā 'bhāvō vidyatē sataḥ .
> ubhayōr api dṛṣṭō 'ntas tv anayōs tattva-darśibhiḥ ..

> [That which is unreal cannot come to be.
> That which is real cannot cease to be.
> Those who know truth, see clearly between these.]

Bhagavad-gītā, 2.16

200. HOW TO TEST A QUESTION?

After examining the question and the answer you expect to it, if you find that they are in the objective plane, then reject them. Because that question and its answer cannot take you beyond relativity.

But on the other hand, if the question and its answer lead you to the subject, the Absolute, accept them; because they take you to the source, beyond the relative.

27th July 1951

201. LIFE, THOUGHT AND FEELING DEFINED

> Existence conditioned is 'life'.
> Consciousness limited is 'thought'.
> Peace expressing itself is 'feeling'.

Happiness is something beyond mental pleasure. It means tracing the source of happiness you have enjoyed, to your real nature.

The incessant pursuit of objects of pleasure by man and the real source of all that pleasure are clearly illustrated by the simple story of a dog. The dog got a dry bone and began to munch it hard, for blood. This munching bruised its gum, and a few drops of blood came out. The dog immediately tasted this blood and thought it came from the bone. So it began to munch the bone harder, and more blood came out of its own mouth. This again the dog drank, until at last it was exhausted and left the bone.

Exactly the same is the condition of man, who hunts after objects of pleasure, encouraged by the glimpses of pleasure he occasionally seems to enjoy immediately on contact with them. Like the dog, man also takes the object to be the source of the pleasure enjoyed, and pursues it with still greater avidity.

But the moment he comes to understand aright, that it was his own real nature of Happiness that he was enjoying all along in the name of pleasure, the pursuit of objects stops altogether; and he becomes Self-centred and eternally happy.

The illustration of the beetle and butter also proves the same thing. [See note 148.]

202. WHAT IS THE GOAL OF ALL DESIRES? 'DESIRELESSNESS.'

Though desire is a prelude to worldly pleasure, yet you enjoy pleasure only when that desire ceases – that is, when you reach the stage of desirelessness.

Your desire for the object causes your body and mind to be incessantly active in order to get the object, and the activity continues until you achieve your object. But when once the desired object is achieved, the activity – having no other object – naturally ceases. The body and senses get relaxed, and the mind refuses to function.

At this stage, you are absolutely desireless. It is then that your real nature of Happiness shines by itself. Soon after, when your mind begins to function again, you connect the happiness experienced with the preceding object.

Happiness dawned only when desire changed into desirelessness. The goal of all desire is Happiness. Since Happiness is achieved only by desirelessness, desirelessness is the goal of all desires.

203. BEWARE OF HAPPINESS IN SAMĀDHI.

A jnyāna-sādhaka who has heard the Truth from his Guru, in the course of his attempt to establish himself in the Truth, may sometimes be casually thrown into a nirvikalpa state, with its sense of intense happiness. But he should be extremely careful not to get caught or fascinated by the enjoyment part of the experience. Otherwise it might enslave him, and thereby retard his progress.

204. HOW DOES VĒDĀNTA INFLUENCE ONE'S LIFE AND ACTIVITIES?

The mind is responsible for all worldly activities. Therefore the question comes to this: 'How does Vēdānta influence the mind?'

The mind cannot exist by itself, but only on some stronger support. Formerly, the ego served to support and direct all the activities of the mind. But when the ego is no more, the mind has only the absolute 'I'-principle to depend upon, and on that background the mind can never go astray.

The Vēdāntin always lives in strict conformity with the laws of the state, society, community, etc. He finds nothing to be gained by going against them. On the other hand, by obeying these laws he at least sets an example to the ignorant people, to whom it would do immense good; because these laws tend to bring about human justice, and this in due course would lead one to divine justice, which is Peace itself.

Looking from another angle of vision, you see that when you stand as the witness in all your activities, you become disinterested and free. This disinterestedness is clearly and naturally reflected and expressed, in all your activities.

205. THE GOAL OF ETHICS

Ethics has always unselfishness as its goal. But witnesshood takes you even further, and makes you selfless or egoless. So when you stand as the witness, you have actually transcended all ethics.

Ethics belongs to the realm of the mind alone, and the witness stands beyond it. So one who has reached the witness does not stand to gain anything by following the laws of ethics. He, however, observes them mechanically, through habit, just to set an example to the ignorant.

206. AT THE SAME LEVEL IN WHICH YOU GET ATTACHED, YOU CAN NEVER GET DETACHED.

Detachment is to be gained not by being detached from a few of the objects perceived, but from the whole world of objects which manifests itself in that level, as an integral whole.

In other words, you are to become detached from that level itself. This can never be achieved by confining yourself to that level alone. Nor is it possible to become detached from all objects separately, one by one.

Therefore, the only means to gain complete detachment is for the subject to take his stand in a higher plane or level, and from there view the world. Then you will see that the former world – with all its questions arising in its own level – altogether disappears.

This is how attachment in the dream world is transcended, by the subject changing over to the waking state.

207. THE HEART IN DIFFERENT PLANES

The spiritual heart is of no gross material stuff and so cannot be located in space. Still, to satisfy the lower adhikāris in the gross plane, it is conventionally located in the right hand side of the chest.

But in the subtle plane, the heart is the integral 'I'-thought, forming the centre of all thoughts. And beyond it, the heart is the right Absolute.

208. VISUALIZATION

Visualization is there when the effect that is produced in seeing is produced by the depth of understanding.

30th July 1951

209. ASTROLOGY – ITS FIELD AND EFFICACY

Asked about the relative efficacy of astrology, Gurunāthan said:

It is a process of calculation and application of mathematics, in establishing the relationship of cause and effect, reduced to the terms of their source: 'time'. In these calculations, many other things have also to be taken into consideration. If all these are given due consideration, the predictions will be mostly correct.

Still, facts relating to the body alone can be thus predicted successfully – facts regarding the 'sharīra-yātra' (the 'journey of the body') as they technically call it. Even here, sometimes it goes wrong, whenever Consciousness from beyond the realm of the mind brings to bear its influence upon the activities of the body, either directly or indirectly.

For example, when a Sage's thoughts in any way intervene from beyond the limitations of time, the predictions fail. Therefore, with regard to the life of yōgins or sādhakas progressing under a Sage, good astrologers usually refuse to predict anything. Here, something other than the body element, from beyond the body level, comes into operation.

> balī puruṣa-kārō hi daivam apy ativartatē
>
> *Yōga-vāsiṣhṭha* [unverified]

This means: If your free will becomes predominant in your activities, you gradually transcend your prārabdha-karmas [conditioning influences from the past].

210. HOW DOES UNSELFISHNESS HELP YOU TO TRANSCEND THE MIND?

Every time you do an act in strict conformity with ethical laws, you know on the surface that it takes you to the unselfish part. But if you examine the same act carefully, you will find that every such act takes you even further – to the real background, beyond the mind's plane.

This glimpse of your real nature expresses itself as pleasure, when you come back to the mind's level. But this you immediately attribute to the mind's activity just preceding it. Hence you miss the spiritual values of the communion with your real nature.

In every act called good or virtuous, there is a grain of self-sacrifice, however small.

211. CAN MIND LEAD ME TO REALIZATION?

We speak of 'instinct', 'reason', 'intuition', 'over-mind', 'super-mind', etc. In all these, mind persists and you have not gone beyond it.

For realization, you have to reach the general background of all these: which is pure Consciousness or Peace. From any stage except the first, namely instinct, this background can be attained directly and with the same result.

But evolution by itself, continued to any extent, will never take you to this background – your real nature.

31st July 1951

212. SOME SAY THAT REALIZATION IS SELFISH. CAN IT BE SO?

Some people, from their own relative plane, say that realization of Truth is selfish. Here, 'self' evidently means the lower self or the ego. This statement is made without understanding the true significance of realization.

Realization means the annihilation of the ego or the lower self. If any act is to be called selfish, the lower self should remain over, to claim the fruits of the action. But here, it is the death of the lower self that takes place. Nothing remains over to claim the fruit, nor are there any fruits capable of being enjoyed.

To call this 'selfish' is a contradiction in terms. It should really be called 'Real-ish' or 'Truth-ish', not 'selfish'.

213. HOW CAN I PROVE THAT I EXPERIENCE PERFECT PEACE IN DEEP SLEEP?

Gurunāthan: However, you will admit that you do not experience anything of the opposite of peace by way of activity or unhappiness in deep sleep. Well, that is the characteristic of Peace.

Now we will take another approach. Would you not get annoyed if you are suddenly woken up from deep sleep?

Disciple: Not if anything pleasant is offered on waking up.

G: But, at the moment of being disturbed from sleep, would you not be annoyed?

D: Yes.

G: Then, on being given something pleasant on waking, you are really taken back to the essence of the deep sleep state again, though you appear to be in the waking state.

Further, you love deep sleep so much that if it evades you for a few days consecutively, you even take to drugs to induce deep sleep. This also shows that you get Happiness in deep sleep.

After a hard day's work, you feel quite exhausted (or unhappy). But after a night's deep sleep or deep rest, you feel much refreshed and rejuvenated. All this you could certainly have gained from nowhere else except the preceding deep sleep state. This also shows that deep sleep is the source of happiness or refreshment.

214. WHAT IS THE MINIMUM EXPERIENCE NEEDED FOR SELF-REALIZATION?

If you experience the Truth at least once in the waking state, as it is experienced in the nirvikalpa state, that is enough to establish you in the Absolute.

Your conviction should be such that even a thought is not needed for you to stand in the Truth.

215. WHAT IS THE KIND OF EXPERIENCE THAT IS REALLY HELPFUL FOR REALIZATION?

It is not helpful at all taking you to a sphere of which you know nothing.

But if, after you have been taken there, you feel that it was familiar to you all along, that alone is really helpful. There, you must feel that it was always your own sphere.

This is exactly what happens here. You are shown the thing best known to you, the 'I'-principle. Usually, it manifests itself in a medley of impediments. So your familiarity with it is not in the least affected, and your conviction always stands at the highest. It is exactly like embracing a long lost child of your own.

3rd August 1951

216. LOGIC HAS ITS OWN LIMITATIONS. WHAT ARE THEY?

Lower logic is divided into *inductive* and *deductive*. Both of them concern themselves only with objects assumed to be existing, and deal with evidence and facts distinct and separate one from the other.

But when the very existence of the world – gross as well as subtle – is disputed and has to be proved, neither of these approaches helps us. Because here, the 'I'-principle or subjective Awareness is the only thing admitted to be existing. Here, it is the higher logic alone that can help us in the proper manner. Lower logic can never do it.

To the ordinary man, the only evidence available regarding the existence of the world is the evidence offered by the five sense organs. It is 'evidence' that is taken up here, and examined to show that it does not prove the world at all. But it proves only sense perceptions, or the senses themselves. In other words, the evidence proves nothing but the evidence. Therefore, it is no evidence at all, as far as the fact to be proved is concerned.

If you assert that the world exists, it is your burden to prove that it does. The opponent has only to deny it, until the existence is proved beyond doubt. Ultimately, even if you give up all argument and say 'I know the world and so it must exist', that also cannot hold good, because you cannot know any object except through one of the sense organs. When this is so, it proves again that it is that sense perception or sense alone that is known, and not the object nor the world.

217. YOU SAY RELATIVE KNOWLEDGE IS MEMORY ALONE, HOW IS IT?

When do you really know? You say you know a thing only when you are able to remember it. If not, you say you do not know.

Knowing has no connection with the object. It is pure knowledge alone.

So memory plays a very important part in making you believe what you are not.

218. MENTAL KNOWLEDGE AND EXPERIENCE

Mental knowledge is of the surface. But the heart is deep. When knowledge goes deep, it becomes one with the heart and is experience.

5th August 1951

219. A THING DOES NOT EXIST. HOW?

Question: It is said the wall has no length, height or thickness. Similarly, body has no weight, height, etc. How is this proved?

Answer: When you stand as wall, no thoughts regarding its height, length and thickness occur to you. It occurs only to that one who objectifies or sees the wall. Or in other words, these qualities come into existence only when one thinks of them. The wall, standing as wall, can never objectify itself or think about itself. If it tries to do so, it ceases to be the wall for that period of time.

Similarly, when you stand as body, you have no conception of any height or weight of that body. They do not exist then, so far as you are concerned, and you do not feel that they exist either. Therefore you are pure, unqualified Existence – both when you stand as anything, and when you do not stand as anything.

The body has no right to speak of itself. It is only he who sees the body that can and has a right to speak about it. So anything standing by itself can have no quality distinct and separate from it.

Without seeing length, you cannot know it or speak about it; and to see it you have to stand separate from it. When you separate yourself from length, it ceases to exist. Therefore objects and their qualities cannot exist together; since they are but separate objects from the standpoint of yourself, the only subject. All qualities are but superimpositions on the subject. You are the only subject or perceiver, and all else are but objects.

No object can exist independently of the subject, and two objects cannot exist simultaneously. Life consists in your perceiving objects in quick succession, but you perceive them only one at a time. This incessant change alone makes life possible. And the change itself is made possible only by the illusion of memory, which makes the non-existent appear as existent.

The body does not exist, either when you stand separate from the body, or when you think about the body.

220. WHAT IS MEANT BY RELATIVE EXISTENCE?

All questions relating to the Absolute can be explained only by illustrations from the world, where both parts are objective. The example of the pot and the earth is taken up here as an illustration, in order to answer this question.

The pot has no existence independent of the earth of which it is made; or in other words, the pot's existence is derived from the earth, which has a relatively more permanent existence. Similarly, objects have no existence independent of the self or the 'I'-principle. That is, the existence of the world is only relative to the subject 'I'.

Here, the 'I' is not gross like the earth in the illustration. Still, the 'I' is much better known than anything objective or gross. The existence of this 'I', though not apparent to the senses, is accepted by all persons alike.

Everything else has an existence only in relation to this 'I'. Things depend upon varying proofs to establish their existence. But the 'I' alone stands in need of no such proof at all. It is self-evident (svayam-prakāsha) – self-luminous.

221. WHAT IS REAL EXPERIENCE?

Consciousness stands as pure experience, without an experiencer. When I come to know a chair, I realize the existence of a something called Consciousness, distinct and separate from the chair. The chair becomes only instrumental towards directing my attention to the Consciousness.

That is the 'I'-principle, pure Consciousness.

222. 'When I say 'I am the body', it means 'I am not the body.' How to explain this paradox?

After hearing the Truth from my Guru, even if I constantly take the thought that 'I am the body', it cannot harm me.

Because the thought 'I am the body' consists of two parts – 'I' and 'the body' – the one distinct and separate from the other, according to the Truth already grasped. So, constant repetition of the thought would only mean alternately taking the thoughts 'I' and 'the body', several times. Every time you think of the body, you are objectifying it and showing it as separate from the 'I'; while the 'I'-thought can never be objectified.

So, every time you repeat this thought, 'I am the body', you are actually only emphasizing the separateness of the body from the 'I'. This really means: 'I am not the body.'

223. Can institutions help the spread of Vēdānta?

A great philanthropist from America once came to Gurunāthan and had a talk with him. He told Gurunāthan that he had come ready to finance any institution Gurunāthan would like to start, to propagate Vēdānta. He offered a fabulous amount to start work immediately.

To this Gurunāthan replied at once: 'I do not want to start any institution; and if anybody were to ask my advice, I would only discourage him. Such institutions very soon miss their goal, and get involved only with the means. Thus they degenerate into mere worldly institutions, with many of their attendant evils. Look at the institutions supposed to have been started by Shrī Shankara himself, with great hopes and with his blessings. What was the position of Shrī Shankara himself, and where are those institutions now? Institutions are generally stumbling blocks to the attainment of real spirituality. They foster desire for leadership and unhealthy competition.

'Vēdānta or Truth can be communicated only through personal contact with a Sage. This could be done only individually, and for this no institution is needed at all. If anybody wants spiritual instruction, I am here ready to give it. In that respect, you may take myself as an institution, if you so wish.'

224. SIGNIFICANCE OF WAVING THE LIGHT AND BURNING CAMPHOR DURING PŪJA BEFORE THE IMAGE

Waving the light means: 'Though I take Thee to be a form, Thou art really light and so am I.' It is this thought that is intended to be inspired by the waving of the light during pūja.

The camphor, with its sweet fragrance, quickly burns out; and leaves no trace behind. This is intended to symbolize the burning of the ego before the Absolute; without leaving any trace behind, even as a samskāra.

225. CAN PŪJA HELP ONE TO THE ULTIMATE?

No, not completely. But it can take you a long way towards the Ultimate. Pūja to the Absolute is done in four progressive stages.

1. *Gross pūja:* This is the ordinary pūja done by the organs of action to the Absolute.
2. *Oral pūja (japa)* is pūja done by word of mouth to the Absolute.
3. *Mental pūja (meditation)* is pūja done by mind to the Absolute.
4. *Self pūja (Ātma-pūja or samādhi)* is pūja done to the Absolute by one's own self. Here pūja is done by the self to the self. You are still in mental realm and pūja can take you only so far.

Beyond even this, you are in your real nature, which you can visualize only with the help of a Kāraṇa-guru in person.

11th August 1951

226. WHAT IS THE FIELD OF SCIENCE?

Science starts upon the basic error of giving independent existence to the world of objects, leaving the subject and the thing nearest to it – the mind – to themselves. Science examines only remoter things.

227. HOW ARE ACTIVITIES RELATED TO THE SAGE?

The Sage has both worldly and spiritual activities. To him, both are recreations, each in relation to the other (on an equal footing).

228. ACTIONS

According to the shāstras, actions are of two kinds, sinful and virtuous. You have to transcend both these before reaching liberation. The sins have to be washed away by virtue, and finally virtue has to be surrendered to the Absolute.

Then alone does one become eligible for liberation, according to the shāstras.

229. THERE IS HAPPINESS EVEN IN MISERY, OR ANY OTHER FEELING. HOW CAN THIS BE PROVED?

We often pay our hard earned money to witness certain plays (like *Nalla-tangaḷ*), pathetic from start to finish. So one is actually courting anguish. This clearly shows that there is something of real pleasure even behind that anguish.

Similarly, there is a state called 'viraha-mādhuri' (sweetness of separation) which devotees usually long for. *Rādhā-mādhavam* is a typical instance of this. It is true that Rādhā was wailing at her separation from Kṛiṣhṇa and was expressing her longing to get back to him. But really she did not want to get him back so soon, even if he was prepared to come. She was really enjoying a greater degree of happiness, in the longing itself, than she could expect from the fruition of the longing.

It is a sort of love which never wants actual union, but only wants to continue longing, without actual fruition. Fruition however ends the enjoyment. But happiness felt in the longing is purer, intenser, and of much longer duration than that felt in fruition. In such longing, one is really enjoying oneself, but without knowing it. This is clear from the fact that one does not like to be disturbed from or to forget that longing.

This shows that Happiness is the background of apparent misery, and similarly of all emotions and feelings.

You have necessarily to discard all objects before experiencing Happiness. But in the case of misery, you have steadfastly to cling on to the objects as long as the misery lasts. The objective world must disappear for Happiness to come into being, and it must appear for misery to do so. When misery is divested of all objects, it gets transformed into Happiness itself.

Similarly, when seeing is divested of form, it gets reduced to pure Knowledge or Consciousness.

230. WHY DO MOST BHAKTAS DISLIKE ADVAITA?

A bhakta generally does not like to become one with his iṣhṭa-dēva. He is prompted only by the enjoyment aspect of his contact with the iṣhṭa-dēva, himself standing always separate. He fears that by becoming one with the deity, the enjoyment would cease.

But he is mistaken. So far, he had been enjoying his iṣhṭa-dēva only as an object, or was only getting reflected enjoyment. But when he becomes one with the iṣhṭa-dēva, he ceases to be the enjoyer in the ordinary sense of the term, and becomes Happiness itself.

14th August 1951

231. WATCHING AND EXAMINING THE MIND (A YŌGIC EXERCISE). HOW IS IT POSSIBLE?

Shāstras prescribe an exercise to watch and examine the mind. For this purpose, the subject needs the help of an instrument, and the only instrument available is the mind itself. It is not possible to watch and examine the mind by the mind itself. The real subject also cannot examine it, because then the mind ceases to be mind. Therefore the exercise, as such, is spiritually futile.

232. HOW CAN AN OBJECT BE THE CAUSE OF AN EMOTION?

An object cannot become manifest by itself. How then can it stir up any emotion in you? If an object is known to be non-existent, even the idea cannot reasonably occur afterwards. Therefore no object can create an emotion in you. Understanding this in that manner establishes you in your real nature.

233. How can worldly experience lead one to advaita?

When you see a thing, your seeing and the form seen become one and stand as knowledge. Then only is the experience complete, and then you cannot even say that you saw.

You stand as seeing itself, or Knowledge. The object seen is also seeing. Thus the seen and the seeing become one in you, the Knowledge. Therefore, the experience of seeing a thing is pure *advaita*.

The seeing appears to be split up into the seeing and the seen. But this is impossible, and therefore *dvaita* is never experienced.

You depend upon your knowledge alone, to establish that you see a thing. When you know a thing, the thing is covered by Knowledge, or it is Knowledge expressing itself in the form of the thing; or, to be more accurate, Knowledge expresses itself. This is pure advaita, and is the experience of all.

When Knowledge dawns, the object disappears completely. You say you perceive a thing only when the perception is complete. Then the object loses its objectivity and becomes one with you. This is nothing but advaita.

'When you say you perceived an object, the object is not there and you are not elsewhere.'

234. When am I free?

'When the thought that you are "That" becomes the flesh of your flesh, the blood of your blood, and when that thought courses through your veins quite naturally and effortlessly, you may be said to be free.'

16th August 1951

235. What is the significance of vishva-rūpa darshana?

'Vishva-rūpa', as seen by Arjuna, was not all-comprehensive as the name signifies. The vishva-rūpa was really composed of the sāttvic, rājasic and tāmasic elements. The purpose of showing this to Arjuna was to convince him of the supremacy of the sāttvic over the two other elements, and to help him to establish himself in the sāttvic. The running away of the rākṣhasas in fright showed the rout of the rājasic element before the sāttvic.

Vishva-rūpa is the all-comprehensive world picture. It is the picture of an eternal present; because the future is also seen there, as in the present. The background of all that vishva-rūpa is Lord Kṛiṣhṇa himself.

We see only an infinitesimal part of it as the visible world. In the vishva-rūpa, the subject and objects are both perceived. It needs divine vision to see that as a whole.

236. STATEMENTS IN THE SHĀSTRAS

These are of two kinds – absolute (nirapēkṣha) and relative (sāpēk-ṣha). The relative statements are to be interpreted only to the extent needed in order to reveal their intention; and they are not to be taken as absolute statements.

For example, the examination of gross objects from the relatively higher plane of the sense organs reveals that they are but senses themselves. This finding is true only in its own plane, and it has no application in any other.

237. WHAT IS THE NATURE OF THE SHĀSTRAIC APPROACH TO THE ABSOLUTE THROUGH THE GODHEAD?

For example, take Lord Nārāyaṇa. The conception of Nārāyaṇa, according to the shāstras, is developed in four stages.

1. *Viṣhṇu-nārāyaṇa*, the Lord of Vaikunṭha, is the first in the order. It corresponds to a man identifying himself with the gross body in the gross world.

2. *Pada-nārāyaṇa* is the one next above, with a subtle body in the world of ideas. It corresponds to a man in the dream state or in deep contemplation.

3. *Vibhūti-nārāyaṇa* is the one higher still, in the deep māyā upādhi, giving infinite strength to both the Nārāyaṇas below for their work. It corresponds to the man in the causal body in deep sleep

or avidya, ever refreshing and strengthening him for the other two states of activity. All these three have their own separate names, upādhis and functions.

4. *Ādi-nārāyaṇa* is the highest of all, devoid of all upādhis and functions. It corresponds to the kūṭastha, in the turīya state of man. It is called by a name only when we look at it from down below. Reaching that state, it stands nameless, unmanifested, and Absolute. Then alone does the jīva, who proceeds along this path, reach the ultimate Truth.

Those who are satisfied by any of the first three Nārāyaṇa realms get stranded there, and perish along with those realms themselves; because they are mere manifestations and as such perishable. But the Ādi-nārāyaṇa, the last of the four, stands alone beyond all upādhis, shining in his own glory.

It is in this light that any Godhead should be accepted as a means to liberation; and the aspirant should proceed right through to the unmanifested, where alone he reaches the Absolute and attains liberation.

238. WHAT IS THE ORIGIN OF THE HINDU SCRIPTURES AND HOW TO READ AND UNDERSTAND THEM ARIGHT?

The Hindu scriptures are of four classes: *Shrutis*, *Smṛitis*, *Purāṇas* and *Itihāsas.*

Shrutis are the highest, consisting of the four Vēdas and the Upaniṣhads. They are dominated by ten of the Upaniṣhads, which are called the *Dashōpaniṣhads*. The Upaniṣhads expounded the ultimate Truth, mostly in the form of bold assertions of direct experiences of the authors themselves. The Vēdas describe different kinds of rituals for the attainment of varying degrees of worldly happiness. This is also in the form of assertions, unsupported by any reason or argument.

When these were first expounded, people were so docile and faithful that they took these assertions as gospel truths and lived according to them. But as centuries passed, people became more inquisitive and began to question these assertions in the Shrutis. This perceptible change in the general outlook demanded a closer and more reasonable interpretation of the Shrutis.

As demanded by the times, the new interpretations came forth in the name of *Smṛitis*: rationally explaining the practices and their aims, and establishing rigorous rules of conduct in the application of the rituals enjoined in the Shrutis. The authors of these Smṛitis were often great ruling kings and sages. These Smṛitis were in their turn accepted and obeyed implicitly for several centuries by the people. But when the general intelligence developed still further, the people began to question the Smṛitis also.

Then came the *Purāṇas* with innumerable stories and anecdotes, explaining how the fruits of actions were strictly awarded in conformity with the Shrutis and Smṛitis, in the form of experiences in heaven, hell or earth. This continued to appeal to the faith of the people and keep them at their duty for several centuries more. But the Purāṇas also in their turn began to be criticized.

Then the *Itihāsas* were written, as further explanations of the very same Truths discussed in the shāstras just mentioned. These were mostly in the form of attractive stories, telling of highly emotional incidents and sublime morals, like the epics of *Rāmāyaṇa*, *Mahābhārata*, etc.

In studying any of these works, it should never be forgotten that the primary object of all of them is only to explain the statements of absolute Truth expounded in the Shrutis. To attain this end, the lower works employed several means of illustration: such as stories, anecdotes, etc. These are not to be taken as true in themselves at all times, but to be accepted only for the purpose of establishing the Truth expounded in the Shrutis.

When that Truth is understood and assimilated, the means adopted have necessarily to be discarded or forgotten. Nobody dares to carry on his shoulders the canoe which helped him to cross the river. You know how foolish and embarrassing that would be.

The doubts or difficulties or conflicts arising in any one of these classes of writing are sought to be explained by resorting to the next higher class of work.

But, after systematically studying these works, including the *Dashōpaniṣhads*, an earnest disciple once quite legitimately asked his master how two different processes of creation, described in two of the important Upanişhads – the Chāndōgya and the Taittirīya – could be reconciled.

Answer: Strictly speaking there was no creation at all. But, at a lower level, it may be answered in a different way. The key to progress, in any form of spiritual enquiry, is to go from the particular to the general. Every aspirant is confronted with a world of infinite diversity. He has to reduce this diversity into some form of generality. Then alone can he reduce the whole world further, into its ultimate source.

The object of the order of creation described in the Upanişhads was only to help the aspirant to reduce or dissolve the world, in idea, to its very source in the order of the particular system of creation he was inclined to accept. The method was considered quite immaterial, so long as it helped one to reach the source. The enunciation of the order of creation was not intended to establish the reality of the world or of creation at any stage; hence the enunciation of more than one order of creation.

This method of dissolving the diversity of the world, by degrees into the most general, was followed literally by the yōgic sādhakas. Some of the usual practical methods adopted by them were panca-kōsha-prakṛiyā, panca-bhūta-prakṛiyā, stūla-sūkṣhma-prakṛiyā, etc.

When diversity is transcended in any manner, a spark of Truth from the lips of the Guru is sufficient to take the aspirant to the right Absolute. This shows that when any conflict arises at the highest level, only the Guru remains there to solve it and lead you on.

239. IS THERE ANY SPIRITUAL VALUE IN A PRAYER TO A PERSONAL GOD?

Prayers are often made by devotees for the attainment of pleasure or its objects. Here, God is taken only as a means for attaining the object, which is considered much dearer than God himself. This position is deplorable indeed. You do not get any spiritual benefit out of such prayers or fulfilment of desires.

240. APPARENT IRRECONCILABILITY OF PURĀṆAS

Each Purāṇa describes its own presiding deity to be supreme and all the rest to be subservient to it. How is it possible to reconcile this position?

'Brahman' or the 'Absolute' is considered to be the background of all Godhead. Each God is conceived in the Purāṇas from two different standpoints. One as the unmanifested (kāraṇa-brahman) and the other as the manifested (kārya-brahman), both being denoted by the same name. Between these two, the unmanifested alone is real and acceptable, while the manifested has only a relative existence.

In each Purāṇa, its particular presiding Godhead, though called by the same name as the manifested, is to be understood as the one unmanifested Absolute. As such, all other manifested Godheads have to pay obeisance to their background, the Absolute. This is what is described in all the Purāṇas.

Viewed in this perspective there is no difficulty in harmoniously reconciling all the Purāṇas.

Unqualified brahman	nirvishēṣha-brahman
Qualified brahman	savishēṣha-brahman
Unmanifested brahman	kāraṇa-brahman
Manifested brahman	kārya-brahman
Unconditioned brahman	aparichinna-brahman
Conditioned brahman	parichinna-brahman

241. HOW TO IMPART ENLIGHTENMENT?

The ignorant man alone is to be enlightened through logic and argument. The ripe aspirant is to be enlightened only through tattvas.

> yuktyā prabōdhyatē mūḍhaḥ prājñas tattvēna bōdhyatē
>
> *Yōga-vāsiṣhṭha* [unverified]

9th September 1951

242. HOW TO MEDITATE?

If you want positively to meditate upon something, without losing sight of your real centre, meditate upon the ultimate perceiver. Then the perceived and the perception both disappear; and the perceiver stands alone without being a perceiver, shining as the Absolute.

This can be done in two ways:

1. Meditating as the witness of thoughts.
2. Meditating as the witness of feelings.

16th September 1951

243. WHAT IS THE SIGNIFICANCE OF THE SAHAJA STATE?

You are established in what is really meant or what really happens when you say that you know or that you love. By knowing or loving, an object is actually brought nearer and nearer to your own self, until at last it merges in you as Consciousness or Peace. Love and Consciousness pure always annihilate the ego.

In statements such as 'He who sees…', 'He who hears…', 'He who thinks…' etc., the unqualified 'he' is the absolute Reality itself. He who is able to realize this, is in the sahaja state.

Even after realizing that what you have seen is a rope, it is quite possible to see the snake in the rope with all its details. But you can never be frightened by that snake, because you know full well that it is your own creation. This is how a Jnyānin in the sahaja state sees the world in the Self, but is in no way affected by it.

Shrī Caṭṭampi-svāmi (a Sage contemporary of Shrī Ātmānanda) often used to say: 'All this is the manyness of the One'.

Shrī Shankara: 'Perception of an object is but oblation to the fire of knowledge.'

Gurunāthan: '*One* is the Truth. What you call two is not two but '*one-one*', and three but '*one-one-one*', and so on. The word 'two' makes you forget the one, which is the real background and substance of all numbers. But when you say 'one-one' it serves the same purpose as two, but does not make you forget the Reality. 'Two' does not really exist at any time.

So also, look at all objects without forgetting their common background, the 'I'-principle or Consciousness. This is the sahaja state.

244. WHAT IS THE ROYAL ROAD TO TRUTH?

And what is the purpose of *karma-yōga*, *karma-sannyāsa*, *rāja-yōga*, *bhakti-yōga*, etc.?

All these are usually supposed to be mārgas (means) to the attainment of the Truth. But in fact, no mārga or course of practice or exercise by itself is capable of leading one to the Truth. Hearing the Truth from the lips of the Guru alone is the means to realization or jnyāna. That is the royal road to Truth.

For one who has attained jnyāna this way only recently, any of the mārgas described in the shāstras, if practised in the light of jnyāna already attained, will be helpful in establishing oneself firmly in the sahaja state.

Without this preliminary attainment of jnyāna, no amount of effort by itself in any of the mārgas could be of any avail to establish one in the Truth. Shrī Kumaḷi-svāmi is himself a living example of this. (Shrī Kumaḷi-svāmi was a great yōgin disciple of Shrī Ātmānanda. Refer volume 3, pages 217-9).

So these mārgas acquire meaning and are of practical usefulness only after one has gained jnyāna from one's Guru. But all of them prepare the ground beautifully well even before hand.

Karma-sannyāsa is concerned only with renouncing the actions of the body, the senses and mind – purely in the dualistic plane and that only as far as it is possible to do so. *Rāja-yōga* strives to discover the potentialities of the mind to the maximum – all from the dual plane alone. Both these methods take no thought of the Absolute. Similarly, the *bhakta* also moves only in the dualistic plane, and does not dare to think of the Absolute.

Of all these mārgas, *karma-yōga* alone has an advaitic goal called 'naiṣhkarmya-siddhi' – i.e. to be engaged in all the activities of body, senses and mind, and at the same time to be convinced beyond all doubt that you are neither the doer nor the enjoyer at any time, but only the ultimate witness or Truth itself.

This really constitutes the life and activities of a Sage. This way of living is natural and agreeable. It can well be said to be the highest, and it is devoid of any effort or artificiality.

The karma-yōgin is directed not even to entertain the thought that he should achieve 'naiṣhkarmya-siddhi'. Because even that thought makes him a doer and brings in so much of attachment.

To become established in the witness, the independent existence of objects has to be denied in full. This stand alone is complete. Looking from this stand, all attempts at doing good to humanity in this ephemeral world become quite meaningless.

16th September 1951

245. HOW TO SHOW THAT THE 'I'-PRINCIPLE IN ME AND IN ALL IS ONE AND THE SAME?

You say the 'I'-principle in '*me*'. What is this '*me*'? Is it the body, senses, or mind? No. Because these are not there in deep sleep, and still the 'I'-principle is there all alone.

So the '*me*' means the 'I'-principle itself; and it comes to this. The 'I'-principle is indivisible and is only one. Duality is only in manifestation – namely 'body, senses or mind. Beyond this, there cannot be any duality, since there is nothing there to be distinguished from another.

Therefore, the 'I'-principle is unique, and the objects alone are different.

23rd September 1951

246. EXPERIENCE – WHAT IS ITS SIGNIFICANCE AND GOAL?

The fact that *you experience* needs no proof. But the mistake is made only in specifying the objects of experience. What is it that you experience?

The progress from the illusion of the world to pure objectless experience is usually made in three distinct stages.

1. The first and the lowest is that you experience the world or objects. But this is easily disproved since no object can be experienced as such.
2. The next stage is that you experience the knowledge of the object. This also becomes impossible, since there cannot be any

knowledge of an object whose existence cannot be proved by experience.

3. The last and the real stage is that you experience only pure, objectless knowledge, or the Ātmā itself, or experience itself.

So in every experience, objective or otherwise, it is only this pure knowledge or the 'I'-principle that is really experienced. This experience is my real nature. It expresses itself in all the activities of the mind, senses and body.

But the word 'experience' is indiscriminately and wrongly used in connection with all the activities of the *non-ātmā*, and called 'experiences' of the mind, senses and body. This makes one forget the real nature of experience or Self. And out of this forgetfulness of the Reality springs up the world of objects.

If you forget the real nature of experience and then view the realm of the mind and body as such, everything there will appear independent and real. But if you look at everything without forgetting the real nature of your experience, everything will appear to be nothing other than Experience itself.

There is a saying that: 'The damsel of māyā never dares to appear before anyone who knows her.' Likewise, objects will never appear as objects, to one who knows them to be real experience or Ātmā alone.

247. HOW TO DESTROY THE ILLUSION OF OBJECTS?

Two different approaches:

1. Destroying the immediate object alone, allowing the samskāras to linger on. This is a partial solution prescribed only to the lower adhikāris.

2. But the uttamādhikāris are instructed to examine the objects now and here, and it is shown that they are nothing but the 'I'-principle. This leaves behind no samskāra whatsoever.

248. HOW TO THINK ABOUT THE ABSOLUTE?

Answer: Strictly speaking, it is impossible to do so. Spiritual sādhakas are often asked to think of the Absolute. The Absolute is clearly beyond all thought, and therefore it is impossible to think of it directly. There is no need for that sort of thought either, because you are always that. In order to think of the Absolute in any manner, you have to objectify it.

You need only to eliminate yourself from all that is non-ātmā. When that is done, your real nature as Ātmā, which is self-luminous, shines all alone in its own glory.

Therefore, what the sādhaka is actually asked to do is only this. In the guise of thinking of the Ātmā, think of all that is non-ātmā, all that constitutes mind, senses and body, and eliminate them from yourself. When left alone, you stand as Ātmā.

Inert instruments can never think of the self-luminous 'I'-principle. So you should never attempt to speak or think of this 'I'. But if ever you happen to think of this 'I', then just eliminate the thinking part alone, which is inert, and you remain as you are.

Shrī Vidyāraṇya's exposition of this Truth takes you only to the tether end of witnesshood, and leaves you still as a witness. But you should go even a step beyond the witness, to the ultimate Reality itself – proving that there is nothing else to be witnessed and that you are all alone: the Absolute.

26th September 1951

249. REASON – LOWER AND HIGHER

Lower reason: Silently makes reference only to your own [personal] experiences.

Higher reason: Makes a silent reference only to the very being in you, and the endorsement comes spontaneously from within.

250. HOW DO I KNOW THAT I HAVE STRAYED AWAY FROM MY REAL NATURE?

Answer: You have not strayed away.

Question: Then who wants to know the Truth?

Answer: The mind or the ego.

All illustrations used in the course of spiritual talks have to be immediately applied to the subjective sphere and their significance realized.

The 'I'-thought is not the real 'I'.

Eliminate the thought aspect completely from the 'I'-thought, and what remains alone is the real 'I'-principle.

29th September 1951

251. WHAT DOES A GURU DO FOR A DISCIPLE?

It is something which a disciple need never bother herself about, and which the intellect can never grasp.

You need only know that a Guru takes you from the phenomenal to the Absolute. You will be able to get a glimpse of it only when you rise higher and higher. From the level of the mind, you can never conceive how it takes place. Much less understand it.

Your question is purely from the mind's level. So give it up. Do not try to solve it, for the time being. Ultimately, you will come to the position that the question was not necessary at all.

How can a virgin understand the pangs of delivery until she becomes a mother herself? No amount of inference will be able to take you to the Reality.

252. SENSES COMPARED TO COLOURED SPECTACLES

Your senses are a sort of coloured spectacles, before your Consciousness. They colour the vision completely and create a world.

So the only thing needed is for you to remove the coloured spectacles of your senses and mind; and then you will see the Reality, in its nakedness and full glory.

253. REASON AND HEART – THEIR RELATIONSHIP

They are not watertight compartments at all. Both of them radiate from the common centre, the 'I'-principle, and you can reach that 'I'-principle through either.

If you reach it through the heart, you will find the reason also present there; and vice versa.

Reason includes the heart element also. The shāstras bear testimony to this. Reason or vidyā is represented in the shāstras as the spouse of the Absolute. This feminine aspect, attributed to the personification of reason, amply proves the prominence of the heart element present in it.

254. Why the traditional injunction of secrecy in talking about the Truth?

Spiritual sādhakas are strictly enjoined by the shāstras not to speak the naked Truth to purely worldly minded persons. Truth suffers thereby. Such listeners interpret it only in the customary, objective relativity in which alone they live. They find it impossible to reconcile the Truth this way. So they begin to ridicule Truth itself. This naturally drives them to perdition. You must try to avoid such a catastrophe at all cost.

255. Why do I feel that I do not know my real nature?

Answer: The 'I'-principle does not ever feel and does not make a complaint either. It is always the mind that feels. The mind is incapable of knowing my real nature. Even when the mind turns its attention to my real nature, the mind loses its own form and gets merged in Consciousness – my real nature.

Before you can say you feel, you must necessarily perceive that feeling. That perceiver then must certainly be beyond that feeling function. You are that, the 'I'-principle.

Love becomes divine when personality is not emphasized (Upaniṣhad).

256. (A visitor asked) How to give up wrong identification during eating?

Answer: Though you think you are eating, when the body is eating, still you also know or perceive the eating.

Identification is usually made only after the function. During the function, you stand as the function.

So, after the eating, stand as the knower of the eating; and then you are saved.

257. HOW DOES REMEMBRANCE PROVE ME?

Remembrance of any past incident consists in recollecting all that is connected with it, including also your own body and personality as part of the incident.

You cannot remember anything but your actual perceptions. So you must have definitely perceived your personality also, during the incident. This perceiver could be nothing other than your impersonal Self. So every act of remembrance proves you alone.

It was the mind that was in activity, and again it is the mind that remembers later. The mind silently gets the information from the witness, which alone was present during the incident.

Going deeper, you will find that memory itself is a misnomer. Because the mind can never bear witness to the mind itself.

Here follows an incident (not a story) of a lunatic cured by the witness thought.

258. A LUNATIC CURED BY THE WITNESS-THOUGHT

Once, in August 1950, when Shrī Ātmānanda stayed in Bombay for a couple of days on his way back from Europe, he gave audience to a good number of spiritual enthusiasts who flocked for short interviews with him. Among them was an educated young Parsi gentleman who was a lunatic for the past twenty years. But he had occasional sober moments, for an hour or two every day. Fortunately, it was during one of those sober moments that he came for the interview. As soon as he was led in and seated, Shrī Ātmānanda asked him: 'Well, what is it that you want?'

Visitor: Well, Sir, I am not come for any spiritual instruction. They say I am a lunatic, and I too believe it, more or less.

Shrī Ātmānanda: Sorry, I am not a doctor myself. You must go to some doctor and take advice.

Visitor: No Sir, I have tried all that in vain. I heard that you are a great divine, and I am sure you can help me out of this malady.

Shrī Ā: No, you are mistaken. I am not a saint and I have no powers to help you in this. Please go and seek remedy elsewhere.

Visitor: No Sir, I am desperate. I shall not return without getting something from you.

Shrī Ātmānanda was in a fix. The gentleman's face did not show any signs of disorder and he felt compassion for the man. So Shrī Ātmānanda asked him, rather abruptly: 'Well! What is your ailment?'

Visitor: They say I am a lunatic.

Shrī Ā: Is it true?

Visitor: Yes, it is true, more or less.

Shrī Ā: How can you say so?

Visitor: Because I know it. I cannot think about anything consistently for some time.

Shrī Ā: How do you know that?

Visitor: Well, I know that. I can see my mind running from object to object, in quick succession.

Shrī Ā: But are you that changing mind, or are you that knowing principle which never changes?

Visitor: Of course, I am that knowing principle.

Shrī Ātmānanda retorted with some force: 'Be that knowing principle always, and don't worry about your mind.'

The gentleman opened his mouth wide and sat aghast for a minute, and said with luminous satisfaction: 'Yes! Yes! I have got it. I want nothing more from you now. Allow me, Sir, to go, and I shall write to you from home.'

Shrī Ātmānanda: 'Yes. You may go and be at peace.'

He went home straight and wrote to Shrī Ātmānanda regularly, after three days, one month, three months, six months, one year, and three years (the last being in August 1953) – all equally assuring that he was leading a steady, happy, contented and prosperous domestic life with his dear wife and children, of course with hearty endorsements from each of them regarding his normality.

This was indeed a miracle of the ultimate witness. Shrī Ātmānanda had only just helped him to direct his own attention to that talisman in himself and he was saved.

29th September 1951

259. HOW TO PROVE THAT THERE IS NO IGNORANCE IN DEEP SLEEP?

After waking from deep sleep, we make two spontaneous assertions:

1. 'I was at peace'; and
2. 'I did not know anything.'

These two statements refer to the very same experience, one positively and the other negatively; and therefore they cannot be different. The second is, in fact, only a paraphrase of the first. The second statement means only that 'I did not know anything other than the positive experience of deep peace in deep sleep.' So, there was no causal body present there at all. [There was no body of unconscious potentiality, implying an unmanifest world.] This proves not the existence of ajnyāna [unconsciousness], but its non-existence, in deep sleep.

Another approach: That which precedes is said to be the cause, and that which succeeds the effect. Here, the time element is essential to make this distinction possible, and to establish causality. But standards of time differ fundamentally in the waking state and in the dream state; and in deep sleep, time does not exist at all. Where there is no conception of time, neither causality nor a causal body can exist. For this reason also, there is no ignorance in deep sleep but only deep peace, undisturbed by any other experience.

Understanding deep sleep correctly in this way, you find the 'I'-principle there, in its real nature. This 'I'-principle shines incessantly, through all states. So when you say you wake up from deep sleep, it is wrong; for your deep sleep, as your real nature, continues without a break. That is to say, you never come out of the 'I'-principle.

All the worlds created by you in the waking and dream states are withdrawn into you in deep sleep. The world as such does not exist in deep sleep, but only as the pure 'I'-principle.

260. How can I be one with Consciousness?

1. They cannot be separated, even for a moment, even in idea.
2. Both stand as the ultimate perceiver or subject; and can never be objectified, not even in idea.

The doer or enjoyer is consciousness, appearing limited by 'buddhi' or 'generic mind'.

In the presence of Consciousness, the mind, senses and body – which are really dead matter – function as though they are not dead matter, just like iron filings getting enlivened in the proximity of a magnet.

When the mind is proved to be Consciousness itself, samskāras die out, and the mind no longer continues as mind.

261. What is my relation with action and inaction?

Action depends upon inaction, and inaction upon action, for their very existence. This is impossible; and so both are non-existent, as such. Therefore, I stand transcending both.

Any particular feeling, pursued to its very source, suddenly disappears; and you will be thrown unawares into your real nature of Peace.

262. What is Vēdānta?

Vēdānta is not a system at all. 'Vēdānta' means the 'end of knowledge'. It is Truth alone, pointing to Truth.

It has no quarrel with any religion. It only says to all religionists: 'Dear friend, so far as you have gone, it is all right. But please come higher still.' Vēdānta does not belong to any particular religion, but transcends all; and is in fact the fulfilment of all religions. It is Vēdānta alone, remaining as the background, which gives life to all religions.

Even after realizing Vēdānta, one could very well continue his worldly life as before, being to all appearance a member of the old religion to which he formerly belonged. But to himself, he has transcended all its boundaries and he can no longer be claimed by it.

So experience of Vēdānta really makes one a better Hindu, or a better Christian, or a better Muslim, as the case may be.

Thus the Sage is the fulfilment of all religions.

30th September 1951

263. WHAT IS MEMORY? (At the mind's level)

At the mind's level, we have to take it that the witness silently witnesses the events and subsequently transmits the information to the mind. The mind in its turn identifies itself with the witness for the time being, and poses as if it were present during the past act referred to.

But when the mind is engaged in a thought, it is never possible for it to witness this very thought simultaneously.

264. WHAT IS THE COMPOSITION OF THE EGO?

It is the ego, which is a crude mixture of body and Consciousness, that takes both the thoughts:

1. I am the body (objectively), and
2. I am Consciousness (subjectively).

In the first thought, the Consciousness part of the ego is ignored, and the body part alone emphasized. In the second thought, the body part is ignored, and the Consciousness part alone is emphasized.

1st October 1951

265. WHAT IS THE NATURE OF LOVE IN ITS APPLICATION?

If you love another for his or her gross and external qualities alone, that love is of the lowest type.

But if you love the other knowing that it is the life principle alone in the other that you love, then that love becomes sublime.

And lastly, if you love the other knowing that it is that which transcends the attributes – body, senses and mind – that you love, there the otherness vanishes at once. That love is the most sublime, and is the Absolute itself.

The ordinary man believes the object he desires to be real, and to be the source of the pleasure he enjoys. But the Sage sees objects as mere pointers to the Self.

266. How is Truth experienced?

According to the traditional path, it is believed that the Truth dawns upon the sādhaka as a mark of divine grace, after a prolonged practice of manana and nididhyāsana, after first hearing the Truth from the Guru.

But under a Guru who has established himself in the natural state and adopts the direct path to the Truth, it is quite different. He is Truth itself and knows the Truth. He stands in need of no grace from elsewhere to lead his disciple to the Truth. He knows well how to tell the disciple what the Truth is and can safely take him direct to it, here and now.

But the disciple has of course to make some effort after that – to establish himself in the Truth thus realized, and reach the natural state.

2nd October 1951

arthād arthāntaraṁ yāti cittē madhyē tu yāsthitiḥ
nirastamananā cāsau svarūpa-sthiti rucyatē

Yōga-vāsiṣhṭha [unverified]

Means: Between two thoughts I am in my real nature. To be deeply convinced of it is alone needed to establish you in the Absolute.

In thoughts, you allow yourself to be limited by yourself.

… prāṇann ēva prāṇō nāma bhavati, vadan vāk, paśyaṁś cakṣuḥ, śṛṇvan śrōtram, manvānō manaḥ; tāny asyaitāni karma-nāmāny ēva …

[Seen as living in itself, it gets to be called 'life';
as speaking, 'speech'; as seeing, 'sight';
as hearing, 'sound'; as thinking, 'mind'.
These are only names of functions, attributed to it.]

Bṛihadāraṇyaka Upaniṣhad, 1.4.7

Means: Mind and senses are but names of functions. *Sat*, *cit* and *ānanda* – when manifested – become life, thought and feeling.

267. HOW IS THOUGHT NON-EXISTENT?

Thought is non-existent whether looked at from the lower or the higher plane.

Looked at from the 'I'-principle, thought gets transformed into Consciousness and ceases to exist as thought.

Looked at from the lower plane, the gross objects being proved to be non-existent as such, thought – which is supposed to be their subtle form – becomes a misnomer. And thus also thoughts are non-existent.

268. UPON WHAT DOES THE WORLD DEPEND?

The world depends upon the subject alone. The world appears exactly in terms of the stand taken up by the subject.

When you are subjectively transformed, after hearing the Truth from the Guru, the apparent world also undergoes a corresponding transformation; until, at the last stage, the subject and the object both stand as one in pure Consciousness, the 'I'-principle.

3rd October 1951

269. THE NATURE OF THE UNDERSTANDING OF THE SAGE AND OF THE ORDINARY MAN

If you say that you do a thing, the Truth is that you do not do it. It really means that you stand beyond both doing and not doing.

We first go beyond the three states to discover the 'I'-principle; and then looking from that stand, we see that the 'I'-principle expresses itself in all the three states and even beyond them. Thus the jīvan-mukta expresses himself in all the activities of the body, senses and mind.

But to the ordinary man, a jīvan-mukta appears only as another ordinary man, exactly as the Absolute appears to the layman as objects perceived by the senses.

270. IS THERE TIME IN DEEP SLEEP?

In deep sleep there is no conception of time.

But on waking, you take your concept of time from the waking state and try to apply it to the deep sleep state, and hope thereby to bind deep sleep. This is impossible.

So deep sleep is in fact not bound by time at all.

271. WHY DOES A SAGE NOT SERVE HUMANITY?

Answer: Why don't you serve the humanity you found existing in your dream? The Sage gives the waking world and its humanity only the same degree of reality as the dream world itself.

The question arises out of utter ignorance of what liberation is. Service, as you say, is motivated always by love (of course conditioned) for your brother. The Sage sees his brother not as an object to be loved as you do, but as one with himself in essence; because the Sage stands always as the absolute Reality which is also the background of the whole world. Therefore, the Sage loves his brother as himself.

What greater service and sacrifice can you conceive of, than this one of becoming one with the entire world?

The Sage is already established at the centre which you aspire to reach by all your laborious service and sacrifice, but which you invariably fall short of, somewhere on the way.

4th October 1951

272. *BHAGAVAD-GĪTĀ*, 4.18

> karmaṇy akarma yaḥ paśyēd akarmaṇi ca karma yaḥ .
> sa buddhimān manuṣyēṣu sa yuktaḥ kṛtsna-karma kṛt ..
>
> [One who sees actionlessness in action,
> and action only in actionlessness,
> is wise among men. Throughout all actions,
> he remains impartial and complete.]

In the verse, 'karma' should be understood as 'action'; and 'akarma' as 'actionlessness', not as the negative 'inaction'. He who sees, in action as well as in actionlessness, a certain changeless principle –

the 'I'-principle standing behind both but not connected with either – is verily the wisest and the greatest of yōgins.

Now taking each part separately:

1. He who sees actionlessness in action – or the changeless background, the 'I'-principle, behind every action – gets established in the ultimate Reality.
2. But when the body, senses and mind are apparently actionless, if you blindly superimpose that actionlessness on the 'I'-principle, that amounts to action and that binds you. So you have to guard against that kind of superimposition. If you begin to claim action or actionlessness for yourself, you bind yourself.

A new approach: Action proceeds from inaction, and inaction proceeds from action. So both are non-existent as such.

'All the world is relative. I am the only Absolute.'

273. WHAT IS THE ORIGIN OF MEMORY?

Suppose on seeing a chair, the thought arises in me that this is 'the-chair-that-I-sat-on-yesterday'. This, as you see, is an integral thought. It cannot be split up into parts.

But the illusion of splitting it up into parts alone brings in memory to victimize you and make a fool of you. 'That-I-sat-on…' is only a qualification of the chair, which can never be separated from the chair in that integral thought. That qualification does not denote in fact any previous function.

274. HOW DOES THE WORLD COME INTO EXISTENCE?

In the creation of the world, it is ideas that get solidified into the gross world. Immediately, it assumes independent reality and begins to react upon the mind itself.

275. PAST IS PAST ONLY IN THE PRESENT.

Because the thought, 'as though of the past', occurs only in the present.

276. LONG PRACTICE MAKES EVEN WRONG APPEAR RIGHT. (A story)

There was a palace cook who usually diluted the milk for the king, keeping a portion of the milk for himself. The king got accustomed to it and believed it was pure milk. Subsequently, a new cook came and gave the king pure milk instead. This upset the king's stomach. At first, the king thought that the new cook was in the wrong and scolded him for negligence. But eventually the king understood that the old cook had regularly cheated him.

This is exactly the nature of our view of the Reality. We are so accustomed to its perverted form that we take the *form* alone as real and take no note of the substance. At last, when the Truth is revealed to us by the Guru, we look back and recognize our long-standing mistake.

277. WHAT IS SECOND CHILDHOOD?

You are first born into this world as a child in ignorance. Subsequently, on reaching maturity, you hear the Truth from your Guru and are liberated. Then you become a *child in knowledge*, never to change.

So only a Sage can really be said to have a second childhood.

5th October 1951

278. YOU RENOUNCE ONLY FOR SUBSEQUENT ABSORPTION IN FULL. WHY?

True renunciation is renunciation of 'objects' from your 'Consciousness of objects', leaving you as 'Consciousness pure'. Looking from there, you see 'form' to be nothing other than yourself; and so you absorb all objects into yourself and rest in Peace, as you do in deep sleep.

So also, physical renunciation is intended only to take you to the Reality, in the first place. Looking back from there, you see the objects renounced as nothing other than the same Reality. And so you readily absorb them all back into your self. Then alone do you attain real Peace.

This shows that the renunciation begun in the manner of the ordinary sannyāsin has to be undone in the end. Then why begin this anomaly at all, if it could be avoided without prejudice to your realizing the Truth?

279. WHO CAN REALIZE THE TRUTH?

Only he who has heard the Truth from a Kāraṇa-guru, with earnestness and sincerity. All the shāstras say: 'Thus far alone can we say. The Guru alone can give the rest.'

Ācāryavān puruṣō vēda

Chāndogya Upaniṣhad, 6.14.2

It means: He who has a Guru alone knows.

280. WHAT IS RHYTHM?

Constant and continuous repetition of a word or a set of words amounting to a mantra creates a harmony both inside and outside the individual. The external harmony thus created expresses itself as happiness, sometimes in the form of 'rhythm' used in poetry. This, to be effective, should be spontaneous and untrained, and is found only in inspired poetry. It is the reflection of the perfect harmony experienced inside by the poet himself. This alone attracts the readers generally.

This is the mystery of the Sage's writings as well. Because they spring from the harmony of Truth, which is his natural element always. In the Sage's writings, very little is said and much is left unsaid. But what is left unsaid by the Sage is often more alive and forceful in creating the ultimate effect. What is left unsaid instructs the reader more effectively than what is actually expressed in words.

7th October 1951

281. WHAT IS PAURUṢHA? (The quality of being a puruṣha, the inmost core of oneself)

All conscious and deliberate activities of mind and body are subject to *pauruṣha*. Pauruṣha has a tinge of independence about it. It is opposed to destiny. A man who has not the capacity of thinking deeply about his future meekly submits to destiny. Destiny governs only the bodily and mental activities of man. All the rest is governed by paurușha alone.

Paurușha is the 'being' beyond the mind, inclined to activity.

282. WHAT MAKES ONE A TRUE ASPIRANT?

It is one's earnest desire to get to the Truth that prompts one to search for it. This desire is nothing but the direct function of the heart. All your conscious efforts, even though actuated by reason, follow only the course chalked out by this heart.

Therefore, every seeker of the Truth expresses his heart sufficiently well. At last, when the seeker following the path of reason reaches the citadel of Truth, he finds the heart also there in full and as one with reason and himself.

So Truth is visualized by the harmonious blending of the head and the heart, in Peace.

13th October 1951

283. WHAT IS REAL BONDAGE?

When the mind is thinking or feeling, you always stand as the witness. But when you talk about these very thoughts or feelings sometime later, you apparently change your stand and pose as a doer. You do not make any distinction between these two functions, and you attribute both these activities to the 'I'-principle. This is real bondage.

284. WHY DOES CONSCIOUSNESS THINK IT IS SOMETHING OTHER THAN ITSELF?

This is a question very often asked. Now, examining the question itself, we find that it is asked from the position that such an identification exists. And this question has also conceded the existence of body, senses and mind, besides that of Consciousness transcending all these.

Consciousness and everything other than Consciousness exist in two different planes. When we look from the plane of Consciousness, we find there is nothing other than Consciousness, and there this question cannot arise.

When looked at from the mind's plane and conceding the existence of both world and Consciousness, it has been proved that Consciousness can be there only as witness. The witness witnesses only perceptions, and not objects. It has also been proved that perception is nothing other than Consciousness itself. For this reason also, the world is an illusion and the question cannot arise.

The question cannot arise in Consciousness, since the world is not there. Nor can it arise in the mind's plane, since you cannot drag down Consciousness to the mind's level and make it part of the apparent world.

15th October 1951

285. What is the nature of thoughts and feelings?

Thought rises in Consciousness, rests in Consciousness and sets in Consciousness. Therefore, it is nothing other than Consciousness. It consists of the content and the boundary.

Now, examining thought with the mind itself, the mind perceives only the boundary, and calls it thought. Examining it closer, the mind crosses the boundary and enters the content of thought. But, to its amazement, the mind finds itself lost and merged in the content of thought, which is nothing but pure Consciousness.

Thus, the thought endeavouring to examine the content of thought is no thought at all, in the strict sense of the term. Because its object is Consciousness itself, which can never be objectified; and in the attempt the mind dies and gets transformed into Consciousness itself.

Similarly examining feelings, the mind gets merged in Peace itself. Thus thoughts and feelings are nothing other than my own real nature – Consciousness and Peace.

286. HOW TO RISE FROM THE GROSS TO THE ABSOLUTE THROUGH ANY SENSE ORGAN? (e.g. the hearing organ)

An 'idea' is conveyed to us by one or more words in any language. The same 'idea' is also capable of being conveyed to another in another language. Thus, the idea is the same, though its upādhis or languages are different.

Therefore, this 'idea by itself' has no language of its own, and the language does not go into the make of the idea. It only expresses itself in the gross or the subtle, through any language. Unexpressed as it is, it is languageless.

All ideas are similarly reducible to the languageless idea. As languageless ideas, there is nothing to distinguish between each other, except the samskāra that you started the enquiry each time from a particular idea. Therefore, languageless ideas cannot be many but only one.

Transcending the samskāra regarding the origin of this enquiry, the languageless idea stands as the ultimate Reality. The following are the definite stages [from left to right], in the progress from the gross to the Absolute.

Vaikharī	*Madhyamā*	*Pashyantī*	*Parā*
Gross	Subtle	Witness	Absolute
Gross idea	Subtle idea	Languageless idea	Absolute
Gross mantra	Subtle mantra	Essence of mantra	Absolute
Gross form	Subtle form	Form generic	Absolute
...	...	...	...

The third and the last stages are one and the same, but for the samskāra that the third has some distant relationship with the preceding two stages.

21st October 1951

287. WHAT IS INSTINCT?

Long practice of any voluntary action naturally becomes mechanical; and degenerates into instinct, which is involuntary.

22nd October 1951

288. HOW TO KNOW CORRECTLY?

Only if your knowledge of your own Self is correct, can you hope to know anything else correctly.

It is our experience that our physical activities do not stand in the way of our thoughts and feelings. Similarly, it is possible for me as witness to be always knowing – even when the body, senses and mind are functioning. Merely note this fact and become deeply convinced of it. Don't attempt to objectify the witness by thought.

> *Sat* is that which is incapable of being even thought of as non-existent. I alone am the one such.
>
> > [asad brahmē 'ti cēd vēda svayam ēva bhavēd asat .
> > atō 'sya bhūd vēdyatvaṁ sva-sattvaṁ tv abhyupēyatām ..
> >
> > If it were found that all there is
> > does not exist, then one's own self
> > could not exist to find this out.
> > The self cannot become what's found.
> > Just what one is in truth oneself
> > must be acknowledged at the start.]

Shrī Vidyāraṇya, Pancadashi, 3.25

289. WHAT HAPPENS WHEN YOU LOVE AN OBJECT?

When you love an object, the object is outside and the love is inside you. They can never meet, as they are.

The contact is established inside, where the gross object is represented by its subtle form or thought. So the real contact is only between your own thought and your own feeling. Hence it comes to mean that you love only yourself, always.

290. HOW CAN I BE DISPASSIONATE?

You *are* dispassionate, even now.

1. When you are desiring any one particular object, you have practically renounced everything else, except that one object.

Now, examining that particular desire more closely, we find that in the moment of the desire, you renounce even that particular gross object, in favour of its thought-form. Because the gross object has no access into the mind's realm, where alone the desire exists. Therefore, you desire only your own thought-form, which is nothing other than your own Self.

So you desire only yourself, and are always in perfect dispassion. Know this, and you shall be free.

2. It is a fact that you gladly renounce everything you profess to own or desire, with a whole world of objects including even your much loved body. And that, without even a moment's notice, you go into another state. In that state, you readily accept a new body in a new world, to be later renounced likewise.

   This shows beyond doubt that you are not attached in the least to the objects in both the states. Therefore, you are always in complete dispassion. Know this, and you shall be happy.

20th November 1951

291. WHAT IS IT THAT MANIFESTS?

Every perception, quality or attribute wants a permanent background for its existence. This background is the Reality itself. To denote the Reality, we give it a name. But still this background remains as that which transcends senses and mind.

It cannot be called unknown. I say it is even more than known, not by the senses or mind but by Consciousness or the 'I'-principle. Thus the background of everything is the one Reality itself.

When you say that the unknown exists, it means that you have known it.

When the mind says that there is something transcending the mind, the mind itself transcends its realm and, standing as pure Consciousness, knows that something as Real.

292. KARMA-YŌGA ACCORDING TO THE *BHAGAVAD-GĪTĀ*

Action consists of doership and enjoyership. In karma-yōga, you are first asked to renounce by thought the fruits of your actions. This helps you only to annihilate the enjoyership. The more important aspect, namely doership, has next to be dealt with.

Both these could be transcended only by knowledge of the Truth.

29th November 1951

293. DIFFERENT DEFINITIONS OF MIND

1. *Yōga-vāsiṣhṭha*: The mind is that which oscillates between consciousness and inert matter.
2. *Upaniṣhad:* The mind is only the name of a function (vṛitti-nāma).
3. *Svāmi Vivēkānanda:* The mind is not a substance in itself, but only that standpoint viewed from which the Absolute appears diversified, as the manifested world.
4. *Gurunāthan:* Mind is Consciousness itself, appearing limited.

294. WHAT DOES SELF-LUMINOUS MEAN?

Self-luminous means that which does not need the help of another light to manifest itself or prove its existence.

You know you exist. So the 'I'-principle alone is self-luminous. The world is all dead matter. You cannot say it exists until you lend the light of your own Self to manifest it. It can shine only by your light. In other words, the world has only a borrowed existence.

The 'I'-principle alone has an original or independent existence. Whatever is not self-luminous can have only a borrowed existence.

295. WHAT IS THE APPARENT VARIETY IN FORMS?

There is no variety in forms. You say there are many forms and you use the word 'form' to denote all forms – this form, that form, etc. What is that 'form' which is common to all forms? It is changeless and therefore beyond the realm of the mind.

So you simply use the word 'form' and drag it down to the realm of the mind and make it stand for what it is not. Things extraneous to form are brought in, to create variety in forms. Form is one and the same. It is changeless, and hence beyond the realm of the mind.

Therefore form, when rightly examined, is the ultimate Reality itself. Hence there is no variety in forms. Likewise, there is no variety in other sense objects as well. Thus man is the ultimate Reality, tree is the ultimate Reality, flower is the ultimate Reality.

The sound which is common to all sounds knows no variety, just as form which is common to all forms knows no variety. So you can never speak of various forms or various sounds. Without going into the generic sound, you cannot invent a name. *The generic in all cases is the ultimate Reality.*

The generic in you naturally refuses to be limited in any way, and so you always bring in generic names. The generic subject sees the generic object, and the particular subject sees the particular object only. It is the generic that always manifests itself. But the mind has a peculiar self-deception, and it somehow chooses only the particular. That is how the world appears.

Suppose there are several forms impressed on a surface of clay. In order to perceive the different forms, the basic idea of clay has first to be forgotten. But we invariably ignore the fact that without the clay, none of the forms can exist. In other words, without a changeless background, diversity cannot exist.

The general rule by which the enquiry into the Truth of this world proceeds is '*from the particular to the general*'. So, in order to explain the variety in objects and perceptions, we have to get to the background and then look at the apparent variety. Then we see that the variety vanishes altogether.

Viewed from another angle of vision, we see that objects first sensed by the senses are immediately transformed into knowledge when known. Then all objectivity and variety vanish and Consciousness alone remains.

All our suffering is created by our being captivated by variety, and our forgetting the background on which the variety appears.

296. WHAT IS THE RELATION BETWEEN DEEP SLEEP AND THE WAKING STATE?

It is often stated that a man wakes up from deep sleep on hearing a sound, meaning thereby that hearing the sound was the cause of his waking up.

No one makes use of senses or mind in deep sleep, because they are not there. So the sound could not have been heard in deep sleep. And when it was heard, he must certainly have been in the waking state. An experience definitely belonging to the waking state can never be said to be the cause of the waking state. So the statement is wrong, and it is not the sound that woke him up.

Usually you wake up from the deep sleep state and you cannot find a cause for it. Why can you not assume that you likewise came to the waking state, and heard a sound? Why do you want a cause for the waking up?

297. THE KṢHAṆIKA-VIJNYĀNIN'S AND THE ADVAITIN'S POSITIONS

According to the kṣhaṇika-vijnyānin, the conception of jnyāna is a mere idea. It is not self-luminous. The kṣhaṇika-vijnyānin believes that the conception of Ātmā is an illusion, like the ring of fire appearing by the rapid movement of a lighted torch.

The torch by its movement appears at different points in rapid succession. Evidently, in relation to the ring of fire, the torch is more real.

But the kṣhaṇika-vijnyānin admits that there are many such ideas (torches). Who can make a comparison between these several ideas? The perceiver alone and not any one of the several ideas. Therefore, the advaitin says that the holder or the perceiver of the several ideas alone can compare them and come to a conclusion. That perceiver must be self-luminous, in order to do so.

That is Ātmā. That is the real 'I'-principle. Whose ideas are they? My ideas. So I am the holder.

298. REALIZATION AND ESTABLISHMENT

You hear Truth from the lips of your Guru. Following the words, their sense and their goal – which is the Ultimate – you rise from level to level, from body to mind and from there to Consciousness. On thus hearing the Truth from one's Guru, the understanding of the Truth is *immediate, instantaneous and complete*.

Soon after, you come back to the body-idea. The Truth that is heard from the lips of the Guru takes the disciple from level to level to the ultimate Reality. In order to get established there, the disciple has to remove innumerable obstacles. The knowledge of the Truth that he has acquired from the Guru helps him to overcome all obstacles. When this is done, realization is complete.

299. BEING AND BECOMING

Being and becoming cannot go together. When you are striving to become the Truth, you are admittedly away from Truth; and when you are in the being or Truth, there is no need for any striving at all to become the Truth.

When you are at the centre, manifestation is not perceived; and when you are at the manifestation, you are outside your centre.

So the 'I'-principle and the manifestation can never meet.

300. WHAT DO I LOVE?

You say you love your wife. But suppose she passes away and you are left alone near her dead body, at the dead of night. It creates in you not the feeling of love as before, but a creeping sensation from head to foot. This shows that before her death you were not extending your love to that inert body part still lying before you, but only to the life principle in it which has already left the body.

This 'life principle' can easily be proved to be changeless consciousness, which knows no birth or death. Your real nature is changeless Consciousness. Therefore, it is clear that you love only yourself, even in the form of other objects or persons.

Hence the Upaniṣhad says [*Bṛihadāraṇyaka* 4.5.6]: 'A man does not love the wife for her sake, but only for the self in her; and the wife does not love the husband for his sake, but only for the Self in him.' When Happiness comes, the mind dies.

1. The Self is objectless love or Peace. Love for self is degraded, compared to pure love or the Self.
2. It gets more degraded when it becomes self-love.

3. This gets further degraded when it becomes love for objects. But still, love is there. Get back to it in its purity.

So, to reach your real centre, the 'I'-principle, you have to retrace the whole course from objects to the Self, in the reverse order. If, in your love of objects, you are able to emphasize love, you will easily get to the love aspect or the peace aspect of Reality. Just as, in your Consciousness of objects, when you emphasize Consciousness, you get to the Consciousness aspect of the Reality.

You love things for yourself. So you love the Self more than anything else.

301. THE ORDER AND EFFECT OF MANIFESTATION

The Reality is manifest as Consciousness first, and Consciousness manifests the object next. If one thing is said to manifest another object, the first thing is really manifesting itself, as the background of the second. The rock manifests itself as the background of the image. Thus, Consciousness manifesting perceptions means that Consciousness remains as background and perceptions appear and disappear in it.

When you see a chair, it is admitted without saying that the space all round is lighted up by the gross light. But this light, by itself, is not perceptible to the naked eye except in relation to some object; and so it is not usually noted or emphasized.

Similarly, the presence of Consciousness is most essential to make any perception possible. Therefore, the manifestation of any perception first proves the existence of Consciousness, and only next proves the object lit up.

Unless you are self-conscious it is never possible for you to be conscious of objects. But the self-consciousness part is usually ignored. It is that Consciousness that has to be emphasized.

> dēhābhimānē galitē vijñātē paramātmani
> yatra yatra manō yāti tatra tatra samādhayaḥ
>
> [When bodily conceit has passed
> and truth of Self is realized,
> whatever states the mind may reach,
> all mind is there absorbed back in.]

Shrī Shankara tradition, Dṛig-dṛishya-viveka, 30

yadi dēhaṁ pṛthak-kṛtya citi viśrāmya tiṣṭhasi .
adhunai 'va sukhī śāntō bandha-muktō bhaviṣyasi ..

[If separating body out,
you stand at rest in consciousness,
then here and now you come to peace
and happiness, where you are free
from all restraining ties and bonds.]

Aṣhṭāvakra-samhitā, 1.4

Even after separating yourself from the body, the mind may still continue, but it is always found functioning towards the Reality (inward).

302. WHAT IS ADVAITA VĒDĀNTA?

Examining the three states, we find that the 'I'-principle is changeless, and that changelessness, happiness and knowledge are its characteristics.

This, in short, is the whole of Vēdānta – which has not only to be understood, but also lived in right earnest.

303. WHAT HAPPENS WHEN THE GURU TALKS TO THE DISCIPLE?

'It is the Truth that speaks the Truth to the Truth. That is the Truth about it.'

When the Guru talks to the disciple, it creates a deep conviction in him regarding the point at issue; and he becomes more and more attached to the Guru.

1st February 1952

304. APPEARANCE IS ALWAYS DECEPTIVE.

It is our daily experience that we hear the thunder long after the lightning. But the fact is that both occurred simultaneously. Therefore, just at the moment when we hear a sound, there is no corresponding sound actually in existence. It has already undergone change and disappeared.

So even in the gross world, we see that no perception is true, as and when it appears.

305. IT IS OFTEN SAID: 'THAT IS THIS.' WHAT DOES IT MEAN?

Concepts of time and space, 'then' and 'there', added to a thing = 'that'.
Concepts of time and space, 'now' and 'here', added to a thing = 'this'.

Take away space and time from both, and what remains over is neither 'that' nor 'this'. It is Ātmā, which transcends time and space.

2nd February 1952

306. CONCENTRATION

Concentration is relevant only when it is assumed that the mind is by nature distracted. But the fact is otherwise. The mind is always concentrated. But, for argument's sake, let us say that the mind is distracted. Two ways of approach can be adopted to achieve concentration.

1. Applying the mind continuously to any particular object or ideal and thereby trying to rise above distraction. The concentration achieved by this means is only temporary.
2. Examining the mind itself and discovering that it is never distracted, since it can never take two thoughts simultaneously. To know this deeply takes you even beyond concentration, a long way towards Reality.

307. FALSE IDENTIFICATION – HOW DOES IT WORK?

The activities of body, senses and mind are not self-dependent. The 'I' alone knows thoughts. But the 'I' does not express itself. Therefore, to correlate two thoughts, the mind is utilized. The mind identifies itself with the 'I' and works in the name of 'memory'.

It may be said, from the sphere of duality, that the individual jīva imbibes experiences from the witness of the states. But it may be asked: 'Is this possible?' It is. If the jīva can claim the *sat-cit-ānanda* aspect of the Reality, why not this?

On listening to the Guru you realize the Truth, *now* and *here*. You have only to cling on to it, in order to take it to *then* and *there*.

308. THE WAKING SUBJECT CANNOT DISCUSS DREAMS.

All questions about dreams are easily disposed of. The waking subject who audaciously puts forth the problem is most incompetent to do so, as he himself is entirely absent in the dream state. Moreover, the dream state is no dream state when actually experienced. It is then a clear waking state to the dream subject.

The three states are considered by the shāstras as *upādhis* to the witness, and as *qualities* to the jīva.

> sthūlavuṁ sūkṣmavuṁ kāraṇam ennatuṁ
> mūlamāṁ cittinuḷḷōrupādhi trayaṁ
>
> [The 'gross', the 'subtle' and the 'causal':
> at root, all three of these are just
> expressions of consciousness.]

Eṟuttacchan

5th February 1952

309. 'WHO IDENTIFIES?'

'Who identifies?' is a question sometimes asked. Identification is the parent of doership. The question presupposes a parent even to identification, and puts a doer before it.

In the question, Ātmā and anātmā are both considered to be real and on a par with one another. That should not be. Anātmā is only an illusion, and all questions come out of that illusion alone.

8th February 1952

310. THE CONTEMPLATION OF THE WITNESS ASPECT

When the mind's attention is directed to the silent witness, the mind has to get into tune with the nature of the witness and become silent also, or be dissolved in the witness. (Mechanical acting is mind becoming solidified, so to say.)

The advantage of the witness aspect is that it removes the basic error. So that aspect of the Reality is the best suited for contemplation.

10th February 1952

311. WHAT IS THE TAINT OF THE NIRVIKALPA STATE?

Something inevitably draws you out of that state. That must evidently be the feeling that you went into it by your own effort. Therefore it is transient.

Moreover when you come out of it, you again see a world unexplained; because something of the world remains in you still.

312. BHAKTI AND JNYĀNA PATHS

Bhakti cripples your ego and makes you feel equal to the most insignificant blade of grass; and you conceive your God as the conceivable Absolute. Thus, when your ego is at last lost, you automatically reach the position of the Godhead.

But *jnyāna* takes you up, step by step, by the use of discrimination or higher reason; attenuating the ego little by little each time, until the ego is dead at last. By this process, you transcend mind and duality, and reach the ultimate Reality.

11th February 1952

The ignorant bhakta always chooses to remain as the ego in the dvaitic level; and to do homage to the personal God, as distinct and separate from him.

But the bhakta whose devotion has received an advaitic touch from a Kāraṇa-guru conceives his personal God as Ātma-mūrtī, establishing thereby a direct and permanent relationship with Him. Thus Rādhā's Kṛiṣhṇa was the witness, and Rādhā was the ego. This approach, by itself, takes one right to the ultimate Truth.

313. THOUGHTS

Thoughts may be viewed with equal advantage in three different ways, in relation to yourself. You may choose any one or more of these ways.

1. As pure Consciousness, and so yourself in essence.
2. As shining in your own light, and so pointing to your real nature.
3. As the witnessed, yourself being the disinterested witness.

314. HOW TO FACE EMOTIONS?

You may face your emotions successfully in two ways:

1. By trying to see that you are the silent witness of the emotion, without doing any violence to the system.
2. By trying to see that emotion rises in you, abides in you and vanishes into you; and so is made of your real nature itself.

In either case, emotion fails to do you any harm.

12th February 1952

315. CAN A SAGE WHO HAS LEFT HIS MORTAL COIL BE A GURU TO A NEW ASPIRANT?

No. Never. When a Sage leaves his mortal coil, nothing remains over except pure Ātmā. But if the relationship has been directly established when the Sage was alive, it is enough to lead the aspirant to the ultimate Truth.

The fact whether such a Guru-disciple relationship has been directly established is known only to the Guru. The fact of the regular tattvōpadēsha having been imparted is also not the criterion.

If the disciple has deep love and devotion for the person of the Guru who is a Sage, it is enough. Nothing more is needed for the disciple, by way of sādhana or instruction from the Guru, to reach the Ultimate and stand established there. Shrī Vaṭivīshvarattamma was a living example of this fact.

Even if the disciple is incapable of such deep love and devotion for the Guru at the outset, there is no cause for discouragement. Because the Guru is love incarnate. Even if the aspirant is mentally prepared to make a surrender to the Guru on the body level, and if he has the readiness to listen and act up to the instructions of the Guru at least for the time being, he is provisionally accepted as a disciple. Later on, when the Truth is imparted to him in the regular order, the whole of the Guru goes into the disciple and takes his abode there. It is only then that the aspirant becomes a regular disciple and the relationship is established for ever.

316. WHAT IS SURRENDER?

Surrender, so far as the ignorant man is concerned, is only of upādhi to upādhi, on the body level. But spiritual surrender means surrender of the ego to the Ātmā in one, Ātmā being represented by the Guru.

This is possible only at an advanced stage, when the disciple is capable of cognizing the impersonal. Therefore, real surrender is possible only after visualization of the Truth; and it can never be insisted upon as a qualification for realization, much less for initiation.

It is said: 'The Guru is immanent in all, as pure Ātmā. But he is immanent particularly in the disciple – to a much greater degree, on account of the relationship.'

317. HOW DOES A THOUGHT ABOUT THE GURU, JUST BEFORE EVERY ACTIVITY, HELP ONE?

Question: We usually take just a thought of the Guru before taking to any activity, spiritual or worldly. What is the significance of this?

Answer: It brings the living presence of the Guru to preside over all our activities or to illuminate the whole experience.

318. How can I prevent anything from being superimposed upon me?

Thinking that you are *sat-cit-ānanda* takes you beyond the mere 'this' aspect.

> *Sat* [existence] comprehends all life. Therefore no particular aspect of life can be superimposed upon you.
>
> *Cit* [consciousness] comprehends all thought. Therefore no thought can be superimposed upon you.
>
> *Ānanda* [happiness] comprehends all feeling. Therefore no feeling can be superimposed upon you.

Therefore you stand beyond the possibility of any superimposition – in the form of life, thought or feeling.

319. Activity as a sādhana to get established in Truth

After visualizing the Truth beyond all doubt, throw yourself heart and soul into any activity and lose yourself in it. It is a sādhana in itself which takes you right to the Reality each time. Thus, when you are engrossed in work, you have at the same time renounced the work.

If you can see the entire world – including your own body – as only dṛishya (the see-able), you are free; and you have accomplished what has to be accomplished.

For the ignorant man, 'ignorance of Consciousness' covers up the object; but, for the Sage, 'Knowledge' covers it up. When you know the chair, you do not think of seeing. It is only when you are questioned that you say 'I saw'. But Consciousness stands behind the perception of a Jnyānin, always Knowing without knowing.

It is said: 'The world or the mind carries on its head the instrument for its own destruction.' So also, if properly examined, it can be found that every question carries with it its own answer.

On listening to the Truth from the lips of the Guru for the first time, you unknowingly rise to the highest level in understanding, and visualize the Truth. All that you have to do after that is to go knowingly to the same height and visualize the Truth, as often as possible; until that Truth becomes your natural state.

15th February 1952

320. Reality of states compared

At the lowest level, there are the three states: waking, dream and deep sleep states. Examining them closely, one finds that there are only two states – the deep sleep and dream states. Examining them still further, one finds that there is only the deep sleep state. Examining deep sleep more closely, it is found to be no state at all. The dream and waking states are only appearances on deep sleep.

It is in and through Me that all activities take place. But the mistake is made in the attempt to objectify that non-doer self and its experiences, exactly as in other activities.

16th February 1952

321. 'Why should I live?' or 'Why should I die?'

These are questions very often asked. Each question itself clearly implies the answer that I do not want to live, or that I do not want to die. Reducing the question to its fundamentals, in the most general form, it appears as: 'Why should I?' To this question, nobody is willing to add the implied negative answer as above. Therefore, these questions are irrelevant. Hence, in its particular form also, the question cannot arise.

Mind in its functions moves either forwards to something-ness, or backwards to apparent nothingness. When you are thinking of the ultimate Reality, you can discover that your mind is functioning backwards to a state where all thoughts vanish. It is a retreat into the inmost core of your own being (Consciousness).

19th February 1952

322. Happiness is peace.

Happiness exists only in relation to previous suffering. When that state of happiness continues without being disturbed by unhappiness, it is called deep Peace.

323. SOME DEFINITIONS:

Space is the generic form of objects; and
Time is the generic form of thoughts.

What is 'beauty'? 'Beauty' is personalized when you perceive it. But in itself, 'beauty' is an expression of the Absolute. It is harmony itself and is not perceivable. Knowing 'beauty' as purely impersonal, it can never tempt you, even when personalized. Truth and beauty are one.

When the ego tries to see beauty in the beautiful, both get transformed into the beyond and become beauty itself. By seeing that something is beautiful, you see really that you are beauty itself. For example, you say: 'The boat is beautiful.' But do you see anything other than wood? *No*. Then where is the beauty? Certainly in the seeing, which is illumined by Consciousness. Consciousness is beauty itself.

You say that you *know* and that you *love* another.

Knowledge (in the relative sphere) is becoming one with another with one's intellect.

Love is becoming one with another with one's whole being. So love is relatively deeper. Deeper Knowledge is love.

Direct perception is silent knowing.

22nd February 1952

324. THE DIFFERENT SAMĀDHIS

Yōgins classify samādhis into five classes:

1. *Savikalpa* is visualizing a sense object (usually the form of the iṣhṭa-dēva or an ideal) in the dualistic sphere.
2. *Nirvikalpa* is beyond all doubts, name and form.
3. *Nissankalpa:* Here, desires in embryo cease coming up in the form of sankalpa.
4. *Nirvṛittika:* Here, even involuntary vṛittis (mentations) cease coming up from the source of thoughts, which have been stilled.
5. *Nirvāsana:* Here, even the instinctive upsurge of vāsanas in embryo is stilled.

These are but states of the mind, in the course of the mind getting more and more sāttvic. A yōgin who has just come out of nirvāsana samādhi continues like a dead body, with the mechanical functioning of a gentle prāṇa alone.

Realization of one's own real nature is still beyond, and has to be fulfilled by listening to the Truth from the lips of a Kāraṇa-guru. The sahaja state has to be attained even after that, by being established in the Truth so visualized.

23rd February 1952

325. WHAT IS REAL EXPERIENCE?

Every so-called experience ends or merges in the ultimate 'I'-principle. Or in other words, the 'I'-principle is the only experience.

Feeling is nothing but intense thought. Some say that feeling is beyond knowledge. Yes, beyond superficial knowledge it might be. But who is it that decides? Certainly not feeling, but a knowledge which knows the feeling. Therefore, there is a deeper knowledge beyond the feeling.

But the Truth is different still. You are, beyond head and heart, true Knowledge. Your real nature is the background of both thoughts and feelings. The head and the heart are only different functions of the mind. You know both. In the statement, 'I know I am', it is absolute experience – beyond the head and the heart – that speaks. So real experience may be said to be a harmonious blending of the head and the heart.

25th February 1952

326. WHY DOES ONE LOVE FLATTERY?

Because it is the Self or Ātmā that is flattered, and it really deserves all that and even more. But let not the ego claim it. That is all.

When a work written by a Sage is read by some one, while the Sage is still living, it opens up a direct contact with him. But after the Sage's passing away, this cannot do so. If the desire is deep and earnest, contact through reading will certainly facilitate meeting in person either that Sage, if he is still living, or some other.

327. HOW TO TRANSCEND THE FEELING OF FEAR?

Turn your attention from the fear to the subject ego. Immediately, you see the ego to be nothing but the witness. Thus, you can easily get over the fear and reach the background.

Existence can never be dead existence.

Existence and Consciousness are one and the same thing, viewed from two different aspects.

28th February 1952

Man alone, of all living beings, exists and knows he exists. Animals only know objects.

The dream state is as continuous as the waking state. The deeply impressionable person alone has dreams.

1st April 1952

328. WHAT ARE EXPERIENCES DURING SĀDHANA AND HOW TO INTERPRET THEM?

The following is a typical instance of such an experience of an ideal sādhaka who had accepted 'Lord Kṛishṇa' as his Ātma-mūrti. He had advanced to the extent of having deep and lively visions of Lord Kṛishṇa, talking and walking with him even with a greater sense of reality than the usual waking state experience.

In one particular vision, the sādhaka was led on by Lord Kṛishṇa through a narrow path, with a thorny forest on one side and a steep precipice on the other. At last they came to a narrow streamlet with very little water in it. There was a culvert across it and a small Kṛishṇa temple and tank on the opposite side. Lord Kṛishṇa stopped and asked him, in all apparent seriousness, to bathe in the tank, to go to the temple, to offer prayers and to come back. In the meanwhile, Lord Kṛishṇa promised to wait there till he returned. Without a thought, he went off and did everything as instructed by the Lord.

But when he came back, he found that the quiet little stream had swollen into flood and torrents, and that the culvert had been washed away. Lord Kṛishṇa was still waiting on the other side of the stream. The sādhaka was bewildered at this sudden and dreadful change. Seeing him dispirited and helpless, Lord Kṛishṇa immediately asked him to take courage and jump across the flooded stream. Thus encouraged by Lord Kṛishṇa, he felt strengthened and without any further thought of consequences he jumped across the stream, landing safely beside the Lord; and both returned home.

The incident appears to be insignificant, but the significance is very deep. His readiness to leave the living Kṛishṇa behind, and to go to the temple to worship the dead Kṛishṇa there, clearly showed that he did not recognize Kṛishṇa for what he really was. To prove this to him, he found on his return to the stream that the imitation Kṛishṇa in the temple was helpless to take him across the rushing torrent, while a word from the living Kṛishṇa could perform the miracle in a moment. This incident opened his eyes to the real glory of Lord Kṛishṇa, who was ultimately in him.

It is to avoid such pitfalls that sādhakas are usually prohibited, during the days of their sādhana, from reading any spiritual books other than those prescribed by their Guru, and from meeting any apparent jnyānin or yōgin for the purpose of spiritual conversation.

You cannot recognize a Jnyānin from his appearance or words. But you can rest assured that a true Jnyānin will only send you back to your own Guru for instruction.

329. HOW IS ACTIVITY AND INACTIVITY RELATED TO TRUTH?

From inactivity, you cannot get to the beyond without something active coming to your help. But from the active sphere, you can rise straight to the Ultimate, merely by understanding it aright.

2nd April 1952

330. WHAT IS THE EVIDENCE OF THE HIGHER REASON?

The mind is only an expanded form of the ego. Even in our daily life, there is something in us which stubbornly refuses to accept blindly all that the mind brings in. This is a clear expression of the higher reason in us.

4th April 1952

331. WHAT IS THE TEST OF SPIRITUAL SĀDHANA?

When you are engaged in any mental activity, if there is the least taint of objectivity, then that activity is not spiritual. But if there is no such objectification at all, it is purely spiritual or ātmic in nature. This is one of the tests of spiritual sādhana.

5th April 1952

332. THE MORAL OF '*BHUSHUṆḌŌPAKHYĀNA*'

The story is of a mythological crow (Bhushuṇḍa) in *Yōga-vāsiṣhṭha*. The crow was the form assumed by a great yōgin, who by his wonderful powers managed to outlive the deluges of nature. ['Deluge' here refers to the cosmic deluge in which the whole universe is destroyed, at the end of each cosmic cycle. See notes 378 and 984.]

The moral is that he had to strain himself endlessly to maintain his ego, with the result that he was never at peace.

333. PROBLEMS AND PEACE

Some people say they have no problems in life. This is meaningless talk. It only means that they are mere cowards, who stubbornly refuse to think in the light of evident facts.

Happiness and unhappiness can be conceived of as opposites only when they are considered as definitely limited expressions of Peace. They are usually compared to the obverse and the reverse of the same coin, the coin itself being Peace. If either of these expressions happens to continue indefinitely, its expressionship vanishes and it stands transformed into Peace.

334. WHAT IS THE RELATION BETWEEN DEEP SLEEP AND THE INTERVAL BETWEEN TWO MENTAL ACTIVITIES?

These are really one and the same. They appear different because deep sleep comes in the disguise of a state during which emphasis is placed on its limitation, and its content is ignored. If this prejudice or disguise – which is purely a product of the waking state – is realized as such and thus given up to the waking state itself, what remains over is identical with the interval between thoughts. It is your own real nature.

335. WHAT IS THE TRUTH ABOUT DOING GOOD TO OTHERS?

It is not the nature of the act alone that constitutes its goodness. The test of every act is to see whether it binds you or releases you.

For example, if after giving charity, the thought that you have done a good deed sticks to you, it certainly binds you, though only with a golden chain. It clearly amounts to an evil, so far as yourself and the Truth are concerned. Your ego gets inflated thereby.

It is the mental attitude that counts, in all such matters. You can be really good only on reaching the ultimate Truth, when even the 'good' loses its 'goodness' and becomes transformed into that ultimate Truth.

336. HOW TO EDUCATE CHILDREN?

They have necessarily to be educated at school on '*avidyā*' ['false learning'], relating to all subjects having a wide and varied range; and at home on '*vidyā*' ['true learning'] regarding the real 'I'-principle, the permanent background of all that is taught at school.

337. MEMORY

Memory is double edged. It is a thought like any other thought, and it is a cheat outright. Because it makes you believe that something that never happened, happened.

338. WHERE DID THIS MISUNDERSTANDING START?

The principle involved in the question is causality. Causality is only a synonym for diversity.

The fundamental misunderstanding from which every other misunderstanding originates is the thought that 'I am the body.' This misunderstanding, which is merely a thought form, can never exist in the physical plane. It exists only in the mental plane. In that plane the body cannot exist. Therefore the cause and effect can neither co-exist nor exist in different planes.

Beyond the mind there is no diversity at all. But you are searching for the cause of the misunderstanding in the plane beyond. Or in other words you are trying to establish diversity in the plane beyond, where there is no diversity. Thus if you continue to enquire into the cause of 'avidyā' [false knowledge], you would still be entangled within the boundaries of 'avidyā' itself.

339. WHAT IS THE CAUSE OF ILLUSION OR UNREALITY?

Reality can never be the cause of unreality. So unreality or illusion alone must be the cause of illusion. This is meaningless, and hence there can be no cause for illusion or unreality.

It has been proved already that all that is seen is form, all that is heard is sound, and so on. All that is known is knowledge. Therefore ignorance also, when known, becomes knowledge itself. And when it is not known, there is no problem either.

Misunderstanding cannot know understanding. But, on the contrary, understanding alone can know misunderstanding. When understanding begins to know misunderstanding, misunderstanding becomes understanding itself.

340. WHO DIES?

The body and the life principle are the only two fundamental entities involved in the change called death.

Of these two, the 'body' has always been dead and inert matter, and as such cannot die again. The life principle is always changeless, and so it can also never die.

The life principle does not go into the make of the body. You say you die. How do you know that? Who knows it? You cannot take note of anything without a witness. There can be a witness only when something known is concerned. But you never know death. Between two mentations, there is nothing known, and so the witnesshood also cannot be present.

As far as death is concerned, you simply give a name to the unknown and dismiss it for the time being. Therefore death is a misnomer.

13th April 1952

341. WHAT IS THE RELATION BETWEEN FEELING, DEEP SLEEP AND THE EXPERIENCE OF 'I AM'?

Can I think of any feeling, for example hate? *No*. Hate as such can never be an object of thought. Hate cannot stand divorced from the objects with which it is connected. You cannot conceive of hatred. It can never appear by itself. Thoughts have to be indented upon to lead you on to it; and they themselves suddenly expire, plunging you into the experience called feeling, which is beyond all thought.

It is in the same manner that you think of deep sleep. You think of all things connected with deep sleep, other than deep sleep itself. At last all thoughts expire, and you are left alone in the state called deep sleep.

Similarly, in the thought about yourself, you think about your body, senses and mind – all distinct and separate from you – and dismiss them. When all those thoughts expire, you are left alone in yourself. You are that principle which remains over, even after everything perceivable has been eliminated from you.

342. WHAT IS THE RELATION BETWEEN ACTIVITY AND ITS OBJECT?

> Seeing perceives only seeing,
> Hearing hears only hearing,
> and so on …

Knowledge knows only knowledge, and love loves only love. In short, the instrument utilized is itself perceived by the instrument. So also, you see only yourself in others. The child cannot see a thief in anyone, because there is no thief in the child.

343. WHY IS THERE DIFFERENCE BETWEEN OBJECTS?

1. The answer is in the question itself. It is the word 'why' which creates the question. 'Why' means what is the cause? This presupposes the existence of causality. And causality can exist only if you admit the existence of difference between cause and effect. Therefore, it is absurd to ask for the cause of difference. The acceptance of the principle of causality in the question itself already implies the existence of difference.
2. The question can be solved by defining difference. Difference comes into existence only through time, space and causality. We generally say that time, space and causality are the source of diversity; but to be more precise, we should really say that time, space and causality form diversity.
3. The question can also be solved by proving that there is no diversity at any time.
4. It is caused by the mixing up of one percept with innumerable other concepts which have no connection with that percept.
5. The question is finally solved by proving that all is Consciousness.

344. THE CAUSE OF DIVERSITY

1. In seeking the cause of diversity in general, you posit the existence of such a cause even beyond the world. This is absurd.
2. When the earth is made into a pot, the earth neither vanishes nor undergoes any change. If a child who had no 'pot idea' in it already were to see the pot, it would only see the earth in the so-called pot. Here, earth – which was originally one and still remains one – is split up into two by the mere name 'pot'; and you assume the earth and the pot to be quite separate. This assumption alone constitutes diversity.
3. An object depends upon perception alone. But perception proves only one thing at a time. So two things cannot exist simultaneously. Therefore comparison of things is impossible. Hence diversity is an illusion.

345. How is Truth the background of *sat-cit-ānanda*?

Existence is the only thing that does not go out of existence. So existence is the Truth itself.

Existence cannot be existence without Consciousness. Therefore Truth is Consciousness.

Truth, being objectless, is incapable of being felt. So it is peace that is the background of all feelings.

Therefore Truth is the background of '*sat*', '*cit*', and '*ānanda*' or Peace.

346. The concept of *sat-cit-ānanda*

There are three fundamental human experiences – namely life, thought and feeling. The most generic forms of these experiences are termed *sat* [existence], *cit* [consciousness] and *ānanda* [happiness].

These three names denote only three aspects of the one and the same thing; and that thing is the ultimate Reality.

15th April 1952

347. What is the Truth about bondage?

It is not objects, but only your own thoughts and feelings that appear to bind you. But thoughts and feelings can never bind you unless the ego is present to claim them as its own.

At the moment when thoughts and feelings occur, the ego is not present. The ego comes only after thoughts and feelings have disappeared. Then the ego alone is present, and no thoughts or feelings.

Therefore, thoughts or feelings and the ego can never exist simultaneously; and so you transcend bondage. Hence there never has been any bondage, at any time.

17th April 1952

348. How to attain liberation through 'upāsana'?

The form adopted or visualized in one's 'upāsana' is called an 'iṣhṭa-dēva' or 'saguṇa-brahman'. Iṣhṭa-dēvas are of two kinds: sāttvika-dēva and siddha-dēva. Saguṇa-brahman is the expression of 'nirguṇa-brahman'.

If it is approached with the sole object of attaining liberation, the form you visualize is called a 'sāttvika-dēva'; and if the object of your 'upāsana' is not liberation but only the attainment of powers, your vision is called a 'siddha-dēva'.

Even after visualizing the siddha-dēva, if you change your goal and long for liberation, the siddha-dēva himself becomes transformed into 'sāttvika-dēva' and leads you on. It is the intense desire for liberation that makes even the path of 'saguṇa-brahmōpāsana' sweet and endearing.

As long as you attach an attribute to God, He remains only as a mental concept. And together with the attribute, it becomes a percept.

349. SĀTTVIKA-DARSHANA

Sāttvika-darshana is that in which the forms of the Guru and the iṣhṭa-dēva appear as synonyms of the same Reality. Through sāttvika-darshana, one is taken to the right Absolute; and the statements made in that state will always point to the Ultimate. The following are some such.

1. The world is a world of relativity.
2. The effect is the cause of the cause.
3. Don't you want to see me in my real form?

Darshanas are of two kinds: 'pratyakṣha' and 'sāttvika'. Pratyakṣha is the lower type, being the object of the senses alone, and the result of being guided by a 'kārya-guru' or limited guru. The iṣhṭa-dēva in pratyakṣha-darshana dances only to your tune and to your samskāras.

Saints were mostly yōgins or siddhas. But real Sages were few among them, like Shrī Tattvarayar, Shrī Tāyumānavar, etc.

350. HOW ARE THE 'I'-NESS (AHANTA) AND THE 'THIS'-NESS (IDANTA) RELATED?

The 'I'-ness is the ego, which develops into body, senses and mind. The 'this'-ness is the non-ego, which develops into the world.

But the 'this'-ness can never stand by itself. Therefore, neither reason nor experience allows us to state that objects appear in the 'this'-ness alone.

Therefore both of them appear and disappear on Ātmā, the only Reality.

20th April 1952

351. HOW IS CONTACT WITH THE GURU MADE POSSIBLE?

The mind and its working: When you take a deep thought or feeling, there is a phenomenal reaction – expressing itself simultaneously in the form of attracting other cosmic forces of a like nature, to reinforce your own mind.

As a result, you actualize your own thoughts and feelings and depend upon them all the more. It is in recognition of this principle that you are advised to take only good thoughts at all times. If your thoughts get adulterated with doubts of any kind, they invite the opposite forces as well; and as a result you are often confused or bewildered.

The same principle explains why devotees, artistes etc. attract to themselves, without any effort, other people who think and act in the same way.

It is the very same phenomenon which enables one who is thirsting for the absolute Truth with all earnestness and sincerity to meet the Guru, who is but the embodiment of the absolute Truth in the world.

352. IS THERE ANY RELATION BETWEEN THE BODY AND THE 'I'-PRINCIPLE?

Take for example the figure in the rock, or the serpent in the rope. Is there any relation between the rock and the figure, or between the rope and the serpent? When you reach the rock or the rope as it is, even the idea of the figure or the serpent completely vanishes. There is only the rock or the rope. From the plane of the rock the figure is only an illusion.

Similarly, from the plane of the 'I'-principle, the body does not exist as such. In other words, the body is also the 'I'-principle itself. Therefore, the question of relationship does not arise at all.

353. WHAT IS LAKṢHAṆA?

It is a means to attain the Truth. In the aphorism, 'That is this', it is this process of indication or lakṣhaṇa that comes into play.

'That' means Truth, mixed with 'that time' and 'that space'; and 'this' means Truth, mixed with 'this time' and 'this space'. In the two parts of the aphorism, 'that time' and 'that space' can never be 'this time' and 'this space'; and therefore 'that' can never be 'this' as such. Take away the time and space qualifications from both, and pure Truth alone remains in all its glory.

This process of eliminating the material parts and realizing the Ultimate behind is called 'jagadahat-lakṣhaṇa' or 'bhāga-tyāga-lakṣhaṇa'.

Similarly, in the apparent 'I' – which is a crude mixture of body, senses, mind and the 'I'-principle – see the first three as objects pointing to the last one, the real subject. Thus eliminating the non-real part from the apparent 'I', you reach the ultimate 'I'-principle, pure.

1st May 1952

354. WHAT IS THE PROCESS AND THE LIMIT OF TRANSLATION?

The art of translation is not so simple as it seems on the surface. An idea is first conceived and then expressed in the same language. The structure has to be demolished and reduced to the languageless idea before it is recast in any other language, just like the types in a foundry.

There again, you have first to conceive it afresh, according to the fundamentals of the new language; and then to express it in the words of the new language. Very often, apparently important words and analogies in the original will have to be ignored, and quite new analogies and words accepted to suit the vocabulary and trend of thought in the new language.

But this should come spontaneously and not by effort or choice. So translate only the idea as an integral whole, and never try to adhere literally to the usages of the original.

355. How is knowing distinct from mentation?

A gross object can only be a sense object. Without the senses, a sense object can never be said to exist. Therefore, what is called an object is nothing but a sensation. Likewise, it can be said that an object of thought is nothing but thought itself.

In knowledge, however, there is no such instrument as the senses or the mind. Therefore, to say that I know anything is wrong. There can never be a subject-object relationship in knowledge.

An ignorant man does not draw any distinction between knowing on the one hand and perceiving, thinking and feeling on the other. Thus he superimposes an object on knowledge also.

356. The exercise of putting the mind in the blank state

A yōgic sādhaka once attempted a particular yōgic exercise which he was not authorized to do by his Guru and got into trouble. His Guru had already passed away, and so he came to Shrī Ātmānanda for help. In the course of explaining the position to him, the above question was incidentally taken up and discussed as an example.

Every sādhaka is not permitted indiscriminately to do this exercise. Being an exercise of the mind it has its own dangers, if one goes wrong. It is dangerous to do it without sufficient precautions. Parallel to the thought-force of the individual, there are corresponding cosmic forces of the world; and both are governed by phenomenal laws. To create a blank state of the mind without safeguards, in the middle of the cosmos, is as dangerous as creating an unprotected vacuum in the midst of a high-pressure region.

The only safeguard you have to take in this case is to train your mind in a sufficiently strong course of sāttvic thoughts, capable of warding off other undesirable thoughts that might come in from the cosmic world. Because, when your individual mind is suddenly divorced of all its own thoughts, there is a natural tendency for the thoughts in the cosmic world – particularly those in tune with your other samskāras – to rush in and overpower your mind unawares. The strong walls of your adherence to sāttvic thoughts (thoughts relating to the ultimate Truth) can alone protect you against this catastrophe.

8th May 1952

357. SOME DEFINITIONS

> *Language* is the art of concealing thought.
> *Thought* is the art of concealing Truth.

Transcending or giving up language and thought together with their samskāras, you reach the Truth direct.

Bondage is the conviction that the object remains over, after every experience of knowledge or peace.

Liberation is the conviction that not even a trace of the object remains over, after every such experience.

18th May 1952

358. HOW TO KEEP MY CENTRE DURING ACTIVITY?

The different spheres of an ordinary man's experience are: (1) doing, (2) perceiving, (3) thinking, (4) feeling, and last of all (5) knowing. The first four kinds of activities are always changing, and the last alone is changeless.

Whenever you have an experience of any of the first four types, ask yourself the question: 'To whom is it that the particular experience occurs?' You will see without any difficulty that it is not to the ultimate 'I'-principle, but only to one of its four mediums or instruments. Then why do you worry about them in the least?

Know that you are the knower, always at your centre, and be at Peace. What more is needed?

The instrument and the background can be represented as shown below:

Doing, perceiving, thinking and feeling	Media or instruments
Pure 'I'-principle	Background

1st June 1952

359. THE ILLUSION OF THE SNAKE IN THE ROPE AND ITS APPLICATION IN VĒDĀNTA

This illustration is usually applied in Vēdānta to prove the falsity of the objective universe and the changelessness or Reality of the ultimate subject.

Here, the snake stands for the whole of the objective world – gross as well as subtle, including all thoughts, feelings, and the ego itself. The rope stands for the changeless background or Ātmā, the real 'I'-principle. Therefore, any thought or feeling of doubt regarding the illusion has to be met not by seeking an answer for it in the same plane of illusion, but by seeing the thought or feeling as part of the illusion itself, and as such dismissing it summarily as unacceptable.

It has to be remembered that the apparent 'I' or the ego is decidedly the most vicious part of the objective world; and when it is set aside as such, all doubts and questions cease, leaving you in the Reality itself.

The apparent 'I' as well as the objective world are both superimpositions upon the ultimate 'I'-principle. The rope stands for this unattached 'I'-principle.

At the moment of the experience of pure Consciousness, one is beyond all states. One only expresses it in words in the waking state.

5th June 1952

360. LOVE AND HOW TO LOVE?

All worldly love is mere bargaining and has always its opposite attached to it, ready to express itself when the consideration anticipated is in any way obstructed.

But a Vēdāntin's love alone knows no bargain, and naturally knows no opposite. It is perfect and unconditional; and always in the form of giving and not taking. Therefore, even to love one's own wife or child in the best manner, one has to become a Vēdāntin first. All talk of love in this world is nothing but unadulterated fraud.

So know yourself first. Then alone can you love anybody or anything truly and unreservedly.

361. HUMAN FASCINATIONS AND THEIR REACTION UPON SPIRITUAL PROGRESS

The ordinary man of the world is usually carried away by one or more of three fundamental fascinations: physical, psychological and intellectual.

Those who are victims of physical fascination live contented with their sensual enjoyments alone, and do not seek anything higher.

The second class of people are enamoured of all sorts of imaginary mental pleasures and psychic powers and are lost that way.

The last group of people, who are the incorrigible pandits, profess to be searching for the Truth, and labour hard to bring even the Ultimate within the realm of the intellect. In this vain effort, they fail miserably; but stubbornly refuse to admit their failure, and hoodwink the ignorant man by their superior intellectual powers and shrewd but misapplied logic. From this nefarious practice, they derive a sort of malicious intellectual satisfaction and pleasure, which alienate them from the Truth as long as they persist in this vicious traffic.

These last two types of people, though they start with a faint idea of getting at the Truth, are slowly side-tracked; and deceive both themselves and the ignorant public regarding the ultimate Truth.

362. WHAT IS TIME?

Time consists of its three component parts – the past, present and future. The past and future cannot manifest themselves without appearing first in the present. When they appear in the present, they are also the present and nothing else. Thus the past and future depend upon the present for their very existence, and vice versa. So all are non-existent, and time is not.

'I am' or 'anubhava-mātrātmā' is the source and the end of all experiences, devoid of the experiencer and the experienced.

363. Scope of exercises called spiritual

All exercises involving contemplation or meditation in any manner secure only relative purity of the heart.

If you use right discrimination and reason and examine all your experiences disinterestedly, you get to your centre, which is the inmost core of your being.

To set matters right, you are only asked to give equal emphasis to all the three aspects of your activities – namely perceiving, thinking and knowing – and to recognize that knowing is the only aspect among these which really concerns your own self.

If you continue this practice for some time, you will find the first two material aspects slowly drop away as unreal; and you stand established in your real nature, the Truth.

Therefore, don't fail to see that every activity is recorded in knowledge, your real nature, before another activity commences.

8th June 1952

364. How does the mind react?

The ordinary man is a slave of the mind and follows implicitly its dictates, as long as he is enamoured of sensual pleasures.

But when you begin to turn away from the mind and start looking inward, the mind becomes bewildered and is ready to follow your footsteps faithfully, like a slave.

Vital energy, seeing, hearing, touching, tasting, smelling, thinking etc. are all verbal nouns.

> … prāṇann ēva prāṇō nāma bhavati, vadan vāk, paśyaṁś cakṣuḥ, śṛṇvan śrōtram, manvānō manaḥ; tāny asyaitāni karma-nāmāny ēva …
>
> [Seen as living in itself, it gets to be called 'life';
> as speaking, 'speech'; as seeing, 'sight';
> as hearing, 'sound'; as thinking, 'mind'.
> These are only names of functions, attributed to it.]
>
> *Bṛihadāraṇyaka Upaniṣhad, 1.4.7*

12th June 1952

365. ACTIVITY AND INACTIVITY

Activity and inactivity are ordinarily conceived to be opposite terms. But in fact there is no direct connection at all between them.

Activity and inactivity are related directly only to me, the 'I'-principle, which is their common background. It is only through me that activity and inactivity can even indirectly be connected.

366. EFFICACY OF THE REAL 'I' THOUGHT

If you take to the deep thought, 'I am pure Consciousness', with the emphasis rightly placed on 'I' and not upon Consciousness, it amounts to a regular process of relaxation, and the brain cells do not move in the least. On the contrary, even casual ailments, like a head-ache caused by mental or physical strain, begin to disappear after such relaxation.

It has already been proved that 'I am knowledge or Conscious-ness.' If the meaning of this statement is rightly understood, your stand must have undergone a thorough change. You should be able to apply boldly all the activities of the one with equal emphasis to the other.

Taking 'knowing or shining' as the only expression of Conscious-ness, when you say 'I am shining', you must be able to take it as equivalent to 'I am I-ing'. And when you say 'I know the object', it must mean 'I am I-ing the object.' It will also prove that the object is nothing but yourself.

If I am Rāma, all my activities are spontaneously applied to and endorsed by Rāma. So also, I being Consciousness, I must also be possessed of the only quality of Consciousness – which is shining.

15th June 1952

367. COMMUNISM

Communism is a noble ideal; and if properly understood, sincerely followed and consistently applied, it leads you to the absolute Truth. The essence of its goal is equality, but it is unfortunately misapplied in practice by the modern political communists.

Equality or oneness is the attribute of the Ultimate. It is established only when you reach the Ultimate, transcending body, senses and mind. But the political communist wants to establish equality or oneness in the physical realm, forgetting the impossibility of making bodies equal, or senses equal, or minds equal, or intellects equal. They woefully reverse the order of importance by putting the body first and the intellect last. This is the secret of the failure of their present ideal.

Real equality is possible only beyond all these realms, and the present day communists do not want to go beyond even the body. As such they are at loggerheads with their own goal. Their goal, as they conceive it, is short-sighted and barren.

The vēdāntin alone is the real communist, who clings to his ideal steadfastly and establishes it unquestionably in the ultimate Reality – the 'I'-principle.

368. Is there diversity in emotions?

It is experience that must prove emotion. When you say you were angry some time ago, you direct attention to that period of time in which you suppose you were angry. Examine the experience you had then. Was anger present there then? *No*. There was no anger. Because you cannot separate what you call anger from the 'I'-principle. So during that period you were all alone, and that is what your experience points to. Anger becomes evident as a separate entity only when the function of memory begins its mischievous operation.

Shrī Shankara represents this memory as the veritable māyā.

smṛti-rūpaḥ paratrapūrvadṛṣṭāvabhāsaḥ

[Where memory appears, it forms
a show of something seen before –
a distant something not now here.]

Shrī Shankara, Adhyāsa-bhāṣhya (Introduction to Sūtra-bhāṣhya), 3.1

Memory misrepresents real experience as something that is opposed to Truth. Therefore, it is memory that misrepresents permanent Peace, as transient emotions.

If memory did not interfere, every experience now called 'emotion' would really stand transformed into your real nature – the only experience. It is the wonder of wonders to find that the real nature of even this memory is Consciousness or Peace.

Looking from this stand, we find no means to distinguish between 'emotions', as we call them now. All of them stand reduced to that one Reality or Ātmā, the true nature of them all.

Thus there is no diversity in feelings and thoughts. It is only memory that posits all difference.

19th June 1952

369. TRAINING IN BHAKTI OR YŌGA – HAS IT ANY BEARING UPON ULTIMATE REALIZATION?

Even the iṣhṭa-dēva in vision is only an object of your senses. You take to your sādhana with a fund of stored up samskāras. The conduct of your iṣhṭa-dēva towards you will be in tune with your previous samskāras.

But you attach greater reality to the Lord in your vision than to the objects of this gross world. The more you emphasize the Lord, you are indirectly and unknowingly emphasizing your own personal self as the perceiver. This can never be a help to the attainment of the impersonal.

It is the experience of all Sages who have had dualistic bhakti or yōgic training in their early days that all that training had really been, in one sense, an obstacle to their progress to the ultimate Truth.

370. WHY DO QUESTIONS SEEM TO RISE EVEN AFTER VISUALIZING THE TRUTH?

The mind has usually two distinct kinds of activities.

- One is outward-going and trafficking with the world of the senses, gross or subtle.
- And the other activity is inward-going, seeking the 'I'-principle.

The latter activity is called the higher reason, vidyā-vṛitti, higher logic etc. Listening to and visualizing the Truth belong to the latter.

In its course, objects are no obstacle; and at the goal, there are no objects at all.

All objects belong to the outward-going function of the mind, and naturally all questions also belong to the realm of the mind.

Questions do not belong to him who was listening to and visualizing the Truth. Coming down from there to the world of the senses, you see the senses and other objects all around. Immediately, the mind thoughtlessly thinks that they also are party to the experience you had beyond the mind. This is the secret of all questions.

> vismayaika śarīrāyā māyāyāś cōdya-rūpataḥ .
> anvēṣyaḥ parihārō 'syā buddhimadbhiḥ prayatnataḥ ..
>
> [Only amazement can arise
> from this embodied, seeming world
> that is itself made up of questioning.
> Thus, those who are intelligent
> must look with care, to get beyond.]
>
> *Pancadashī, Citra-dīpa, 139*

It is with the instrument of Consciousness that you visualize the Truth. If you use the same instrument to examine the world also, the world of the senses will not appear to you as such, but will stand transformed into Consciousness.

Therefore, the activity of the senses and mind alone is the source of this world. But these being part of the world itself, the world cannot be said to have any independent source at all.

371. Is there a subject-object relationship at any time?

The 'I'-principle is the only one thing whose existence is never questioned. This is never an object of the senses or the mind.

Regarding this 'I'-principle at the time of experience, no subject-object relationship exists.

During the perception of objects also, the experience is exactly the same. The apparent object gets transformed into the 'I'-principle or knowledge, and stands as one with it, beyond all subject-object relationship.

The activity of the Jnyānin is also the same, but undertaken knowingly. He realizes that no activity vanishes before being recorded or merged in knowledge or the Self. It means that sound, form etc. are never perceived as such, but all of them merge in knowledge.

372. WHAT IS THE RELATIVE IMPORTANCE OF OUR ACTIVITIES?

Usually, man has three different kinds of activities – perceiving, thinking and knowing – the former two being false and the last alone real.

Invariably, the first two false activities alone are recognized in worldly transactions. And the last, but real activity is sadly ignored, though the word 'knowing' is used indiscriminately.

The vēdāntin proves and shows you that even the first two false activities owe their very existence to the third one. You must always bear in mind that when knowledge dawns, perception and thinking vanish.

373. HOW TO RECONCILE THE STATEMENTS: 'I AM THE WORLD' AND 'THE WORLD IS NOT'?

> na mē bandhō 'sti mōkṣō vā, bhrāntiḥ śāntā nirāśrayā .
> ahō mayi sthitaṁ viśvaṁ, vastutō na mayi sthitam ..
>
> [For me, there is no being bound
> nor getting freed. Confusion fails
> to find support, and comes to peace.
> All of this world exists in me:
> where it does not exist as world,
> but as unchanged reality.]

Aṣḥṭāvakra samhitā, 2.18

There is no wave at all in water. In the verse above, Aṣḥṭāvakra asserts first that 'the world shines in me', but only to lift the layman from the mire of illusion.

Immediately, he corrects himself and comes out with the whole Truth. No, the moment the world touches me, it becomes transformed into myself.

So I am alone, and the world is not.

374. What is the remedy for evil tendencies?

It has already been proved that mere mental repentance over one's past evil deeds is no guarantee against their repetition. In fact it only aggravates them. Then how are we to overcome such tendencies?

If we take to evil unknowingly, an intellectual corrective might be of some avail in dissuading us from it afterwards. Most often, we take to such evil activities knowing full well the scope of their consequences, but being unable to resist the stronger cravings of the heart. When the heart and the head are thus opposed to each other, the head is helpless and meekly surrenders to the heart. In such cases no amount of intellectual correction will be of any avail.

It is here that we really need a potent remedy. The heart itself being in trouble, the remedy has naturally to come from the beyond. But beyond the heart, there is nothing but the 'I'-principle – the Truth. Adhering to this 'I'-principle, either by analysis or by elimination, your samskāras drop away, for want of support.

If you have heard the Truth from a Sage, the problem is easy enough. Whenever you find your heart straying away to anything undesirable, just think of the Guru, who is the ultimate Truth, and the heart recoils with a shudder. It will think twice before daring to launch into similar mischief once again.

To one who has not had the privilege of surrendering to a Sage, it is open to approach the goal through the medium of God. Let him take the deep thought: 'I am the son of God and therefore am incapable of being a party to a wrong action.' As a result of this thought, he is unconsciously taken beyond the realm of activity and is thrown into the witness, though he does not recognize it for the time being. Frequent acquaintance with this state, which is so peaceful and captivating, slowly deprives the heart of all its outward-going propensities.

Thus, the heart becomes purified and fit to receive instructions about the Truth from a Guru. Before long, he will come into contact with a real Sage and will be illumined through him.

This is the only law that relates the phenomenal to the Absolute. The heart is always at Happiness which is one's own nature. The heart always takes you to the source and controls even the intellect.

Usually, desire for independence expresses itself only when the mind is active. But that desire itself is in no way independent, nor is the personal 'I'.

23rd June 1952

A thing can prove the existence of nothing other than itself. Sensations can prove the existence of the senses alone, and so on. So you can also prove only yourself.

> yat tvaṁ paśyasi tatrai 'kas tvam ēva pratibhāsasē .
> kiṁ pṛthak bhāsatē svarṇāt kaṭak-āṅgada-nūpuram ..
>
> [In what you see, just *you* shine forth, alone.
> What else but gold shines out in golden ornaments?]
>
> *Aṣhṭāvakra samhitā, 15.14*

375. WHAT ARE THOUGHTS AND FEELINGS?

It is admitted that thoughts and feelings are in myself. It is also admitted that in me, there cannot be anything other than myself.

I cannot go out of myself to know or feel anything, and things from outside cannot come into me. The moment they touch me, they get transformed into myself; and thus I know only myself, always.

Here, thoughts and feelings become objectless. So they are myself alone.

26th June 1952

376. IDEA AND LANGUAGE

For everyone, an idea takes its origin in the mind and it has a generic language of its own. It is this idea, in its own generic language, that everybody tries to express in the spoken or written language.

In this translation, speakers of some languages lay greater emphasis on the idea part, and render it into the language as it comes, considering language only as a vehicle of the thought. Malayalam is pre-eminently such a language.

But the English language sometimes puts more emphasis upon the language and the form of expression. In the application of this artificial restriction, a fraction of the idea is naturally lost.

377. THE STATEMENTS 'THAT IS THIS' AND 'THIS IS THAT' COMPARED

> atāṇitennōtukil ippadārtthaṁ-
> maŕannatil paŕŕukayāṇu cittaṁ
> itāṇatennākil, itil kuŕēkkūṭ-
> uŕaykkayāṁ vṛttimaŕakkayalla .

> [If someone says 'That is this',
> what's meant by 'this' gets there forgotten.
> It gets merged (into the 'that').
> But if it's said that 'This is that',
> the act of thought does not dissolve.
> It just gets further emphasized.]

Shrī Ātmānanda, Ātmārāmam, 1.52

When you say 'That is this', the 'this' as such is forgotten and is merged into 'that'. Or in other words, 'that' explains 'this'.

But when you say 'This is that', the 'that' is forgotten as such and is merged into 'this'. Or in other words, 'this' explains 'that'.

As between the general and the particular, the general can well be said to be in the particular. But the particular can never be in the general. Gold is in all ornaments and can stand independent of them all. But no ornament can stand independent of gold. Thus, relatively speaking, gold alone is real and ornaments are unreal.

Similarly, 'that' – which represents brahman – is real; and 'this' – which represents the world of name and form – is unreal. But the background of 'this', or the permanent part in 'this', is evidently 'that' itself.

378. WHAT IS MEANT BY THE 'DELUGE'?

The 'deluge' is the last refuge after the misguided search, through the cosmological path, for the cause of the objective world. [The 'deluge' here is 'pralaya' – the dissolution of the world into an unmanifested seed form of undifferentiated causal potency, at the end of each cosmic cycle. It is from this unmanifest potency that the next cycle of cosmic manifestation is supposed to be caused. The concept occurs for example in the story of Bhushuṇḍa in *Yōga-vāsiṣhṭha*. See notes 332 and 984.]

The root of this question, as well as of the search, is the acceptance of the principle of interdependence of objects as true. This position is not correct.

Take for example your seeing a cow and a calf in your dream. It is admitted that the see-er, the seeing and the seen are all creations of the mind. So you see the cow, and you see the calf separately. But immediately, you create a new perception that the calf is the offspring of the cow. Thus in fact, the cow, the calf and the relationship between them are three entirely different perceptions related only to the common perceiver, 'you'.

Similarly, the whole objective world and all things gross as well as subtle – including even the 'deluge' and its accredited cause 'mūla-prakṛiti' ['root nature'] – are all objects, and you are the only real subject.

Therefore, if you correctly understand the real significance of the statement that objects have only one relationship and that with you alone, your perspective which enabled you to visualize a 'deluge' disappears altogether.

29th June 1952

379. HOW TO HANDLE A MANTRA?

A mantra is a harmonious sound or group of sounds, with or without a superficially intelligible meaning, but capable of creating and applying some definite and potential energy if properly uttered.

When Truth flows out of a Sage spontaneously, whether in prose or in poetry, it is a perfect mantra. All attempts to correct it in accordance with standards of rhyme or reason are nothing short of sacrilege and mutilate the mantra, sometimes producing even adverse results. Therefore, accept it as such or reject it.

380. WHAT IS THE BASIS OF IDEA AND LANGUAGE?

An idea comes clothed in language. When the clothing is taken away, the idea stands as the ultimate Truth. So much so that language may be said to be the art of concealing ideas, and ideas in turn to be the art of concealing Truth.

Ideas and language have no significance except in relation to feeling in the phenomenal, or except in relation to the ultimate Truth in Vēdānta.

Tears are the expression of a subtler and deeper emotion behind them, and they have no significance except in relation to this emotion. One who sees these tears independent of the emotion that caused them has seen nothing more than 'warm salt water, like the notorious alchemist'. The purpose of the tears is only to express that emotion. He who is capable of seeing the nature of that emotion behind the tears alone understands the real significance of the tears. He alone is competent to comment upon the tears.

Similarly, in commenting upon a vēdāntic text, he alone is competent to do the job properly who has clearly visualized the background or the Reality behind the text and has made it his own.

381. WHAT IS THE INFINITE AND HOW TO UNDERSTAND IT?

The 'infinite' is a conception invented only for the purpose of lifting you from the conception of the finite.

Thus reaching the infinite, you find yourself even beyond it. When one thing is explained and disposed of, the opposite also is automatically explained and disposed of.

382. EXPERIENCE OF HAPPINESS IN DEEP SLEEP – AN ANALOGY

Suppose a bucket is lost in a deep well, and you dive down to the bottom to make a search. You touch the bucket there at the bottom, and come up to the surface. Coming out of the water, you say you found the bucket. But the bucket was really found while you were under the water, where there was no medium to express that experience.

Similarly, Happiness was experienced in deep sleep, but you get hold of a medium to express that experience only after coming to the waking state.

Experience is always beyond the mind. The personal 'I' knows it only when the 'I' comes to that realm of the mind. Still others come to know it when you give it a gross form by putting it into words. But the experience was clearly beyond the mind.

1st July 1952

383. How is Sānkhya philosophy related to Advaita?

Advaita is a perfection of Sānkhya philosophy. Kapila, the founder of Sānkhya philosophy, conceived *puruṣha* and *prakṛiti* as separate entities but remaining identified; and he held that for liberation, the elimination of puruṣha was necessary. So he tried to eliminate puruṣha from prakṛiti. But in so doing, he allowed certain parts of prakṛiti still to cling on to puruṣha. The plurality of prakṛiti was not rightly examined by the sānkhyas and therefore was wrongly attributed to puruṣha. It thus brought in many liberated puruṣhas.

Advaita philosophy, by right discrimination, finds that plurality belongs only to prakṛiti, and that when puruṣha is reached, prakṛiti ceases to be prakṛiti and is transformed into puruṣha itself.

384. What do I know?

No perception ever stops half way, but always ends in knowledge. At the point of knowing, there is neither perception nor the object perceived. Therefore, you know only knowledge.

You say you know a thing because you have seen it many times. It is true, in one sense. Because, every time, you have been brought into direct contact with knowledge and not with the object. Therefore, it only proves that you know pure knowledge.

From that position, you can never be a witness. You witness only yourself. Knowing is not a verbal noun.

385. WHAT ARE QUALITIES AND THE QUALIFIED?

An object, as we conceive it, is supposed to be a mixture of qualities and the qualified.

But on closer examination, we find that qualities alone are perceived, and that the qualified is never experienced. Thus the qualified remains a mere fancy, for want of proof.

Independent of the qualified, the qualities cannot exist. Therefore qualities are also reduced to mere fancy.

Thus neither the perception nor the perceived are real.

386. WHAT HAPPENS WHEN I SEE A FORM?

We usually say: 'I see a form.' What does it really mean? It has been proved that form can never exist independent of seeing, and that form and seeing are only synonyms.

Therefore, the expression 'I see a form' is meaningless. It would be more appropriate to recast it as 'I form a form' ('ñān oru rūpaṁ rūpikkunnu'), thereby showing that there is nothing other than myself in the form in question.

387. HOW TO PROVE 'ALL IS CONSCIOUSNESS'?

Take for example this tobacco case. What is its content? Silver. If you take away the silver from the tobacco case, the case vanishes completely. But the silver remains over, in the guise of another form.

If all forms are removed from the silver, the silver also vanishes, leaving Consciousness alone. Thus we see that Consciousness was the only reality in the tobacco case.

From 'seeing a form', if either seeing or form is separated, then both vanish simultaneously, because neither can exist independently of the other. Therefore both are one, but not as either. Then what is it? When form and seeing disappear, Consciousness alone remains over; and that is the only reality behind it.

Thus everything is permanent as the background, and not as the expression.

2nd July 1952

388. WHERE IS A MYSTIC AND WHERE IS A DEVOTEE, IN RELATION TO TRUTH?

A mystic's position is a very complex and confused one. He has a lot of self-made samskāras. He has to transcend all those samskāras before visualizing the Truth. This involves much strain.

A devotee's position is relatively much simpler and easier. He has transcended most of his samskāras, by his surrender to the iṣhṭa-dēva. Therefore he will be able to grasp the ultimate Truth much more easily than the less fortunate mystic.

389. IS THOUGHT OF CONSCIOUSNESS AN ABSTRACTION?

It might appear to be an abstraction at the outset, when your stand is in the mind's realm alone. But you cannot continue there for long. The object of your thought eludes the mind's grasp; and in the attempt to comprehend Consciousness, the mind itself loses its limitations. Thus the mind ceases to be mind, and stands transformed into that Consciousness itself.

Therefore, the thought of Consciousness, though starting as an abstraction, takes you immediately to the clearest experience of the Absolute.

390. BODY, MIND AND THE 'I'-PRINCIPLE. WHAT IS THEIR RELATIONSHIP AND ESSENCE?

During the period of preliminary investigations in the study of Vēdānta, you are asked to try to separate body and mind from the 'I'-principle. It is only to make you understand the relative values of the terms. Such a separation is not really possible; because, separated from the 'I'-principle, the other two do not exist at all. Therefore they are really nothing but the 'I'-principle. Vēdānta asks you only to recognize this Truth.

From the position of Consciousness, one can say that everything else is not. But from no position can you say that Consciousness is not. Because one has to be conscious of the Truth of that very statement before making it. Therefore Consciousness stands as the background of even that statement.

Hence, even the statement that 'Consciousness is *not*' only proves that Consciousness *is*. Therefore Consciousness is self-luminous and permanent.

391. WHAT IS THE TEST OF THE 'FREE' AND THE 'BOUND'?

If, when you think of Consciousness, the 'I'-thought comes in spontaneously and vice versa, then you are free.

And if, when you think of the body, the 'I'-thought comes in spontaneously and vice versa, then you are bound.

392. CAN THERE BE TWO SELF-LUMINOUS THINGS?

No. The very definition of self-luminous is that which has luminosity as its very nature. There cannot be two such things, because by definition they stand as one. If there are two such things, that principle which knows these two is alone really self-luminous.

Another definition is that self-luminous is that which illumines everything else, including other things which might claim to be self-luminous. If you accept more than one such thing, it would mean that none of them is self-luminous. On that score also, there can be only one self-luminous thing.

393. HOW IS SHIVA CALLED THE 'DESTROYER'?

The function of the faculty called 'higher reason' is only to destroy all that the lower reason or mind has created. Therefore this higher reason or vidyā-vṛitti is verily the destroyer, Shiva himself.

394. WHAT IS THE SIGNIFICANCE OF CENTRE AND CIRCUMFERENCE IN VĒDĀNTA PHILOSOPHY?

The centre is only a position without dimension or magnitude. But the circumference has form, dimensions and magnitude; and is made up of innumerable points or centres. In order to reach the centre from the circumference, you must give up the limitations of form, dimension and magnitude attached to the circumference. Thus the centre is in the circumference and everywhere.

In the spiritual realm, the sense of body or mind stands for the circumference, and the real 'I'-principle for the centre. To visualize the centre, the 'I'-principle, you have only to transcend the ideas of body or mind. Then the 'I'-principle, being there already self-luminous, stands visualized without any further effort.

Therefore, if you succeed in visualizing any one point anywhere in the circumference, it is as good as reaching the centre everywhere. The effort should not be to reach the centre; but to know the centre first, and then to know that you are that.

Ferrier, the French philosopher, says: 'Apprehension of the perception of matter is the subject of metaphysics.' But Gurunāthan improves upon it thus: 'It is only the beginning of metaphysics. Apprehension or knowing is always beyond the mind.'

5th July 1952

395. HOW IS THE MIND THE CAUSE OF BOTH BONDAGE AND LIBERATION?

> mana ēva manuṣyāṇāṁ kāraṇaṁ bandha-mōkṣayōḥ
> bandhāya viṣayāsaktam, muktyai nirviṣayaṁ smṛtam
>
> [It is just mind that is the cause
> of bondage, and of liberation
> also, in our human lives.
> In bondage, mind is tied to objects.
> But, in freedom, mind recalls
> that it is truly objectless.]

Maitrāyaṇi (Maitrī) Upaniṣhad, 6.34.11

The mind has two kinds of activities. One, being extroverted, perceives objects. And the other, being introverted, perceives the real Self or Ātmā.

When the mind is introverted, it comes into touch with the absolute Self, and becomes surcharged with the aroma of Ātmā. In that state, whatever comes out of that apparent mind will be perfect in all its aspects. It comes spontaneously and without a stop. There is no apparent ego to claim any right over any of those statements. Every word or sentence written or spoken by a Sage is of this nature, each being a mantra in itself. It helps to bring you nearer the Truth.

The rest is for you to experience.

396. ART

Every kind of art is conceived and designed to take you, in regular stages, from the phenomenal to the Absolute.

Take for example music. It is the art of taking you to the Absolute through sound. Music, in its gross form, is composed of distinct sounds, harmoniously blended on an apparently changeless background called 'shruti'. This shruti again is audible and gross, but transcends the changes of rising and falling. Leaving the diverse sounds of the music, one has to get absorbed in the unity of the shruti. The purpose of shruti is to show an audible background to represent the inaudible.

Up to this state, the music functions in *āhata*, the audible. From the unity of the shruti, you have to go further still, to the inaudible or *anāhata*, which is the abode of Ātmā. This is achieved by the mind following the shruti and continuing to do so even after the shruti has ceased to be audible. Here, the mind, already divorced of its objects, rids itself of all limitations and merges into the anāhata or Ātmā. Thus you experience the right Absolute through the medium of music.

> Ātmā expresses itself first in *anāhata*,
> which again expresses itself in *āhata*.

Nāda is the generic name for all sounds. It literally pervades all sounds. Through the medium of any art, when you are taken from the āhata to the anāhata, you enjoy eternal bliss. Real art should achieve this without doing the slightest violence to the inner harmony which is the absolute Reality itself. Of course there is diversity in āhata. But in music, it is so skilfully set that it does not do any violence to the anāhata behind it. This is why music so readily appeals to you.

Through the form, direct your attention to the formless light – the Ultimate – called '*oḷi*'. And through audible sound, direct your attention to the soundless *nāda*. These *oḷi* and *nāda* are the two terminating points, when you approach the Absolute through the two distinct paths of form and sound.

arūpamākumoḷiyuṁ
śabdamillātta nādavuṁ
hṛdayākāśamaddhyattil
onnāy˘nilkkunnitanvahaṁ .

[Right at the centre of the heart,
there is an inmost background where
light shines unformed, always at one
with an unspoken resonance.]

Shrī Ātmānanda, Ātmārāmam, 2.9

thayabbalgitamiva nādaprayōgamuṭan-
ēkaśrutīṅkaloru minnalkkaṇakkeyumit-
ekaksarattilorumikkunnapoleyumit-
ākāśasūkṣmatanu nārāyaṇāya namaḥ .

[This subtle background that pervades,
throughout all changing space and time,
is like a changeless harmony
where differences are joined in one.
And it is like a light that flashes
timelessly – in that one single
background drone, which is heard used
in song and music and such arts
that work through resonating sound.]

Eṟuttacchan, Harināma-kīrttanam, 41

6th July 1952

397. YOU SEE THE REALITY ALONE.

When an object is proved to be unreal now, its existence in the past and the future is also proved to be unreal. So an object is unreal from start to finish.

What is the proof of an object? You say you see an object. But you actually see only form. Form is nothing but seeing. So you see only seeing. But did you really see even seeing? No. Because seeing can never exist distinct and separate from you. So you did not see at all. Therefore no object exists.

The fact that you see can alone be admitted. But what did you see? Nothing. Neither form nor anything else. Still, the fact that you saw cannot be denied. Therefore, you are seeing the Reality itself and nothing else.

398. WHAT IS THE TRUTH OF CREATION?

Strictly speaking, there was no creation. Creation is described in the shāstras in two ways:

1. Krama-sṛiṣhṭi (creation in regular order), and
2. Yugapat-sṛiṣhṭi (simultaneous, as in dream).

Of these, the krama-sṛiṣhṭi is disproved and disposed of as illusion by the other, yugapat-sṛiṣhṭi. And yugapat-sṛiṣhṭi, in its turn, is disposed of as illusion by understanding the ultimate Truth.

7th July 1952

399. WHAT DO IDEAS PROVE?

Ideas can only be considered in two ways. One as real and the other as unreal. If you take ideas to be real and consider the fact that you are able to remember them afterwards, you have to admit that you are the store-house or holder of ideas. As the holder, you must be changeless and hence distinct and separate from the ideas. Gradually you will come to realize that ideas only come and go upon the changeless self, and that ideas as such are unreal.

When ideas are considered unreal, since I am aware of them, I stand as the witness of those ideas. Since witnessing is not a function, the witness is always silent awareness or Ātmā. If you take any one activity of the mind, e.g. thinking, you find your role was only that of being aware of the thinking. So you were really the witness of the thinking. You are this with regard to all the activities of the mind. But what the activity is about is unimportant, so far as the witness is concerned.

You might say remembrance proves past thoughts or objects. But remembrance itself is only an activity of the mind. It again proves only your role as a witness. Otherwise remembrance itself would be impossible. And you are the witness of the remembrance as well.

Things are of two kinds:

1. Extrinsic or extraneous to you, and
2. Intrinsic in you.

The second can only be one, and that is your own self or real nature. To discover that, you must cease to be enamoured of everything extraneous to you and emphasize your own intrinsic nature. For example, is 'seeing' extraneous to you or intrinsic in you? Certainly extraneous. Because you can very well continue even without seeing.

400. Is thought the enemy of one's own peace?

Yes, in one sense. If a stranger falls ill, you do not usually feel sad; but if he is related to you in any way, you indeed do. Because you relate yourself to him, at least in thought. Take away thought and you are free, whatever be that thought regarding the world or your own body or mind.

Therefore thought alone destroys your peace.

8th July 1952

401. Heart and prēma

Heart + I am = I am the heart.

Love is the expression of the Self through the heart, and the heart is always wet. It takes you straight to the Self or Ātmā and drowns you in it. Language is dry and is the expression of the Self through the head or reason. It takes you only to the brink of Ātmā; and leaves you there, till the heart rises up to wet reason and ultimately to drown you in love.

So when you begin to discuss love, it is impossible to proceed with the discussion when the heart wells up. Of the different styles in literature, 'shṛingāra' (based on human love) is the one style found best suited to clothe the highest Truth through the message of love or *prēma*. This is why even the Upanịshads have invariably utilized this style to express Truth. The following verse shows the phenomenal ideal of *prēma*.

oruvanuṭanorāḷil snēhamāyālavannuḷḷ-
orunirupamasaukhyadravyamāyāḷutanne
arikilmaruviyonnuṁ ceykayilleṅkiluṁ tān
maruvumorusukhattāltanne duḥkhattenīkkuṁ .

[When someone comes to be in love,
the one who's loved is then a source
of happiness beyond compare.
Then, merely being near that person
brings contentment, even if
there's nothing done. Just in itself
that company brings happiness
and banishes all discontent.]

Mannāḍiyār, Uttara Rāma Caritam, 2.19

9th July 1952

402. WHAT IS AT THE ROOT OF QUESTION AND ANSWER?

Every question proceeds from the answer – which always stands as experience, far beyond the realm of the mind.

Therefore questions are many, but the ultimate and correct answer to all questions is only one, and that is the changeless Ātmā, the Reality. Every question springs from the striving of the mind to bring down that pure experience to the realm of the mind.

403. WHAT IS THE DIFFERENCE BETWEEN *SAT* AND LIFE?

Sat is the greatest generalization of objects, gross as well as subtle; and is the principle of Existence itself. It comprehends both animate and inanimate objects. Life, which is but the first emanation from *sat*, comprehends only animate objects. In this light, *sat* may very well be called a broader view of life.

404. WHAT IS THE SIGNIFICANCE OF ADDRESS? (One end of life)

One's address and experience are the lowest and the highest extremes of one's apparent 'I'.

When you say one's address is perfect, it means that his body identification is so complete. This is bondage of the severest type. The goal of Vēdānta is to release one from the grips of the bondages of this address, and to enable him to identify himself with that permanent principle in him which is beyond any limitation or address.

Address is a synonym for particularization, and liberation is the greatest generalization. Therefore, Vēdānta dispossesses one completely of his address.

10th July 1952

405. MEDITATION

Meditation is yōgic when the mind is concentrated on any one object, or when the prāṇa is controlled in the slightest manner. The latter must be done only in the presence of an experienced Guru. Otherwise it is liable to innumerable pitfalls, which may cause ailments, physical as well as mental.

406. JNYĀNIN'S NIRVIKALPA SAMĀDHI

According to the *Yōga-vāsiṣhṭha*, it is the pleasant coolness you experience as a result of the firm conviction that you alone exist and that you do not see anything or do not see at all.

> yathā prakāśayāmy ēkō dēham ēnam tathā jagat .
> atō mama jagat sarvam athavā na ca kiñcana ..
>
> [This body here shines by my light.
> It's shown by me alone. But then,
> the same is true of everything
> in the entire universe.
> Thus, either everything is mine,
> or otherwise, nothing at all.]

Aṣhṭāvakra-samhitā, 2.2

If you accept the body, accept also the whole world with it. If not, accept neither. What a bold assertion!

407. IS PRAKṚITI REALLY AN OBSTACLE TO SPIRITUAL PROGRESS?

In the early stages of sādhana, when the aspirant is relying upon the lower reason alone, the world of objects appears as an obstacle to his progress.

Gradually, when he begins to awaken his higher reason and begins to rely upon vidyā-vṛitti, everything that appeared as an obstacle before gets transformed into help to lead him on to the Ultimate.

When he takes his stand in the Truth itself, prakṛiti also changes its characteristics and appears as Truth

408. WHAT IS THE MOST CONCRETE OF ALL THINGS?

Concrete literally means real or changeless. Name and form are constantly changing; and their background Ātmā alone is real. Body, senses and mind are changing; and the 'I'-principle alone is changeless or real, through all states and times.

In that sense, the 'I'-principle is the only concrete thing, and all else is but illusion.

409. HOW DOES THE AVADHŪTA PATH WORK?

Most of the avadhūtas take to the visible and are loath to accept discrimination. So they are advised to cultivate an intense aversion to their own body – by discarding it in many ways – and thus to get rid of their attachment to the body. Most of them take to some yōgic practices also, and thereby acquire certain yōgic powers. All this extraordinary conduct makes them admired and venerated by the general public.

But these powers (if not misused) and the practices only prepare the ground for them to listen to the Truth. So they have ultimately to surrender to a Kāraṇa-guru, and take initiation from him regarding the ultimate Truth.

410. WHAT IS 'SPHURAṆA' AND HOW DOES IT FUNCTION?

The natural state of the 'I'-principle in man is unmanifested. This becomes manifest, in the case of human activities, in three distinct stages.

1. The unmanifested state of luminosity itself.
2. Becoming manifest as 'I know I am' or as self-luminosity.
3. Becoming manifested as objects.

The second of the above three stages is not recognized at all by the ordinary man. But the Jnyānin alone recognizes it and perceives it clearly sometimes, before a perception. From the first stage to the second is only a subjective change to 'I am', without losing its identity. This is called '*sphuraṇa*'. It has no object, but it has become self-luminous. That is all. When the 'I'-principle comes to the third stage of perception, it becomes manifested as a jīva.

The statement, 'I am intelligent', is made by the ordinary man and the Sage alike. To the ordinary man, it is nothing short of an integral whole, indivisible and tight. But the Sage splits it up into two distinct parts, the 'I' and 'am intelligent', identifying himself with the 'I' and considering the second part an object or attribute.

The 'I'-principle is pure and attributeless, and is added on to the attribute every time. In other words, the unmanifested 'I'-principle first prepares itself to manifest by adopting the subjective and changeless 'I know I am', then takes on the attribute and becomes clearly manifested.

In place of the three states of luminosity, self-luminosity and illumining the object, love has also its exact parallels in the course of its manifestation.

Pure Consciousness *bōdha-mātra*	Self-consciousness *sva-bōdha*	Consciousness of objects *viṣhaya-bōdha*
Pure love *prēma-mātra*	Self love *sva-prēma*	Love of objects *viṣhaya-prēma*

In all the three aspects, you do not change from your centre. But if you emphasize the seeing or hearing in the third aspect, you become a jīva. And if you emphasize the knowing or witness aspect there, you stick to your centre. If you identify yourself with feelings, you become a jīva; and if you stand knowing the feelings, you stand in yourself.

Jīva is he who thinks or feels, and
Ātmā is he who knows both these activities (and is no 'he' in fact).

411. KNOWLEDGE HAS NOTHING TO KNOW, EXCEPT KNOWLEDGE.

Everything other than knowledge is name or form. The moment you know them they become knowledge itself. So you do not really know anything other than knowledge. Thus the world is not. Then where is bondage?

412. WHAT IS THE RELATION BETWEEN THE LIFE PRINCIPLE AND DEAD MATTER?

Everything perceivable is dead matter. The life principle alone can never be perceived. Therefore the life principle can never be dead matter. Nor can there be any duality or diversity in the life principle. It can only be one. Life transcends perception as well as conception.

Looking from another standpoint, the life principle is the 'is'-ness in everything. From this point of view, there is no such thing as dead matter. Everything perceived is lit up by the Self, and is alive.

13th July 1952

413. THROUGH SOUND TO THE ULTIMATE

The four stages of progression to the Ultimate explained in relation to the path of sound can be applied to any sphere of life. For example:

1. *Vaikharī* can very well be represented by every perceivable expression as body.
2. *Madhyamā* can very well be represented by every expression as mind (inaudible) still with language.
3. *Pashyantī* can very well be represented by the languageless, apparently limited 'I' or witness.

4. *Parā* can very well be represented by the real Self or Ātmā beyond even the limitation of oneness or beyond even the apparently limited 'I'.

Ātmā expresses itself in two realms, namely the mind and the body. The Sage rests at the right end, Ātmā, and sees the other two as mere illusions upon the Ātmā itself.

But the ordinary man remains at the wrong end, the body, attributing complete reality to its form and name, and considering the mind and Ātmā as relatively subtle (less real).

Thus the right perspective assumed by the Sage is reversed completely by the ordinary man. To get to perfection the layman has therefore to reverse his perspective likewise.

Sage's perspective	Ātmā alone real	Mind and body unreal
Ordinary man's perspective	Body and mind both real	Ātmā unreal

414. TO THE ULTIMATE THROUGH DHARMA AND DHARMI

Every perception has two aspects: the *dharmi* and *dharma*. The *dharmi* is the changeless background or existence upon which the *dharmas* come and go. For example we say 'the book is'. 'The book' is dharma and 'is' is the dharmi. Because the '*is*' is everywhere; but 'the book' is only in the book. But it is misunderstood by an ordinary man. He takes 'book' as dharmi and the 'is' as dharma (attribute).

The '*is*' can never be an attribute, because it is everywhere. It alone can be dharmi. If therefore you approach the Truth by way of the 'dharmi', understanding it in the right manner, you get to the ultimate Truth without any difficulty. There the 'is' and consciousness will be found to be one and the same.

Here also, the correct order is reversed, by putting the changeless after the changing. Immediately after every perception, the changeless part '*is*' is conveniently forgotten, and the changing part 'book' alone is emphasized. Correctly, it ought to be said that existence (dravya) expresses itself as book (guṇa). Or in other words, 'Existence books', 'book' being used as a verb. Thus, every existing noun should be considered a verbal noun and its expression a regular verb or attribute. The Sanskrit language emphasizes this usage literally.

Existence is the only dravya (noun). All else is verb or attribute. *Sat* is dharmi and exists in all dharma. But one dharma cannot exist in another dharma. Get to the '*is*' in every perception or find the dharmi in you, and you are free.

In this sense, it is said that Lord Kṛiṣhṇa is to be considered the only male and all other beings females. Looked at from the phenomenal, the world appears as existence, expressing itself as the world. But looked at from the standpoint of Existence, there has been no expression at all.

14th July 1952

415. WHY DOES ONE SEEK TRUTH ELSEWHERE?

Because he does not know that he is himself that Truth.

416. WHAT IS THE TEST OF LOVE?

In your relationship with another, if you can never even dream of any kind of ill-feeling towards that other, that relationship can be said to be bordering on pure love. What is that which you cannot help loving? Ātmā alone.

> ātmāviṅkalatilprīti, prītitān viṣayattilāṁ,
> piṟaykkuṁ viṣayaprīti, yātmaprītipiṟicciṭā .
>
> [In self, what's found is quite beyond
> all mere affection which is felt
> for outside objects in the world.
> Affection felt for outside things
> can be expelled, but not so liking
> for the truth of what self is.
> That can't be given up or changed.]

Bhāṣha Pancadashi, Ātmānanda-prakaraṇam, 26
(Malayalam translation)

417. WHAT IS MEANT BY 'SAKALAṀ DṚŚYAṀ JAḌAM' – 'EVERYTHING PERCEIVED IS INERT' (Upanishad)?

All that you perceive is dead and inert; because in fact you do not see anything. The object, when you seem to perceive it, is dead as object; but is living in the higher sense, as Consciousness.

That which exists can never be dead. Therefore, the material part, which is changing, alone is dead. The existence part of every object is life or Consciousness itself. This is not perceptible and is never dead.

21st July 1952

418. WHO HAS ANY PROBLEM?

You say that you have many problems. But I ask you, have '*you*' really any? When you examine your problems more carefully, you will find that every problem belongs to somebody other than yourself, namely to the body or mind. You, as the real 'I'-principle, have absolutely no problem.

You cannot talk of any problem unless you perceive it. When you are the perceiver, you cannot simultaneously be the sufferer or enjoyer. Thus you cannot have any problem, but you are the witness always. A patient can narrate the details of his disease to a doctor only as the perceiver and not as the sufferer. So the patient is the witness of the disease. Thus you are the eternal witness. This is what Vēdānta wants to impress upon you.

The Truth is now and here. So it is everywhere. If it is not first found now and here, it will be found nowhere else and at no other time.

The utterances of a Sage in the sahaja state are bold and uncompromising, since they directly reflect the ultimate Truth. Thinking along the lines of these bold utterances will itself be a pleasure even on the path, and will take you right to the transcendental.

419. WHAT IS REALIZATION?

Realization is nothing but shifting the centre of gravity or emphasis from the object to the subject in every perception. For example, 'I see the chair.' Here 'I' comes first and 'chair' next. But the ordinary man ignores the 'I' and emphasizes only the 'chair'. Correctly speaking, he ought to be emphasizing the subject 'I' and ignoring the object 'chair'.

The God-given universe is God itself, and can be nothing else.

Invisible means not visible to the ordinary sense organs, but cognized by some higher faculty.

420. WHAT IS THE NEED OF A GURU?

Knowledge is of two kinds: objective and subjective. Objective knowledge of all kinds, relating to objects gross as well as subtle, can be acquired only through objective instruments of the same nature, from the intellect down to the gross body. For this, we readily seek the help of equally objective Gurus – like persons, books, instruments and other appliances.

But, for the acquisition of subjective knowledge (knowledge regarding the 'I'-principle), none of the above instruments nor anything objective shall be of any avail. However, the objective instruments, if properly utilized, do the simple service of proving to you that you are not the body, senses or the mind. They can do nothing more, and your intellect also cannot grasp anything beyond the objective.

The subjective experience of the real 'I' is exclusively the subject of Vēdānta. This can be gained only by personal contact, in an attitude of complete surrender, with a Jnyānin who is established in that subjective Reality. This Jnyānin, though appearing to the ordinary man as embodied, really stands beyond the body, senses and mind – as Ātmā itself. But the disciple, as long as he feels himself embodied, sees the Guru only as a personality. Slowly, the disciple realizes that he is that living principle beyond the body, senses and mind. Then he finds the Guru also correspondingly exalted.

At last, when the disciple, taken thus to the brink of the mind, listens to the words of the Guru explaining the nature of the positive Self, he is suddenly thrown into that supreme experience of the ultimate. It is only then that he realizes the state of the Guru to be that always, whether in apparent activity or inactivity. Thus alone can Truth be ever realized.

Another aspect of the same: You have nothing of your own. Everything you profess to possess is alien to you, acquired from different sources. Your body, your language, your ideas and everything of yours likewise are derived from very many others, each one being a Guru to that extent. All your merit or originality consists in rearranging them in a peculiar manner, calling it 'discovery'.

Every activity of yours is the result of some things you have thus acquired from different Gurus or sources. Therefore, a Guru is essential in every walk of life; much more so in the search for the Truth, since you have to give up all that you deem to possess, before you are let into the ultimate Truth.

> Adṛśyō dṛśyatē rāhur gṛhītēnē 'ndunā yathā,
> tathā 'nubhava-mātrā 'tmā dṛśyēnā 'tmā vilōkyatē

[Source of quotation uncertain]

> The invisible Rāhu is perceived through the eclipsed moon. In the same way the *Ātmā* who is mere experience is perceived through objects.

Translation by Shrī Ātmānanda, Ātma-darshan, *Preface*

In the quotation, Rāhu stands for Ātmā and the moon represents everything perceived (dṛishya). Rāhu or Ātmā is by nature imperceptible to the senses. But Rāhu becomes perceptible only when it comes into direct contact with the moon. Similarly, Ātmā is recognized only when you cognize any object, and direct your attention to the knowing or the witness aspect of the activity.

For example: 'I know the chair.' 'I' is by nature unexpressed. But, in the perception of the chair, if you do take it emphasizing the 'I' or Ātmā in it, the chair only serves to show the Ātmā. Thus utilize all objects as helps to attain the Ultimate.

Every art, science or shāstra starts upon the blind assumption of the basic error that the world, as it is perceived, is real; and it proceeds to examine objects from this stand. But the vēdāntin begs to differ and boldly asks the artist or scientist what he is going to examine, questioning the very reality of the object itself. The vēdāntin calls upon you to prove the object first, before proceeding to examine it.

When you are engaged in examining the fundamentals of anything, you should not allow your past samskāras to come in and taint your judgement. The habit channels of the mind are of course difficult to overcome. So you have to guard yourself strongly against them.

When you are forced to examine what you call an 'object', strictly and impartially, you find that you rely upon knowledge and experience alone for the proof of the object. But knowledge and experience are always within you, and do not go out to meet the so called object. So knowledge and experience can in no case prove the existence of the objects, but only their existence as ideas quite within the mind's realm. Thus the objects admit themselves to be nothing but ideas.

These in their turn are again cognized by that self-luminous 'I'-principle, still further within. By applying the same argument, you see that thoughts and feelings admit themselves to be nothing but that 'I'-principle. Therefore, you see that what appears as an object is nothing but your own luminous Self.

The experienced is always one with the experience. This is applicable in all realms. Identifying yourself with the mind and examining the gross, you find the gross to be nothing but thought forms.

Next identifying yourself with the self-luminous 'I'-principle, you examine thoughts and feelings, and immediately thoughts and feelings are found to be nothing other than that 'I'-principle. Thus the whole world, including your own body and mind, is nothing but your own Self.

> yat tvaṁ paśyasi tatrai 'kas tvam ēva pratibhāsasē .
> kiṁ pṛthak bhāsatē svarṇāt kaṭak-āṅgada-nūpuram ..
>
> [In what you see, just *you* shine forth, alone.
> What else but gold shines out in golden ornaments?]

Aṣhṭāvakra samhitā, 15.14

Perception, thought or feeling is not such at the time of activity. You make it such only after the event. Neither does it exist before the event. Therefore nothing objective ever exists.

421. WHAT ARE STATES?

The states called dream and wakeful, when viewed from the standpoint of the apparent subject, appear only as the wakeful state. A state or experience is styled a dream when its corresponding objects are found to be non-existent.

In that sense, every past experience is a dream; and you have only one experience in the present – the wakeful.

422. HOW IS A DREAM A DREAM?

You say you had a dream, relying upon memory alone. You admit in the same breath that the objects of the dream, including even the dream subject, were all unreal. This shows that memory is no proof of the reality of the objects of the experience supposed to be remembered. If the objects of perception and the organs of perception were unreal, the perception also must be equally unreal.

The mind always works conjointly with the corresponding sense organs. Therefore, when the dream sense-organs and the dream body disappear, the dream mind also disappears. Then the dream perceptions do not have a container to hold on to. Therefore, the dream perceptions are not capable of being remembered in any circumstance. Hence memory cannot prove a dream.

As you wake up from the dream state, you must wake up from the waking dream also. To say that you can now think of your past dream is also wrong. Even to think of a dream you must cast away all that is connected with the waking state, and become a dream subject for the time being.

Prakṛiti (avidyā) carries on its head the weapon with which to kill prakṛiti itself. That weapon is *vidyā-vṛitti* (the higher reason).

423. WHAT IS THE SECRET OF ENJOYMENT?

To say you enjoyed anything, for example music, is wrong.

It is true you started by listening to music. At first you forgot your personal identity and were absorbed in the harmony expressed in the music. But you did not stop there. Through the expressed harmony, you were carried on to the unexpressed inner harmony of the Self and experienced your own Self there.

Coming back, you passed through the very same stages, in the reverse order, and reached the music again. Then you wantonly superimposed the bliss experienced upon the music outside.

The mistake is not in enjoying the expressed harmony, but is only in superimposing the happiness upon some external object – here music. When you say you enjoy any sense object, like music, that object is not present at the time of enjoyment. Nor is the personal 'I', the enjoyer, present. There is only your real Self, in its real nature of Peace.

You utilize music only as an instrument, and abandon it just before enjoyment or experience.

424. HOW DO THE YŌGIN AND THE SAGE REACT, WITH REGARD TO PLEASURE AND PAIN?

When the body suffers, the yōgin, as a result of his incessant practice, takes away the mind from that spot and arrests it elsewhere, thus avoiding the pain. Even when thus separated from the body, the mind has its own sufferings. This sort of evasion does not enrich him, but on the contrary injures him much. Because, later on, he will find it much more difficult than an ordinary man would, to leave off a mind so highly developed and to rest in his real nature. The habit channels of the mind are so difficult to be overcome.

But the Sage views pleasure or pain in quite a different manner. He lets the body or mind enjoy or suffer as it comes; only seeing that it is the body or mind alone that enjoys or suffers and that he – the knower of them all – is not involved in them in the least.

The yōgins, of their own choice, leave the body to itself and labour hard to train the changing mind to expand and acquire powers.

But the one who takes to the jnyāna path leaves both the body and the mind to themselves, and chooses to retreat into his own real nature of Peace within.

425. WHO IS REALLY DOING A DEED?

In the doing, there is only doing and no who (doer) nor deed. In the doer, there is only doer and no doing or deed. And in the deed, there is only deed and no doer or doing.

Therefore the question does not arise.

426. WHAT IS LIBERATION?

You have to gain liberation only from the appendages, viz. body, senses and mind. The officer is an appendage of the man, who is relatively the witness of the officer.

You always desire rest. Real rest comes only from your real nature – Peace. From this background, there is always the trumpet call, resounding 'Go to Peace!' You respond to it *unknowingly*, every time. Thus you go back to your real nature, Peace, after every activity.

This Peace or rest is already in you. You have only to recognize it, and go to it every time *knowingly*. This is liberation. Thus you see that you were never bound.

27th July 1952

427. WHAT IS VICĀRA-MĀRGA?

Vicāra-mārga is the method in which the disciple is directly shown the right Absolute, and the only effort the disciple is called upon to make is to establish himself in that Absolute.

428. TRUTH AND LIBERATION

You actually come into contact with the Truth, as the world, every moment. But you are not enriched by that in the least, until you are told by the Guru about the ultimate Truth in the most unambiguous terms.

Truth can be seemingly transmitted to the ordinary man only by word of mouth. He is taken from the lower to the higher Truth in gradual stages, working up his conviction at every step. To create this conviction, contact through some clear medium is essential.

Hearing and seeing are the most convenient and important of such mediums.

429. WHAT IS REAL LISTENING?

The Upanishads boldly proclaim that listening to the ultimate Truth, over and over again, is the only means to ultimate realization. What is this 'listening'?

Hearing the Truth direct from the lips of the Guru is, of course, the first 'listening'. It is an extremely rare privilege to be in the physical presence of the Guru, repeatedly listening to his words.

But those who are denied this proud privilege of being constantly in his presence can also 'listen'. Thinking deeply over the Truth expounded to you by the Guru, over and over again adducing the arguments advanced by the Guru in detail and every time touching the ultimate experience of the inner Self as you had it the first time, is also virtually listening to the words of the Guru. This is the form of listening adopted by the vast majority of disciples, of course after once having heard the Truth from the Guru in person.

Truth is visualized even on the first listening. Further listening helps you to get established in the Truth.

28th July 1952

430. HOW IS MIND RELATED TO THE OBJECT?

When the mind is taken away from any object, what remains over is neither the known nor the unknown. That can only be the ultimate Reality. Therefore the mind makes the Ultimate appear as the object.

431. WHAT WAS SHRĪ KṚIṢHṆA'S ROLE?

Lord Kṛiṣhṇa is the *Bhagavad-gītā* itself, and the *Bhagavad-gītā* is the absolute Truth. His life (as described in the *Bhāgavata Purāṇa*) is a living commentary on the *Gītā*.

In the whole of his life, we do not see a single instance of his having ever done anything for his personal self. From stealing butter and curds in his infancy to his expounding the ultimate Truth to the Gopīs in the '*Samanta-pancaka*', he had been unique in selflessness.

He is one who has never wept in his life. This shows that its opposite, namely pleasure, was also absent in him. He was beyond both, always at the background.

At the last moment, he blesses even the hunter who shot the fatal arrow at him.

432. How is Consciousness related to objects?

Consciousness has no separate object. So it comes to the realms of the mind and senses, and claims the objects there as objects of consciousness. But when you look deeper, to see how they become objects of consciousness, you have to leave the realms of senses and mind. Beyond the mind, the objects become Consciousness itself, and there all objectivity vanishes.

Every sense organ has a corresponding sense object, and the object of any one sense organ cannot be cognized by any other organ. Moreover, every sense object is of the same nature as the corresponding sense organ itself. Therefore, if Consciousness were likewise an organ and had an object of its own, it could only be of the nature of Consciousness, quite distinct and separate from any other class of sense objects.

The usual statement, 'I am conscious of a thing', is not correct; since a 'thing' can never be the object of Consciousness. What you mean by that statement is only that you are perceiving the thing through the mind in a subtle manner, or that you are mentally conscious of it, or in other words that you can reproduce it in your mind.

When you search for that 'thing' in Consciousness, it is nowhere to be found. It has merged in Consciousness; and the statement ultimately means 'I am conscious of myself' or that 'Consciousness knows Consciousness.' Therefore, Consciousness cannot have any object other than Consciousness.

> ātmānamātmanā kaṇṭu teḷika nī
>
> [It's by the self that self is seen.
> That's what you need to clarify.]

Eṟuttacchan

29th July 1952

433. WHAT IS PRACTICAL REST?

The ideal rest, capable of relieving the exhaustion of days and nights of intense strain, is obtained by putting the mind in what is called the blank state (madhyagatāvastha), for an hour on even less, as convenient.

In order to induce that state you have to refrain from all thoughts – objective as well as subjective. But in the early stages, the mind rebels against it and takes to other thoughts indiscriminately. Then you have deliberately to dismiss those thoughts, one by one. After a sufficient period of such training, you will find that the mind comes to a blank state of absolute rest.

But this exercise should never be attempted, except under personal instructions from a competent guru.

> citraṁ vaṭatarōr mūlē vṛddhāś śiṣyā gurur yuvā
> gurōstu maunaṁ vyākhyānaṁ śiṣyā 'stu chinna-saṁśayāḥ
> [see note 688]

Shrī Shankara, Dakṣhiṇāmūrti-stōtram*, Dhyāna-shlōka 3, at start of Surēshvarācārya's* Manasōllasa

The quotation explains how you really understand anything said by the Guru about the ultimate Truth. You understand only when you are beyond the words, language, ideas, central idea, speaker or listener. At the time of understanding, the teacher as teacher and the disciple as disciple are both absent, both having risen to the ultimate background in apparent silence.

Experience occurs only when the expression stops.

434. WHO IS THE REAL CHILD?

The worldly child, who is a child in ignorance, and the Sage, who is a child in knowledge, are both unattached to objects. The child has not acquired the capacity to think, and the Sage has gone beyond the capacity to think. But the child leaves a slight samskāra behind after every activity, while the Sage leaves nothing behind.

Therefore, the Sage alone is the real child.

435. WHAT ARE THE DIFFERENT EXPRESSIONS OF HARMONY?

The inner harmony of the Absolute is first expressed in:

1. *The language of the soul or Reality* – without in the least losing its essence.
2. Next, it is expressed in the *languageless language of ideas*.
3. Next, in the *language of ideas*.
4. Lower down, it expresses itself or it is expressed in the *language of sounds*, every such integral expression being called a mantra.
5. Still further down, it is expressed in the *language of words*, being the grossest form of expression.

In all these different kinds of expression, the ideal to be maintained is that no part of that inner harmony of the language of the soul should be lost. This is possible only for a Sage, well established in the sahaja state, never slipping out of that inner harmony or real background.

Every thought and word of his is a mantra in its full sense, since the whole of his indivisible Self is in that inner harmony all the time.

30th July 1952

436. HOW ARE THE REAL FLOWER AND THE REAL 'I' ONE AND THE SAME?

The 'flower' is that permanent something upon which all its adjuncts or qualities appear and disappear. So also, I am that permanent something upon which the expressions – like body, senses and mind – come and go.

Everything pertaining to the flower corresponds to the things pertaining to the 'I'. But, giving up all adjuncts from the subject as well as from the object, we find that what remains over is neither known nor unknown, but real; and therefore is nothing but the ultimate Reality.

Therefore, the real 'flower' and the real 'I' are in essence one and the same.

31st July 1952

437. WHAT IS SILENT KNOWLEDGE?

Ordinary knowledge is knowledge '*of this*' (of any object gross or subtle), obtained through a corresponding instrument.

But the silent knowledge or witness has neither a medium, nor is it obtained. Therefore the witness is described as silent knowledge, viewed from the standpoint of the mind or the ego.

The ignorant mind has certain false standards set by itself, and evaluates everything according to those standards. But when the Truth is heard from the Guru, the mind gives up all its previous standards.

Thenceforward the witness, which was so long qualified as silent, ceases to be silent – in the sense that it is the background of both activity and inactivity.

438. WHAT IS INDIVIDUALITY?

Individuality is not what the ordinary man takes it to be. He takes it to be adherence to one's own body, senses and mind; and at the same time he believes that the individuality is changeless. Such an individuality is never possible.

The advaitin seeks that individuality or principle in him which continues unchanged, even when the body and the mind change every moment.

That individuality, if it should be changeless, can only be the real 'I'-principle (Ātmā).

439. HOW TO ASSUAGE HUMAN SUFFERING?

The problem is an illusion. Nobody actually wants to assuage human suffering as it is. Knowledge of human suffering creates a sympathetic suffering in you. It is this suffering in you that directly calls for a solution, and drives you to the habit channel of always seeking causes and remedies in external objects. Thus you attribute the cause of your suffering to the human suffering outside.

A solution could be suggested to this in two ways: objective and subjective.

1. The objective solution seeks to correct the world and its arrangements so as not to allow recurrence of the human suffering. This is not always possible or practicable, because the external objects in question are diverse and often not under our control. It is like attempting to cover the surface of the whole world with leather, in order to afford smooth walking. This is often the way of the ignorant world.
2. The other alternative, adopted by the wise one, is to seek the subjective remedy. Your knowledge of something else was certainly the cause of your pain. But that other something was never in the knowledge or in you. So, examine your 'knowledge of anything' more closely, and you find that it was nothing but pure knowledge. Even when you turn your attention inward, the suffering vanishes. So return to your real nature and you are free.

Correct yourself alone, and do not attempt to correct the kingdom of God – if ever there is one.

440. IS THE 'UNIVERSAL' A SPIRITUAL GOAL, AND DOES IT HELP AN ASPIRANT TOWARDS THE ULTIMATE TRUTH?

No. From the individual to the universal is the cosmological path of progress. But this by itself can never take you to the Absolute. Even when you have expanded yourself to the extent of comprehending the whole universe, you will stand only as the expanded individual by force of samskāras, and therefore you do not transcend individuality.

The universal has also to be transcended in order to get to the Truth. You get at the same Truth by transcending the individual. Then why all this vain labour, to reach the universal?

441. WHAT IS THE EFFECT OF RENUNCIATION?

Renunciation is usually considered as a means to Self-realization, but its effect is just the opposite. When you renounce an object, you actually attribute more concreteness and reality to it than when you are indifferent to it.

Thus renunciation, instead of proving the unreality of the world, makes it more real and frightful, though you are temporarily and conveniently kept away from parts of it.

442. DIFFERENCES IN THE VIEWPOINTS OF EVEN THE UPANIṢHADS EXPLAINED

The Upaniṣhads are all brief records of the expounding of the Truth, to disciples of different standards, by the Sages of old at different times. The general instruction how to approach and understand those Upaniṣhads themselves is to take them all as only formal (aupacārika).

This means that it was primarily only for those to whom it was particularly addressed, and secondly for such others who could not understand anything higher. It was not meant for those who could not understand it, nor for those who could see even beyond.

Svarūpa is the thing in itself, and that changeless background to which attributes are given.

3rd August 1952

443. WHY DID SHRĪ KUMĀRILA BHAṬṬA REJECT THE OFFER OF SHRĪ SHANKARA?

Kumārila Bhaṭṭa was a karmattha and had a guru who followed the vēdic path. He followed the traditional path and had risen well beyond opposites, beyond virtue and vice. The only sin he had consciously committed was deceiving his Buddhist guru. Though it was done not for any selfish purpose, but for establishing the Truth, he decided at last to atone for it by burning his body alive in a flaming pile of paddy husk.

The fire had consumed him almost up to the waist when Shrī Shankara reached him and offered him advaitic Truth. He was quite calm and serene, even in the throes of death, having discarded without a thought all his past virtues. Having transcended the opposites of virtue and vice, pleasure and pain etc., and being able to stand as the disinterested witness even during the pangs of death, he must indeed have risen to the ultimate Truth.

Thus standing as Truth himself, he did not stand in need of it again from Shrī Shankara. Therefore Shrī Shankara was respectfully sent to his foremost disciple, Shrī Mandana Mishra for a spiritual duel, as desired by Shrī Shankara himself.

Kumārila Bhaṭṭa was a staunch advocate of selfless karma. Any path, if followed with sincerity and earnestness even beyond the apparent opposites, takes one to the right Ultimate. *Devotion*, *Vishiṣhṭādvaita*, *Dvaita* and all such paths in due course take you to the same goal of Truth if followed with steadfastness, even beyond opposites, with an eye on the *sat-cit-ānanda* aspect of the Absolute.

Following the expression even beyond name and form, you reach that which is really expressionless, but which expresses itself as apparent objects.

444. WHY IS A SMILE EMPHASIZED IN MEDITATION?

Meditation upon the smile on the face of the iṣhṭa-dēva helps you to the Absolute.

Contemplation of the form of your iṣhṭa-dēva does not help you to rise above body and mind. But the moment you think of his smile, you forget the name and form and are attracted to something higher and more illuminating, namely the consciousness part of it. If you hold fast to the consciousness expressing itself through the smile, you are lead on to the experience of the real Self, in due course.

> nirviśēṣaṁ paraṁ brahma sākṣāt kartumanīśvarāḥ
> yē mandāstē 'nukampyantē saviśēṣanirūpaṇaiḥ
> vaśīkṛtē manasyēṣāṁ saguṇabrahmaśīlanāt
> tadēvāvirbhavēt sākṣādapētōpādhikalpanam

Dharmarāja Adhvarīndra, Vedānta-paribhāṣha, Chapter 8

4th August 1952

445. HOW IS THE YŌGIN'S APPROACH TO THE TRUTH DIFFERENT FROM THE JNYĀNIN'S?

Yōga is a development out of *Nirīshvara-sānkhya* or 'Sānkhya denying God', and is known by the term *Sēshvara-sānkhya* or 'Sānkhya accepting God'. In Sānkhya, prakṛiti is not ultimately disposed of, but is only brought to an equilibrium and rendered harmless. Therefore duality still persists, in the form of puruṣha and prakṛiti, even after the supposed liberation of the individual puruṣha. Acceptance of the position of the existence of several such liberated puruṣhas also retains duality in another form. Therefore the pure Sānkhya never transcends duality completely.

Yōgins always strive to visualize, through the mind, an ideal set by the mind itself. It cannot be denied that every object perceived is lit up by consciousness. Therefore, if the yōgin claims to visualize the Truth in the same manner, he must certainly light up the Absolute also likewise. But with what is it to be so lit up? No, it is never possible. Therefore yōga by itself can never take you to the Absolute.

The means of meditation is also adopted in the jnyāna path. But the disciple has already been told, by his Guru, about the real nature of the Absolute. Therefore, when he meditates upon the Absolute, the mind dies or merges into the self-luminous Absolute.

Some Jnyānins, even after realization, take to meditation as a habit. But they have ultimately to give up this habit also, since it unconsciously tries to limit the Absolute to a state.

Advaita absorbs the witness of the yōgin as well as the witnessed (consisting of the 98 tattvas) into it. Further, prakṛiti is completely destroyed, even before advaita is established.

446. FROM TRIPUṬĪ TO THE ABSOLUTE

1. Knower, knowing and known

   – reduced to –

2. Knowing or witness and known

   – reduced further to –

3. Witness alone, without the witnessed.

5th August 1952

447. 'AHAM' (SELF)

1. "na hanyate" … aham
   Aham means I am the deathless Ātmā.

["na hanyate" means "I am not killed." – probably quoted from the *Bhagavad-gītā*, 2.20. And 'aham' is Sanskrit for 'I'.]

2. aśiraskaṁ hakārāntam
   aśēṣākārasaṁsthitam

[Source of quotation uncertain]

448. HOW IS REALITY IN THE OBJECTIVE WORLD ESTABLISHED?

It is done in two ways:

1. By examining the objective world in an ascending order from the gross to the Absolute. When the gross is examined, it is reduced to mere thought forms, and thoughts in their turn are transformed into pure Consciousness. Thus the world is nothing but the Absolute.

2. By tracing the expression of the Absolute down to the gross world, in the descending order.

   In this process, yourself, the one reality, seems to split itself into two – namely generic thought and consciousness, the perceiver of the thought. At this stage there is no bondage, because there is no other thing in existence except yourself and thought, and your experience is only that you know.

   You see yourself as thought. It cannot be called a thought either, because from the standpoint of Consciousness, there cannot be anything other than Consciousness, and hence there is no thought.

   A thought to be a thought must have an object, and therefore thought can exist only in the mind's realm. In the plane where the generic thought is supposed to exist, consciousness alone obtains to provide an object to thought. But it is called a thought only when looked at from down below.

   This generic thought, which is not thought by itself, next begets innumerable other thoughts and thus the world comes into existence, out of this pure Consciousness.

Therefore, looking from the top or from the bottom, the world is found to be nothing but the Reality.

Ātmā: The unconditioned 'I'.

First emanation: 'I know I am.' The most generic thought. Here I am witness of the generic thought.

Second emanation: Then you come to the particular thoughts – including time, space and causality – establishing the whole realm of the mind. Immediately, you become the 'thinker' in the tripuṭī (of the thinker, thinking and thought).

Third emanation: Further down, you become the 'perceiver', in a world of sense perceptions.

Fourth emanation: Finally, you come down to be a 'doer', in a gross world of bodies and actions.

This is the order in which the unconditioned 'I' manifests itself in different stages. And to return to the same unconditioned state, you have to ascend in the same order, relinquishing the accretions one by one.

449. 'BEING' AND 'VĒDĀNTA' – HOW ARE THEY RELATED?

'Being', which is by nature unmanifested, seems to manifest itself as a mental being in the mind's realm and lower down as a physical being in the gross realm.

This 'being' is Truth itself, but is not experienced as such by all. It is also difficult to conceive of. The world can easily be reduced to thoughts, but the further disposal of thoughts is not so easy.

It is for this that the help of 'Vēdānta' is sought. Vēdānta does its task most wonderfully, by proving that there never was a thought in existence, and that all that ever existed was pure Consciousness, Ātmā alone.

7th August 1952

450. WHAT IS THE EASIEST APPROACH TOWARDS UNDERSTANDING THE TRUTH?

In order that the understanding may be natural and abiding, it has to be based upon your fundamental experiences. For this, you have to begin by examining your ordinary experiences as a layman, gradually eliminating from them all extraneous elements, leaving only Truth behind.

This method alone takes you to the Truth, without any effort or doubt.

For example, examine what happens during your most ordinary perceptions, thoughts or feelings; and prove that in every case it is your own Ātmā, the Self, that is experienced as Consciousness or Peace.

451. What is the difference between 'I' and 'you'?

In the 'you', the 'I' is always present. But in the 'I', the 'you' is not present.

452. Is there renunciation in vicāra-mārga?

Renunciation, like everything else, has two aspects: its form and its essence. Paths like those of karma, devotion, sannyāsa, yōga etc. emphasize both these aspects, sometimes the form even more than the essence.

But for those who follow the path of jnyāna or vicāra-mārga, the essence of renunciation alone is emphasized and the form practically ignored. So much so that an acquaintance of a modern Sage who adopted the direct path for instruction once told him that he wished to accept the path chalked out by him, since it called for no kind of renunciation at any stage of one's life. Because to all appearance the Sage was leading an ideal domestic life.

But to this the Sage replied: 'Well my friend, you are sorely mistaken. It is not the physical renunciation that really counts. If it did, every destitute beggar would be a sannyāsin. He can claim to have renounced much and to possess little.

'But it is that preparedness to renounce everything you possess including your own life – if it is necessary for the attainment of the Truth – that really matters. You can never reach that Ultimate if there is any one little thing in the world which you are not prepared to renounce, in order to reach the Ultimate. That preparedness to renounce everything makes one a real sannyāsin.

Any amount of physical renunciation, without that complete preparedness to renounce everything, makes you only a prisoner in your own self-made mental fetters. You are not much better than a prisoner behind iron bars.

Therefore the ideal of life for one who takes to vicāra-mārga should be inwardly to be a perfect sannyāsin and outwardly to live like a 'man of the world'.

The Sage has renounced his life completely, but has kindly permitted life to cling to Truth for the time being, to be dismissed without notice whenever he chooses. The Sage is always *in* the world but not *of* it.

8th August 1952

453. WHAT IS RASA?

Rasa is that something which descends into the heart and is experienced by the heart.

['Rasa' means 'sap' or 'juice' and hence it indicates the essence or the essential savour of a feeling or an experience.]

454. WHY AM I ASKED TO SEE THE GURU BEHIND ME FIRST (*Ātma-nirvṛiti, 18.5*)?

You are asked first to try to visualize Me behind you, since that centre is not surrounded by any obstacles.

In front of you, you have a forest of worldly objects with which you are so familiar that you believe they have independent existence and reality. In their midst, you will hardly be able to recognize Me, the witness.

In the realm of thoughts and feelings also, it is equally difficult to recognize Me.

But if you succeed in directing your attention to Me behind the mind, you will meet with no obstacles there, and you will be forced to see Me alone. Facing Me, you will transcend all thoughts of body and mind and also the sense of inside and outside.

Then you will recognize that 'I' am in you as yourself, the Ātmā.

Water is always invisible. So is everything. But its existence is never denied.

455. HOW TO VIEW THE EXPRESSION?

Reality, as it is, is unexpressed and imperceptible. Where expressed, it becomes perceptible to the senses or mind. But then the Reality is obscured to that extent. Therefore, do not desire any particular kind of expression, however sāttvic.

Expression is always transient or time limited, and the expression is invariably misunderstood to be the Reality itself. Your goal, however, is always permanent peace or Happiness. And so you must desire the Reality itself, which is always in everything, as the expressed.

456. HOW CAN THE WITNESS OF JĪVA AND THE WITNESS OF ĪSHVARA BE ONE?

The shāstras labour hard, to prove the identity of these two witnesses. But according to our approach, it is comparatively easy to prove.

The only difference between jīva and Īshvara lies in the scope and limitation of each. Each is said to be the witness of its own objects or perceptions. Now, examining the objects of each, we find nothing which is an object of Īshvara alone, and which cannot also be an object of jīva. Thus, their objects being identical, the witnesses alone cannot be different.

Moreover, according to the higher shāstras, Īshvara is but the highest manifestation of the human mind, and is not different from jīva in essence. Or in other words, Īshvara is but an object of jīva. Therefore, their witnesses also cannot be different.

9th August 1952

457. WHY DOES A JNYĀNIN SOMETIMES TRY TO HELP OTHERS IN DISTRESS?

The Jnyānin knows well that the source of all their distress is the fear of death, and he knows that death is a misnomer. So he tries to help them to continue to live in the illusion for a time, only long enough to make them understand that they can never die.

458. WHAT IS THE IDEAL FORM OF CHARITY?

It should be spontaneous, unconditional and prompted from beyond the realm of the mind. It should be selfless.

If, after doing any charity, you continue to pride yourself over it or even think about it, you are really degrading yourself to that extent. If you continue to criticize the way in which the amount was utilized, it means that you have not actually parted with the ownership of the money.

A conditional charity means that you have engaged the recipient as a servant, to do something for you in your absence according to your instructions, expressed or implied.

Therefore, the best way to do charity would be to do it and forget all about it immediately.

459. WHAT IS THE FRUIT OF WORSHIP?

Worship of God ensures pleasures of heaven (dṛiṣhṭa-phala-sādhya).

Worship of the Guru ensures permanent Happiness – including the former, if desired (dṛiṣhṭādṛiṣhṭa-phala-sādhya).

11th August 1952

460. WHAT DO I LOVE?

When love is directed to personal qualities, that love is worldly. When it is directed to the life principle, it becomes sublime. When that life principle is examined, it will be found to be nothing other than pure Consciousness (the Ātmā). Then love is transformed into the absolute Reality.

Let us examine this a little more closely. You say you love a man. Who is the man you suppose you love? Is it his body? No. Because when he dies, you fear even to go near his dead body. Thus you see that your love was really directed to the life principle which was abiding in that body. When that life is examined, it is found to be nothing other than pure Consciousness, which is only one.

Man is incapable of loving anything other than that Consciousness, the Ātmā.

461. HOW IS THE WAKING STATE A DREAM?

By a 'dream' we mean something which is not real. What is Reality? That which does not disappear at any time.

Now, what is there in the waking state that does not disappear? Nothing. Therefore, everything objective, connected with the waking state, is unreal.

But what we have just called the unreal appears all the while. Yes. When the unreal appears as real we call it a dream. Therefore, the waking state is all a dream.

But there is one thing that does not disappear in any state – pure Consciousness, the Ātmā.

462. KNOWLEDGE CANNOT BE A FUNCTION. WHY?

Because nothing can exist by its side to form its object. Therefore, to say that 'I know' or 'I know it' are both wrong. Functioning starts only with the inception of mind and the consequent subject-object relationship.

The sense organs and mind can function only by the consciousness part existing in them.

13th August 1952

463. WHAT DOES THE GURU GIVE ME?

Answer: 'The correct perspective.'

The world and its objects, when viewed through the perspective bestowed by the Guru, appear transformed into that ultimate Reality, just as the brackish and poisonous waters of the ocean are transformed into pure water when they pass through the heat of the sun above.

464. WHAT IS THE SAHAJA STATE?

A Jnyānin, by experiencing the ultimate Happiness, knows that he experiences nothing new and that the limitation he used to put upon Happiness before realization was an illusion. Thus he knows that what one experiences as limited happiness, apparently ensuing from objects, is in fact that unlimited ultimate Happiness itself.

So even if a Sage appears to be leading a normal life as before, he does not see the world as the onlookers see it. Even when the others think that he is hunting after objects of pleasure, he from his own stand is always enjoying his *svarūpānanda*.

A Sage in the sahaja state does not bother himself – as far as he is concerned – with explaining the objective world or its activities. Death for him has taken place long ago, at the moment of his first realizing the Truth. The subsequent stoppage of prāṇa long after and the consequent paralysis of the body, which we usually call death, does not denote the moment of the death of his ego.

The ultimate ideal is not '*not* to see' when objects appear, but to be deeply convinced that the Reality is far beyond both seeing and not-seeing by the senses. You only witness these perceptions, and the perceptions in no way affect you.

Though the eye shows the palace on the backdrop (curtain) on the stage most realistically to you, the intellect from behind tells you it is not real, and you readily accept that correction. So also, though sense organs show the objects to be real, the 'I'-principle – standing behind the sense organs – corrects them and tells you it is all illusion. The Sage readily accepts this position and lets the body and mind continue to function as before, just as he who sees the curtain continues to see the palace on the curtain as before, but does not allow himself to be carried away by the eye's verdict.

You cannot help seeing if you look through the eyes. The only means of avoiding seeing is to cease looking through the eyes. But the Sage does not want to perform that vain labour. He is content with resting in the ultimate Truth, whatever may be the activity the mind and body are engaged in.

We talk ignorantly of the activities of the Sage. It is a clear contradiction in terms. The Sage is that principle transcending both activity and inactivity. So the Sage cannot take to any activity as the Sage; and that which is engaged in any activity is not the Sage. In short, that which is visible to our sense organs or mind is not the Sage. The Sage is invisible and the background of all perceptions – the ultimate Reality. We can in no way reconcile the Sage and the activity we so ignorantly attribute to him.

You say you went to Shāstāmangaḷam in the bus. Except boarding and alighting from the bus you did not perform any other activity. All motion belonged to the bus and yet you say you went, attributing the motion of the bus to yourself who was only a silent witness to the activity of the bus. Still, you claim to have gone to Shāstāmangaḷam. This is the play of ignorance. The Sage does not claim the activity of anything else for himself. He always gives the devil his due and never identifies himself with the body, senses or mind.

Now applying the illustration of the bus subjectively, we find that the bus represents the objective group of the body, senses and generic mind, and 'you' in the bus stand for the real 'I'-principle. Therefore, even when the Sage (the real 'I'-principle) has withdrawn all identification from the objective group, that group is left intact to function as accurately and intelligently as before, under the guidance of the very same 'ignorance' which was guiding it before. What you call 'intelligence' is based upon pure ignorance, which is as much dead matter as the body, from the standpoint of the Reality.

14th August 1952

465. NOBODY DESIRES PURE HAPPINESS. WHY?

Desire is a function of the mind, and pure Happiness is on a level far beyond the mind. Therefore the mind can never conceive or desire pure Happiness. What the mind desires is the one last manifestation just before extinction or merging itself into Happiness.

Take for example the desire for the vision of your 'iṣhṭa-dēva', which usually gives you immense pleasure. Exactly as the vision gives you pleasure, the disappearance of the vision gives you pain; and this is inevitable, as the devotee knows from experience only too well. Thus, the condition just after the vision is dark and dismal, compared to the hopeful, exciting and pleasant condition just preceding it. Therefore, mindful of these two opposite conditions before and after the vision, the devotee naturally longs to prolong the pleasure as much as possible, knowing that the gloom after the vision is inevitable, and that the duration of the vision itself, though pleasant, is not under his control. So his desire for the pleasant feelings, experienced before the culmination of the vision, is greater than his desire for the vision itself, which he takes only as a logical corollary.

Moreover, the mind does not find any glamour in the ultimate Peace, from the standpoint of the mind itself. When you are hungry, what the mind really wants is the disappearance of the hunger, which can only be in Peace. The mind, being incapable of conceiving this Peace, turns to the objective food which is capable of removing the physical hunger. Thus the mind desires always only that preliminary pleasure.

Nobody except the Sage can desire that ultimate Happiness, since all the rest are in the realm of the mind. But the Sage does not desire even that, since he knows he is that already.

466. EVEN ADVAITA HAS ITS PLACE.

bhāvā 'dvaitaṁ sadā kuryāt
kriyā 'dvaitaṁ na karhi cit .
advaitaṁ triṣu lōkēṣu
*nā 'dvaitaṁ guruṇāsaha
*nā 'dvaitaṁ guru sannidhau ..

[* marks alternative versions of the fourth line.]

Shrī Shankara, Tattvopadesha, 87

1st line: bhāvā 'dvaitaṁ sadā kuryāt
You may contemplate deeply on the non-duality when you are not engaged in any other activity.

2nd line: kriyā 'dvaitaṁ na karhi cit
But in your activities there can never be any advaita.

3rd line: advaitaṁ triṣu lōkēṣu
The three worlds can easily be reduced to advaita.

4th line: nā 'dvaitaṁ guruṇāsaha
In the physical presence of one's own Guru, even a Jnyānin feels himself a child before the Absolute. That is the only altar before which an advaitin always falls bowing unconditionally. Advaita is only a pointer to the Guru. You do not reach advaita completely until you reach the egoless state. Never even think that you are one with

the Guru. It will never take you to the Ultimate. On the contrary that thought will only drown you.

Advaita points only to the Ultimate.

> draṣṭra-darśana-dṛśyēṣu pratyēkaṁ bōdha-mātratā
> sāras tēna, tad anyatvaṁ nāsti kiñ cit kha-puṣpavat
>
> [The see-er, seeing and the seen –
> of these, each is pure consciousness.
> With that, reality is found.
> Whatever is not that alone
> is like a flower in the sky;
> it is not really there at all.]

Shrī Shankara

It means: Try always to spot out the Reality in the world. Examine the three parts of tripuṭī separately, and see the Reality in each.

The moment you admit and accept advaita, all illustrations from the world become inapplicable to it and all questions cease. Because, viewed from the stand of advaita, nothing else exists.

15th August 1952

467. WHAT IS THE BEST WAY OF APPROACHING A PROBLEM FOR AN ULTIMATE SOLUTION?

It is best to take your stand, at least in idea, in the deep sleep state and see if the problem arises there. No, the problem does not appear there.

Therefore, all problems are the products of body, senses and mind, and disappear with them. They do not concern you at all.

16th August 1952

468. KNOWLEDGE KNOWS ONLY KNOWLEDGE AND EXPERIENCE EXPERIENCES ONLY EXPERIENCE. HOW?

Your experience alone is accepted as a proof for the existence of anything.

Suppose you see an object. What is your immediate experience? You see and you *can* see only form. But form and seeing can never be outside. They are in the mind itself. Here, a subtle sense organ and a subtle form are created in the mind, and a subtle perception takes place.

This again is not independent. It is established by the knowledge beyond the mind. Beyond the mind, there being neither object nor activity, you can only say knowledge knows knowledge. Similarly, experience experiences experience. Both these statements mean that you are all alone, shining in your own glory, even during so-called perceptions, thoughts and feelings.

I allow myself to be conditioned by time and space, and then perceive the object with the gross instrument of some sense organ. The next moment, I give up the space element, allow myself to be conditioned by time alone, and I perceive only subtle forms with subtle sense organs in the mind. The next moment, I give up the time limitation also and stand alone; and then I am experience or knowledge itself.

This experience or knowledge alone was present in the previous, apparently limited perceptions as well.

469. TIME AND SPACE ARE NOT AND SO THE WORLD IS NOT. (Another approach, assuming time to exist)

Time: Does it exist inside or outside you?

If it is outside, your thoughts and feelings – which are all inside – cannot be affected or conditioned by time, and further, time must be perceptible to the sense organs. This is not so. Therefore time must necessarily be inside the mind.

Next examining in the same manner if time exists in the mind, it is not perceived by the mind either. So we find it is neither there but further inside you.

Beyond the mind there is nothing but the 'I'-principle, and time cannot be there. Therefore time as time is not; and if it exists, it is Ātmā itself.

Space: Do you perceive space? If so, with what organ? If you say 'with the eye organ', it can perceive only form. Space is not form.

So space is never perceived outside; but is inside, just like time. Therefore space is also not; and if it exists, it is Ātmā itself.

470. Do you see man?

You will be tempted to say yes. If so, please define man, without reference to any of his attributes.

You find it is impossible to define man, or any other thing in its generic sense. A thing, in its generic sense, is the *sat* or Ātmā itself. It can never be perceived.

To make it perceivable, you superimpose name and form upon this '*sat*' and say you see the thing. But you see only the superimpositions; and never the thing, which is pure *sat* and not perceivable.

Therefore, nothing is ever seen, heard, touched, tasted or smelt. The '*it*' is the end of all senses, or that permanent background into which all senses merge. In Sanskrit, it is called in reference to each sense by different names, literally meaning the end of each sense perception (namely nādānta, rūpānta, gandhānta, sparshānta and rasānta), each being significant of its source.

Thus, the generic is the only one that is the *sat* or *dharmi*. You do not perceive the generic and do not perceive anything but the generic. *Dharmi* is the Reality and *dharmas* all come and go. Thus, that which is the predicate in all worldly transactions is proved to be the real and only subject of everything.

This shows how Vēdānta or a vēdāntin is really a spiritual atom bomb; and it is no wonder that intellectuals tremble to approach it, for fear of blundering into the Right. You are the only noumenon, everything else – from intellect down to the body – being the phenomenon.

471. Beauty

Beauty is Truth itself and that is yourself. Every object as object is uncouth and ugly, being opposed to and separate from yourself, the Ātmā. But sometimes you project your own self upon some particular object and call it beautiful, however uncouth it otherwise is.

You can never superimpose anything upon nature, since that superimposition also forms part of that nature itself.

17th August 1952

472. HOW ARE DREAM AND WAKING STATES RELATED?

The lower shāstras attribute greater reality to the waking state, on the ground that unlike the dream state, it repeats itself. This statement is made in the waking state, from a stand clearly partial to that state.

Examining these two states impartially, we find that what we now call the dream state was a pure waking state when experienced, according to the so-called dream subject who alone experienced that state.

So there was no dream state in fact, but only another waking state, with nothing objective in common with the former waking state.